D1010432

Hard Lessons

Hard Lessons

The Promise of an
Inner City Charter School

Jonathan Schorr

Ballantine Books

New York

A Ballantine Book
Published by The Ballantine Publishing Group

*This publication was supported in part by a grant from the Individual
Project Fellowship Program of the Open Society Institute.*

www.ballantinebooks.com

Library of Congress Cataloging-in-Publication Data
Schorr, Jonathan.
Hard lessons / Jonathan Schorr.
    p.   cm.
ISBN 0-345-44702-6
1. Charter schools—California—Oakland—Case studies. 2. Educational
equalization—California—Oakland—Case studies. 3. Education, Urban—
California—Oakland—Case studies. I. Title.

LB2806.36 .S35 2002
371.01—dc21   2002018424

Book design by BTDnyc

Manufactured in the United States of America

First Edition: September 2002

10 9 8 7 6 5 4 3 2 1

*To Alex, Malory, Asia, Ronrico, Jasmine, and Nazim,
with all their possibility and promise.*

*And to the heroes called parents, grandparents, and
teachers*

Including and especially my own.

Contents

Introduction

Better Choices, Better Chances

Some journeys defy measurement by clock or map.

It takes only twenty minutes to travel the ten miles from Skyline High School in the hills of Oakland, California, to Castlemont High in the "flatlands." But in that brief time and scant distance, one spans the chasm between a world where hope flows unguarded, and a world where it is measured out in miserly drops.

In the world of the hills, a child who tries hard at school may look forward to a share in the grand riches of this nation. Fine choices, fulfilling work, prosperity, and security await. This child will learn to think of diplomas and skills as pathways.

In the world of the flatlands, those choices go dry like an arid riverbed. The schools that might carry a child to opportunity and comfort are too rare here. This child will learn to think of diplomas and skills as barriers.

The dividing lines between these worlds depend on neighborhood, which in turn depends largely on wealth and race. A board of education draws those lines, and for the most part decides which school the child will attend.

In 1999, a group of parents assigned to lesser schools decided that they would no longer go where they were told. They may have lived among impoverished people, but they refused to accept impoverished choices. They seized on the hope of a new kind of school, believing that they could create their own choices. This book tells the story of the schools they built.

•   •   •

Skyline High School perches on the ridgeline of a range of hills a few miles from the eastern edge of the San Francisco Bay. Students arrive at this, Oakland's best-performing public high school, before the morning mists have lifted. Clad against the chill in padded nylon Starter jackets or polyester fleece, they gather on the concrete pathways that snake through the campus. Like the million-dollar homes nearby, the school enjoys magnificent vistas, overlooking rolling slopes of golden grass and the aptly named Redwood Park. "Located in the Oakland hills," the school's mission statement says, "Skyline High School offers students an extraordinary opportunity to learn in a diverse and challenging environment."

In Oakland, income closely parallels altitude. Oakland may be known as a black city, but the area surrounding Skyline is two-thirds white and Asian. In 1990, at the census, a quarter of the households in the neighborhood boasted incomes over $100,000, putting them in the city's richest 5 percent. Even then, long before the dot-com boom sent real estate prices skyward, the typical home in the area sold for $350,000—twice the city's median home price. Now, homes in the hills fetch more than $2 million.

Skyline was built in 1961 to serve the children of the hills. That arrangement, however, could not survive a decade in which Oakland became a city populated mostly by minorities, and deeply conscious of racial equity. Today, Skyline is racially integrated, though less so economically. Fewer than a quarter of its students come from poor families, but half the students are black, and a quarter are Asian; white and Latino children each account for an eighth of the enrollment. While Skyline is no academic powerhouse, a child—black, white, Asian, or Latino—can get a decent education there. The school, which enrolls about 2,300 students, posts scores at the national average in math, and slightly lower in reading. In one recent year, half of its seniors took the SAT, the college entrance exam, earning an average composite score of 956—just shy of the national average of 1,016. One hundred and twelve students there took the

Advanced Placement test, which measures whether high schoolers have learned enough to skip a college course, and about sixty of them earned passing scores. Every year, Skyline sends a handful of kids to the nation's leading colleges. It is a place where the American dream—rewards for hard work—remains alive.

Skyline, however, is not the province of true privilege. To find that, one might drive for a few minutes along lanes that wind through redwood forests, ending up at a cozy campus discreetly concealed from the street. At a private academy called the Head-Royce School, a different sort of educational reality prevails. Of seventy-four seniors, seventy-four took the SAT last year. Their average score was 1,375—more than 400 points higher than Skyline's. Most students at Head-Royce take more than one Advanced Placement test, and earn passing scores on 86 percent of them. "This year, students of color make up 35 percent of the student body," a school pamphlet reports. Few of these students are poor; despite the pamphlet's statement that "the School makes a strong commitment to financial assistance," 86 percent of Head-Royce families pay the full fare: $14,450 per year, plus "additional fees for books, elective art classes, class trips, and tennis lessons." For those with the good fortune—in both senses of the word—to attend, elite colleges and exciting career choices beckon.

While Skyline may have a hard time competing with offerings like those, it stands far beyond other public high schools in Oakland. As one descends into the "flatlands"—the section of town between the hills and the bay—curving, picturesque lanes give way to gridded, numbered streets and avenues. Houses crowd together; apartment buildings begin to appear. The trees thin out, replaced by chain-link fences and asphalt. This is the Oakland of public imagination— black and brown, impoverished and listless. Instead of quasi-mansions with three-car garages, one sees board-ups, shambles, vacant lots. These empty lots tell the story of the last half century here—of an economy still reeling from the disappearance of ship-building and auto manufacturing after World War II. In East Oakland, once a solid working-class community, the Victorian homes remain lovely, but they have become backdrops for urban gunplay. For a generation, mayors have announced, Hoover-like, that prosperity is just around the corner. In East Oakland, storefront rescue missions woo those who hope that Jesus is better at keeping promises.

On Foothill Boulevard, which marks the edge of the flatlands, a billboard on the side of a store reads, "If you are addicted to drugs get birth control—get $200 cash." The ad's sponsor is Children Requiring a Caring Kommunity, or CRACK, whose campaign to prevent unwanted, drug-addicted babies has been attacked as a scheme to sterilize poor black women. The billboard does not explain that the birth control in question is usually permanent tubal ligation.

Continue down the avenue, past the welter of storefront missionary churches and liquor stores: True Life Baptist; Black and White Liquors; New Life Church of God in Christ; Uhuru House, the "regional office" of the African People's Socialist Party; Joe's Liquor; Giants Liquor; Homeboy's Grocery; Prayer Mission Pentecostal Church; Seminary Market Liquors; Fairfax Liquor; Fairfax Lighthouse Deliverance Center.

After a mile or so, an expanse of blond concrete comes into view. Once, a General Motors plant sprawled across this vast plaza. Now, in the middle of an endless parking lot, sits a large, boxy two-story building. The sign, missing a letter, reads EASTMONT MA L, but that is out-of-date. JCPenney and Mervyn's, the commercial anchors, left years ago. As the economy here decayed, the mall shriveled. Now it's called Eastmont Town Center, and mostly houses social and medical services paid for by the government: a dialysis center, a welfare-to-work office, a military recruiter, and a handful of other nonprofit services. A few marginal businesses hang on—offering manicures, religious trinkets, bean pies, "hoisery."

Farther down the street stands Castlemont High School, amid homes where poverty and single parenthood are the rule. Plenty of people in Oakland can remember when Castlemont was good, when children from middle- and working-class neighborhoods could get a decent education there. Back then, they reminisce, "The Castle"—it did actually look like a castle—was architecturally lovely, too. By century's end, though, the school was integrated only in the sense that African-American and Latino children shared it; there were 13 white children among the 1,798 students. The school's mission statement claims that "Students attending our school can expect to receive the highest quality education in all areas of academic interest and personal need," but that is a lie. In 1999 the district devised for each school an "accountability dashboard," showing academic performance as a series of little gauges. By every measure, Castlemont was running on empty. Students reading at the national average: 8 percent. Students with grade-point averages below C: 58 percent. Days of suspension assigned: 1,785—almost exactly one per student. Percentage of students completing the coursework required for admission to the state university: 17. The average grade in those courses: D-plus. Average SAT score: 708. (Students get 400 points for signing their names. Head-Royce's score was almost twice as high as Castlemont's.) Castlemont's reported drop-out rate was 10 percent annually, but that is statistical sleight of hand. In one recent year, Castlemont had 868 ninth graders and 167 seniors.

Perhaps the saddest indicator of all was the Advanced Placement tests. Under fire for failing to offer AP courses at its poorer high schools—a potent "equity" issue for African-American and Latino parents—the district began providing the classes at Castlemont, and steadily beefed up enrollment. But enrollment is not education. In one recent year, seventy-eight Castlemont students took AP tests. Four passed.

Children at Castlemont, however, face more urgent fears than educational failure. Frequently, the school has been a dangerous place to spend time. According to a survey covering one year there, 81 percent of students have seen or participated in a racial fight, and 22 percent have witnessed or participated in six or more such fights. The school employed a remarkable fourteen security guards, who spoke openly about their fears for their own safety.

Every other inner-city system in the country faces comparable schooling woes. At times, however, Oaklanders have felt like they had it a bit worse than everyone else. They felt that frustration when Jesse Jackson called Oakland a "national laughingstock" over Ebonics, a policy passed by a unanimous school board which stated, quite clearly, that students would be taught in ghetto street language. They felt it when the school board then paid a public relations "consultant" $100,000 to explain to the national media that the Ebonics policy didn't really mean what it said. They felt it when the board decided to spend another $100,000 on corporate logos for the district and its high schools, claiming that the old logo—an oak tree—looked too much like broccoli. (The incident, memorably, led a disgusted former Oakland superintendent to wonder in the newspaper, "Why don't we just bend over and say, 'We're mooning America'?") Parents felt frustration when the district admitted that its teachers were absent more often than its elementary students. They felt it when, in a poll of large cities, Oakland parents' satisfaction with their schools ranked second-lowest in the nation. And they felt it when the superintendent was toppled following a scandal in which the district secretly and illegally hired private investigators to root out embezzlers, and to film district gardeners using their district-owned tools to run private businesses. (It didn't help when the district explained it had broken the law and hired the private eyes because going to the cops would have made the matter public and—of all ironies—given the district a bad reputation. Nor did it help that the scheme came to light when the cops discovered the private investigators videotaping on school grounds and put them in handcuffs.)

Yet, for all the problems particular to Oakland, places like Castlemont exist in every one of our nation's great cities—New York, Philadelphia, Los Angeles, Detroit, Houston, and a score of others. At Castlemont and its kin, the American dream lies dormant and lifeless. That dream rests on the notion that in America, parents—even the poor and the immigrant—can send their kids to good free schools, and see them emerge equipped to prosper and thrive, to vault the barriers of poverty into a more comfortable life. For many Americans, it is this invitation, this preference for merit over caste, that makes our country better than others. All those bright prospects depend, of course, on public schooling. A commodity as universal as tap water, public education ought to serve rich and poor alike, enabling each to go as far as his or her gifts might allow. Yet at schools like Castlemont, one wonders whether that opportunity is still available. Like every school, Castlemont has plenty of teachers who care deeply, and plenty of parents and students who strive to make schooling work. Yet the numbers leave little doubt: an address in the Castlemont neighborhood amounts to an educational death sentence.

Castlemont's depressing statistics highlight a larger truth about American education. The real problem, which Oakland shares with every other major city, could be expressed in a single sentence: in America, race and income determine, with disturbing precision, how well children perform in school. This simple equation has scrawled graffiti on the pedestal of the American dream. Given a few key pieces of data—the parents' income, their own level of education, and their skin color—one can predict, with unsettling certainty, how the child will fare in school. A RAND study estimated that such family characteristics account for more than two-thirds of achievement differences. The equation is so well understood, in fact, that some experts have predicted the performance of ghetto schools based on the demographics of their students, and suggested rewarding those that surpass the expected low level. It is as if the gap in the education of rich and poor were a natural law, like gravity.

As a teacher and then as a writer, I observed the perverse workings of that equation close-up. In 1990, as a twenty-two-year-old fresh from college, I stood before my first class of inner-city ninth graders. Struggling at first, I became a better teacher in time and, after a few years, moved on to pursue my other professional passion, journalism. In the summer of 1998, I took time off from my work as an education writer for the *Oakland Tribune* to track down my first students. It proved a humbling, sobering experience. Now twenty-two years old, these newly minted adults often found the doors of life—of fulfilling careers and comfort—closed to them. Many had not completed high school. A few told stories of triumph over hardship, but most spoke in flat tones of dead-end jobs, unemployment, and boredom. A handful were entangled in a world of cops and jails, after acts of violence at once galling and banal.

In 1999, in my reporting on schools for the *Tribune*, I heard the frustration of parents, teachers, and children daily. It was hard for me to escape the sense that something was deeply wrong. A call resounded, righteously and achingly, from the hallways of schools like Castlemont: the call for something better.

One evening in January, as I was preparing to leave work after a rainy, unseasonably warm winter day, I got a phone call that offered a taste of hope. It was well timed. The nation, just then, was gripped by the car-wreck spectacle of the president's impeachment and the horror of the Balkan slaughter. At Castlemont, students were contending with an on-campus stabbing, which avenged a savage beating which in turn avenged a series of racially charged rumbles. The troubles at Castlemont underscored problems plaguing Oakland's entire school system. The district had revealed that week that some 60 percent of its high schoolers were flunking algebra, a course required for graduation. The low passing rates should have surprised no one, considering that the district hadn't recruited enough trained math teachers to fill all the classrooms, and was producing videotaped lessons to take the place of competent teachers. Thanks to truancy, though, a lack of kids matched the lack of teachers. Attendance in algebra classes that I visited ran as low as seven students in one case and zero in another.

The call that brought a whiff of promise came from a community organizer working for an unusual, formidable coalition of mostly working-class black and Latino families. Together with parents from his organization, he was hatching a plan to open a raft of charter schools. If the plan succeeded, it would do more than mark a declaration of independence for parents who had long felt voiceless before the school district monolith. It would also transform Oakland—a city of 400,000 residents and ninety schools—into a laboratory for one of the most exciting new ideas in education.

The charter concept, unknown just a decade earlier, aimed to re-shape the landscape of American education. It was the darling of politicians from Honolulu to Boston facing voters who suddenly, for the first time in history, had named education as their most pressing concern—above even crime and the economy. Politicos from right, left, and center rallied to this fresh idea, assuring that charters would spread like milkweed. At that time, in 1999, just seven years after the first charter school opened, the majority of states had ap-proved charter laws, and some 1,700 such schools had sprung up. (By 2001, some 2,400 charters in thirty-four states would enroll more than a half million students; George W. Bush, who had cam-paigned on a platform that included charters, was to make them key to his education plans once in office.) Opponents raised angry objections, arguing that charters would speed the "privatizing" of public schools, and would do little to help the great majority of chil-dren, who likely would never attend charters. The naysayers, how-ever, were largely drowned out. With their rapid growth, charters were sure to affect the course of American education, especially in the places where schools performed worst. Yet, for all the excite-ment, pollsters reported that most Americans had no idea what charter schools were.

The charter idea was based on a simple concept: independent public schools that were required to get results, rather than follow bureaucratic rules. A group of people—perhaps teachers or parents—could devise a concept for a school. They would write that plan into a document called a charter, which would include goals that the school would be held responsible for achieving. The local school board or state then might approve the charter, allowing the school to open. If the school failed to meet its goals, the same agency could shut it down. The charter school would be largely exempt from the regulations that govern other schools, but it would have to obey the basic rules that make public schools public: it could not charge tu-ition, could not discriminate in admission, and could not teach reli-gion. It would be funded with per-student public funds, as if each child carried a check for several thousand dollars, and could carry that check to either a district school or a charter. Parents would be free to choose the best school in their community, while school districts would have to do just like any other business: offer good service if they hoped to attract customers.

Teachers' unions ranked among the most vociferous critics of charters, which was ironic, because the nation's most influential teacher union leader had played midwife to the charter idea. The term "charter" first appeared in 1975, thanks to Ray Budde, an educator who proposed setting not schools, but individual teachers, free from the bureaucracy.[1] Yet it didn't become widely known until it was adopted by Albert Shanker, the late president of one of the major national teacher unions. Even Shanker, however, did not envision the form charters eventually took: public schools almost entirely separate from the system. According to the dictionary, the term "charter" means a document in which government grants rights to the people, and this was precisely what later advocates hoped to accomplish. Charters were direct descendants of the boutiqueish alternative schools of the 1960s and 1970s, but unlike those schools, charters would exist completely separate from the system. Charters could be created brand-new, or existing public schools could convert into charters. Yet charters, as the people who dreamed them up hastened to note, were not in themselves a strategy for better classroom instruction. They simply combined freedom of methods with accountability for results.

Despite attacks from unions and others, the charter concept proved extraordinarily popular. It made sense that charters would win a hearty welcome from politicians of virtually every stripe, because the concept bore no ideology of its own. On the contrary, it provided a blank slate on which to sketch the school of one's dreams. For conservatives, charters spoke to ideals of small government, free enterprise, competition, and entrepreneurship. For liberals, they called to mind the beloved alternative schools, and promised freedom of instructional practice. Charters eschewed bureaucracy, replacing hidebound rules (the Education Code in California, for example, filled 1,937 pages) with a do-or-die performance promise. In a nation where four out of five school superintendents faulted politics and bureaucracy for pushing talented leaders out of education,[2] a school without constraints held promise. Moreover, charters raised the hope that sluggish school districts would leap to improve before all their students—and their money—walked out. The most passionate advocates believed that every school should be held to such performance promises, or that whole districts should be "charterized."

Success for the charter concept, however, was far from assured. Each school would be only as good as the ideas behind it, and the talent with which those ideas were executed. And closures of bad schools—with all their attendant pain—were an essential element of the plan. Parents would have to be smart shoppers; school boards would have to be tough but fair evaluators. Charters would have to share the wisdom they gained, and school districts—despite all the fierce talk of competition—would have to listen. In all, it was an optimist's shopping list.

Charters stood as one part of a wider movement in education called "school choice." The most modest visions of choice advocated allowing parents to choose among existing district schools. More ambitious and controversial notions included vouchers, a 1950s brainchild of economist Milton Friedman, which would let families spend public education funds at any school, including private and religious ones. Touted, of late, by an odd marriage of conservative business types and impoverished inner-city parents, vouchers applied the traditional free-market concept to education. Voucher fans said they would deliver a twin benefit, immediately allowing poor kids to attend better schools while pushing the public schools to improve through competition, under the threat of watching their enrollment, and funding, drain away. Parents would seek out the best schools; good ones would thrive and bad ones would shut down. Opponents doubted the market would work that way. They suspected private schools would select the highest-scoring students and most engaged parents, while the remainder would languish in weakened, last-resort public schools. Critics also derided the spending of public funds at religious schools as an abandonment of the Constitution.

Charters did an odd dance with vouchers. To opponents of both, charters were simply a resting point on the slippery slope toward vouchers—a subtler strategy to discredit the public system. To their defenders, however, charters represented a vision of school choice that was still public, still answerable to the taxpayers for its results and its use of funds. If charters prevailed, there would be no need for the controversial vouchers. Without another option, vouchers and other nonpublic choices would win.

Charters—and school choice in general—represented the latest turn in a hundred-year-old cycle of pronouncements of dismay over the state of America's public schools, followed by reforms intended to solve the problem. At the dawn of the twentieth century, the "problem" was that the nation was a poppy field of tiny school-houses, with little agreement on how they should operate. Experts called for larger, more uniform schools, with teachers and curriculum under the command of big, hierarchical, professional, "rational" systems, and massive changes ensued. In the early part of the century, the typical high school enrolled a hundred students; a comparable school at the end of the century had a thousand. Between 1930 and 1980, the number of one-room schools plunged from 130,000 to fewer than 1,000.[3] And the reform cycle continued. In the 1950s, for example, with the launch of the *Sputnik* satellite by the Soviets, America declared itself woefully behind in the brain race. Then, in 1983, the influential report "A Nation at Risk" announced that the previous wave of reform had failed to prevent crisis. "If an unfriendly foreign power had attempted to impose on America the mediocre educational performance that exists today, we might well have viewed it as an act of war," the report said. "As it stands, we have allowed this to happen to ourselves. We have even squandered the gains in student achievement made in the wake of the Sputnik challenge." Once again, academics, politicians, and businesspeople demanded more from the nation's schools. And a welter of reforms did flow forth. A mere (and incomplete) list of strategies aimed at reform and equity in the second half of the century suggests the scale of the effort: the National Defense Education Act in the fifties; the Great Society equal-opportunity changes in the sixties; the alternative schools of the late sixties and seventies; curriculum reforms, new math, integration, busing, Title I funding for poor children, school-based management, whole language, cooperative learning, and—most recently—an intense focus on testing and "accountability," which meant rewards for low-scoring schools that improved, and consequences as harsh as closure for those that did not. Many of these reforms brought benefits for students. None triumphed in erasing the gap between poor and affluent children.

Yet, the country deceived itself when it looked back for some lost golden age of education. By most important measures, the story of American schooling was an almost unbroken march of advancement. At the beginning of the century, barely one in ten American children completed high school; by World War II, the majority still dropped out. By 1999, 83 percent of children earned high school diplomas. Over the twentieth century, likewise, illiteracy was crushed like polio. In 1870, 20 percent of whites and 80 percent of blacks could not read; by 1979, those numbers were 0.6 percent and 1.6 percent. It was true, of course, that by some measures, American children at the dawn of the twenty-first century lagged behind their counterparts in other industrialized nations. They didn't work as hard, or know as much, as they might have. Yet for the large majority of American children, education nonetheless blazed a path to opportunity, comfort, and the pursuit of happiness. And for all the doomsaying in the fifties, eighties, and nineties, the United States had become the most prosperous and powerful nation in the world, whatever the faults of its schools.

Yet now, American schools were being asked to do something no society had ever done: to deliver an academic education to virtually every child. Gone was an age, dominated by agriculture and manufacturing, when low- and semiskilled labor yielded livable incomes for millions of adults without high school diplomas. Gone was a time when serious thinkers on schooling suggested that elementary school teachers "ought to sort the pupils" into vocational, industrial, or academic tracks "by their evident or probable destinies."[4] Gone was a time when education experts attacked "schooling the masses in precisely the same manner as we do those who are to be our leaders" as a threat to social stability.[5] For the first time in history, every child needed a good education. But America had not yet met that need.

The real problem—the one that gnawed at the nation's soul—was a divide between educational haves and have-nots distressingly closely tied to race and class. Once, the gap between rich and poor, between white and black and brown, had been shrinking. Now, it was growing again. Nationally, in reading and math, black and Latino twelfth graders performed almost exactly the same as white eighth graders. Whites were almost twice as likely as blacks or Hispanics to have completed college, and more than three times as likely as blacks to take an Advanced Placement course. Hispanics were four times more likely than whites to drop out of school. Differences in wealth added to the inequity; among twenty-four-year-olds from low-income families, only 7 percent had completed college, while among their counterparts from high-income families, 48 percent had. In places of concentrated poverty—urban neighborhoods like the one around Castlemont—school failure was the norm. And while poor whites and rural communities also suffered serious educational ills, the situation was most glaringly obvious in the urban ghetto. The majority of black children attended inner-city schools, in places like the Oakland flatlands. The consequences shamed any person of conscience. Although the world's richest country, America imprisoned a higher proportion of its citizens than any other nation. Perhaps the country could afford, economically, to write off a sizeable population as a loss. But could it afford that choice morally?

Evidently, for most people, the answer was no. America again had directed its attention to its education problem, and the response, for many reformers, was charter schools. There was an irony here, however. The twentieth century had opened amid great certainty, among a new class of education experts, that improvement lay in bigger schools within bigger, more uniform systems. Now, in the century's sunset, a new wave of reformers wanted to improve schools by making them smaller and freeing them from the giant systems that now dominated public education. (Indeed, such systems, with their democratically elected overseers, had come to be seen as synonymous with true "public education.") To observers in places like France, where education is largely controlled by a central government, the charter idea might have seemed bizarre. Already, America had vested control of education in its cities and towns. Now, the individual schools would hold the reins? Moreover, the idea was a bit shocking: after a century of research on how to educate children well, each school would be left on its own to find its way?

Yet the idea held appeal—the freedom, outside the bounds of bureaucracy, to establish a public school of one's own. This story, burgeoning in Oakland and across the country, deserved telling. It was my good luck to be in the right place to tell it, and to search for answers to the vital and pressing questions it raised: Would these schools offer the sort of academic quality, and the safety and friendliness, the parents hoped for? Would these schools play favorites in admission, or would they play fair? Would they bring improvement in the "regular" schools, or would they steal the motivated, involved parents who drove reform efforts? Every one of these questions pertained not just to the handful of charters I planned to observe in Oakland, but to the entire charter movement.

Over nearly three years, I watched from the inside as an embryonic idea grew into real schools with real children. It is important to note that charter schools may spend their first year, or few years, in a traumatic fight for survival. Indeed, some evidence indicates that charter schools establish themselves academically only after that initial period is over. All the same, those early years are profoundly formative, revealing much about a school's identity and what makes it work. The birth and early years of these schools in Oakland offered essential lessons, in both the unique strengths and complexities of charters, and in the Herculean difficulty of creating an urban school. And perhaps more than anything else, this experience taught that independence from the system, by itself, does not forge schools that answer the needs of our most ill-educated children.

During these three years, I was fortunate to get to know the people whose stories are told in these pages. Lillian Lopez and William Stewart are devoted parents in different parts of town—veterans who have battled the system to find decent education for their children. Each plays a crucial role in the founding of the two schools that make up the core of this story. Nazim Casey, a brilliant and utterly lovable child, contends with more woe and hardship than any youngster should have to face, while genuinely trying to do right and to learn. Laura Armstrong, a tough and passionate educator, fights her own employers to establish a school in the way she believes right. Valentín Del Rio, a first-time teacher, struggles to give his students the education they deserve, even when no one will guide him. And Eugene Ruffin, the CEO of a school management company, attempts simultaneously to win political change, make money, and educate poor children.

In their stories are lessons about building the schools that our children need.

PART I

Rage

Chapter 1

Reality

The rage in Lillian Lopez had been burning for some time.

Her anger began with her neighborhood, the Fruitvale district of East Oakland, the city's greatest Latino stronghold. She didn't want to live there anymore. For nearly a quarter century, she had worked at one good position after another in the corporate offices of Wells Fargo Bank; certainly, between her income and her husband's, they could afford to move to a safer, quieter area. She endured the blast of the boom boxes, the screeching cars that made the front bedroom no good for sleeping, the unswept streets. But the hardest part was being scared. Her two younger boys, with their typical walk, their typical clothes, their typical haircuts, looked so much like every other boy in the neighborhood—even she, driving down the street, would mistake other people's children for her own. One day, she feared, gangbangers with guns would make the same mistake. She couldn't even let her children ride bicycles on the sidewalk, for fear of the speeding cars turning "donuts" in front of the house. But her husband, Jose, refused to abandon the neighborhood. "This is Mexican town," he declared, and he wasn't about to call a moving van to take him away from his roots.

The deepest daily wellspring of anger for Lopez came from her search for a decent school for her boys. In those days, she had no notions about creating a new school, nor even that it was possible—she just wanted to find a place where her two younger children could get an education. Her oldest son, Martín, now twenty-seven and born long before her marriage, had enjoyed a relatively easy journey through private elementary and then public middle and high school. But by the time she married Jose and had her next son, Chipito, times—and schools—had changed. Lopez enrolled Chipito at Jefferson Year-Round Elementary, the neighborhood public school. It was a decision she would come to regret.

For starters, Jefferson had run out of places to put children. Designed to house some 700 children, Jefferson had burgeoned to more than 1,100—and in bad years, that number might jump by another 600 or so. California's grim recession had left it with the most crowded classrooms in America, and struggling Oakland had not built a new school in thirty years. Yet in the Jefferson neighborhood—a mostly poor area dominated by Latino, Southeast Asian, and African-American families—the population had swelled during that time. Bereft of new building funds, the district had responded to the rising tide by hauling one portable classroom after another onto Jefferson's weathered, cracking blacktop playground. The more the numbers of children grew, the more playground disappeared, until the campus—which sprawled across two unbroken city blocks—resembled an odd little city, with narrow, isolated alleys between the yellowish-tan trailers. The gaps between adjoining portables were covered by plywood, which eventually decayed, opening holes big enough to admit rats, or in some cases, children. The innumerable hidden spaces let graffiti artists work with little fear of interruption.

Yet even with the extra classrooms, Jefferson was still overcrowded, and sought to accommodate the high numbers of students by running year-round. This solution depended on a complicated system of four staggered calendars, so that one "track" of kids would attend during another group's vacation. The plan had succeeded in thoroughly annoying parents, some of whom had children on various tracks, but had failed to solve the crowding problem. There were still too many kids, and select unfortunate "rover" teachers were forced to move their entire classrooms every month— bulletin displays, phonics charts, art supplies, and all—to classrooms vacated by other teachers. Jefferson, with thirteen rover teachers among a staff of fifty-one, had it worse than any other school in Oakland. And somehow, there didn't seem to be many alternatives. In 1992, a handful of parents from that crowded part of town had created an independent public middle school called a charter school. But for most teachers in the district, that felt like heresy—like an abandonment of public education as they knew it. Anyway, things hadn't worked out well in that school, and few wanted to try the experiment again.

Chipito struggled at Jefferson. Like his father, he spoke little English. By the end of his kindergarten year, the school notified Lopez that he would be held back. Dissatisfied, and with few friends at the big public school to help with child care, Lopez enrolled him at a private school attached to a small local college. She was happy, briefly, but then Jose lost his job at a local bakery, and they no longer could afford the school. She moved Chipito again, to a Catholic school with lower tuition costs. There, she knew he was not being challenged, and she confronted his teacher. Her protests served only to make her a hated figure at the school, and the administration warned her that if she didn't like their methods, she could take her money and leave. At the end of the year, the nun in charge told her, "I think that you and Jose would be happier elsewhere."

With Chipito entering fourth grade, Lopez returned to a Jefferson in chaos. A cadre of parents was demanding the ouster of the principal and was holding the school's budget hostage. When she joined the parents' committee, Lopez was told that as an outsider she was not welcome in the discussion. The dispute devolved, as Lopez watched, into a fistfight between a parent and a teacher. Things got even worse when it came time for the Lopezes to enroll their youngest son, Alex, at Jefferson. The kindergarten teacher did not show up on time for class most days. The first-grade teacher was a "rover." The second-grade teacher's mere presence sent Alex—who usually liked school—into tears. Shortly into the school year, the teacher was fired amid allegations that he had, without permission, been taking students home with him.

While the fruitless search for a decent education stoked Lopez's fury, other events left her shaken and desperate. Chipito, entering sixth grade, wanted to attend the public middle school, Calvin Simmons, with his friends. He had the support of his father, who did not want to spend money on a private school. Lopez didn't like the size and impersonality of the middle school, but gave in to the wishes of her husband and son. A month into the school year, following an argument over a girl, a gang of young toughs attacked Chipito in front of the school. They knocked the boy to the ground and began kicking him. Chipito escaped and pounded at the school doors, seeking sanctuary, but no one answered. He was not seriously injured, but for Lopez, the locked doors were even more galling than the beating itself—evidence, to her, that the school did not care about her child. Later, she learned that the boy who led the beating on her son had been jailed at juvenile hall, now implicated in a shooting. Lillian Lopez's most frightening fantasy had just come home.

In a wrenching decision, Lopez uprooted her children and moved to a small town called Delhi (pronounced DEL-high) in California's rural Central Valley, transferring to work at the local Wells Fargo office. There was talk that Jose might follow, but he never did. It was not a classic separation; she remained committed to her marriage, though she was angry Jose didn't move with them. And the safe, placid new community seemed, to her eyes, perfect. But the rural idyll crashed on the first day of school, when Chipito came home and addressed his grandmother, who had come from New Mexico to help with the move. "Grandma," Chipito asked, "what's a wetback?" As Lopez's hopes of small-town peace evaporated like a mirage, Chipito added, "They've been calling me a beaner, too."

It didn't end there. At the polls on election day, a man in line in front of Lopez pointed her out to his wife and murmured, "Now they're letting *them* vote!" Chipito, then ten, suffered from chronic stomachaches all year, which Lillian chalked up to the separation from his father. Finally, she faced the undeniable: the move, her last resort, had failed. At the end of the school year, she and her boys returned to the dirt and the noise of the Fruitvale, and the chaos of Jefferson. It was the single worst moment of her life.

• • •

Hope dawned for Lillian Lopez on Saturday, September 27, 1997, at St. Elizabeth's Church. A week earlier, when she was registering Alex for catechism class, a friend and fellow Jefferson mother had mentioned there would be a meeting about improving the school. Lopez had agreed to attend, but she had been to many meetings about Jefferson, and she went to this one reluctantly, expecting to hear nothing new. An intense, plainspoken woman with a reddish tinge to her dark hair, Lopez wore her moods like a banner. And just now, her mood was bleak. She couldn't figure out how to find an acceptable school for her children and keep her marriage going at the same time. She didn't expect to find an answer at St. Elizabeth's.

That morning, seventeen parents crowded around a beaten leatherette-covered table in a long, narrow room tucked into the church convent. Mothers and fathers sat in couples, mostly, which drew Lopez's notice; typically, a mother or father came to school meetings without a partner. All were Latino; many were Mexican-born. To Lopez's happy surprise, the meeting was unusual from the start. In contrast to all her previous school meetings, no district administrators attended this one, which permitted a free-flowing and honest conversation. Parents, not bureaucrats, drove the agenda.

Behind the Saturday gathering was Oakland Community Organizations, a coalition of churches and families that worked for all sorts of improvements, from speed bumps on busy streets to small classes in crowded schools. Estela Cerda, a nervous, slightly uncomfortable Jefferson parent, opened the meeting. She offered OCO's "credential": a statement that the organization represented some thirty-five local churches, with an active membership of thirty-two thousand people. After a brief prayer, Matt Hammer, a professional OCO organizer with wire-rimmed glasses, asked his first question, in Spanish and then in English. Standing by a giant flip-chart pad of paper on an easel, he called on the parents to speak candidly about their schooling concerns.

"Tell me about Jefferson," said Hammer, an intense, slender white man with a trim goatee. "Give me some characteristics."

He didn't need to ask for complaints; they came, slowly at first, then with increasing speed and animation until parents were talking over each other. The bathrooms are dirty, one mother offered. Some said their children were too disgusted to use the bathrooms at all. "My daughter holds it all day," one said. Hammer wrote at the easel. There were other complaints: The water fountains don't work. The school is filthy. The school is too crowded. Kids lose whole days of education while the "rovers" move. The school isn't secure. The gates to the yard are unlocked and the fences are torn. Anyone could get in. And, as if it were just one more item in the litany, parents charged that the kids don't know how to read.

A fire was starting, and Hammer opened a can of gasoline. He asked the parents whether they knew that there were schools within the Oakland district—in wealthier neighborhoods—where children were getting a very different sort of education. He showed bar charts representing test scores at various schools, which OCO had pried loose from the district's research office. Jefferson looked like a one-story cottage on the chart. In richer, whiter neighborhoods, the performance graphs were skyscrapers. In those other schools, enrollment typically was less than four hundred, and there was no year-round school—and no roving. Hammer noted that this was the age of Proposition 209, the end of affirmative action. If these were the differences in achievement, he asked the parents, what happens when your kid has to compete against those kids for admission to the University of California?

His strategy worked. The complaints mounted: The children don't have books. They don't get homework. When they do, nobody checks it. There's no discipline. The teachers don't dress professionally. In Mexico, the parents charged, problems like Jefferson's would be unheard of. Hammer pushed the comparison with Mexico. The parents agreed they had given up better schools by coming to America. They complained that American schools advanced children to the next grade even if they hadn't mastered the material, while in Mexico, *"si no sabe, no pasa"*—if you don't know, you don't pass. In Oakland, parents saw signs that the school system was patronizing them. Their children brought home good grades from their teachers, but low scores on standardized tests. The system was telling them that everything was fine, but they knew their children couldn't read. Those who moved to private schools or to other cities saw those suspicions confirmed: in new schools, their children— supposedly in good shape in Oakland—flunked.

Hammer stepped in to steer the meeting again. On the easel, he drew two columns, headed "real" and "ideal." Above the headings, he drew a stick figure, with a foot planted on each side. The complaints filled the "real" column. Now, he wanted to fill in the ideal. "If we're going to be an effective group of leaders here—that's what we are, leaders, that's why you came to this meeting—we're going to have to develop a vision of an ideal Jefferson, of where we're trying to go," he said, his voice brimming with earnestness and provocation. "So close your eyes for a minute and think about how Jefferson is supposed to be." He saved special emphasis for the final word: "Dream."

After a few moments' pause, he took up the marker. "So, describe to me that ideal Jefferson," he said.

The list, essentially the opposites of the first column, read like a basic bill of rights for children: Clean bathrooms and halls and playground. Classes taught by permanent teachers, not endlessly rotating substitutes. A safe school. Homework, assigned regularly and corrected. A school staff that listened to and respected the parents, and treated the children well. By the hour's end, the parents were hooked. They agreed to meet again, and promised to bring other parents along.

For Hammer, the moment was a gift. The fuel he needed for a new school initiative was plentiful at the St. Elizabeth's meeting, and the articulate and angry Lopez registered as strong leader material.

Moreover, the parents were assembling just the sort of list of complaints that, when focused and narrowed, would become a powerful list of demands. Under his plan, parents soon would present that list to school administrators and politicians in front of an audience of hundreds or perhaps thousands of OCO members. In front of that kind of audience, the big shots would have a hard time doing anything other than promising immediate changes.

Hammer had organized the meeting that morning after careful strategic thought. OCO sought to make change by transforming anger over injustice into action. Here, that meant making education better. OCO was fresh from a series of victories over the district that had led to the creation of new high school programs, and had pushed forward class size reduction in the early grades. Now, OCO was turning to a new battleground: the quality of a half dozen overcrowded, low-performing elementary schools where many of its members had children. As always, Hammer approached the situation strategically, which led him to choose St. Elizabeth's as his rallying point. Hammer wanted to provide a haven outside the school where they could organize before doing battle with the district. The church, a sprawling and friendly compound of mission-style buildings and palm trees, was ideal—an institution deeply trusted by the parents.

Hammer's strategy, of soliciting concerns and helping to turn them into an action plan, had deep roots. His organization, OCO, was started in 1973 by a pair of Jesuit priests who were trained in Chicago by Saul Alinsky, the community organizer. The priests had roamed Oakland, knocking on doors and gathering residents' concerns to build an agenda for community action. A quarter century later, the coalition stood three dozen churches and thirty-two thousand members strong. Yet its mission remained unchanged: helping people—particularly the poor and dispossessed—to advocate for themselves by working together. Citizen "leaders" found and organized other leaders, a step in what Hammer called "making real the democratic promise." A generation after the Jesuit priests, Hammer was emulating those pioneers.

For Lopez, the hour with Hammer and the other parents was

revelatory. Accustomed to superficial meetings run by school administrators, she had never been challenged to think deeply about
schooling and how to make it better. Now, she was struck with the
sense that her battle for a decent school held new promise. Lopez
trailed Hammer around the church, brimming with ideas and questions. Perhaps, she thought, things would begin to improve for her
children. And perhaps her marriage would be saved.

The meetings continued, and Lopez joined OCO, quickly rising to become a spokeswoman for the school effort. After meeting regularly
for two months, the parents narrowed their complaints and desires
to a tightly focused statement, which Hammer recorded on the easel
paper: They would work with teachers, administrators, and other
parents to make Jefferson a clean, safe environment that offered an
excellent education. The OCO parents tore the page off and delivered
it to the new principal at Jefferson, whose name was Mike Hopkins.

• • •

At first, when the OCO parents broached their idea for improving
Jefferson, Mike Hopkins managed a warm reception for the plan. It
wasn't until later that he quietly set out to kill it.

At the time, in fall 1997, Hopkins was nearing the end of his third
decade as an employee of the Oakland Unified School District. An
affable man with black hair in a ponytail, a prodigious belly, and a
ready, high-pitched laugh, Hopkins had entered education as a teacher
in 1968, and after only four years became an assistant principal. In
1975, he was promoted to principal, and over the next quarter century, he captained schools throughout the city, from the toughest
neighborhoods in the "flatlands" to the toniest in the affluent hills.
Eventually, he got promoted to the administration building, where
he worked as personnel director for six years, until a new superintendent sent him back to serve as a principal again. In 1996, when
he was fifty-six and preparing to retire, he came to rest at Jefferson.

A year later, when the upstart OCO parents came knocking, Hopkins regarded them warily. Initially, he had no real problem with Matt Hammer or his efforts. He even posted the flip-chart mission statement on his office wall. But Hopkins had survived numerous struggles for power in a bureaucracy that often was compared to the Soviet system, and he talked about protecting himself with exaggerated, mafia-esque melodrama. Privately, he remarked that he hoped the younger, skinnier man understood his implicit warning: "As long as you're not my enemy, we can talk—I'm not gonna sabotage you," was the way Hopkins later described it. "And if you screw me over, my favorite expression is, I know where you live. And I got some bigger, badder boys working for me than you got working for you."

For Hopkins, a key part of the job at Jefferson was keeping watch on the enrollment numbers, which would grow until the district decided the school had reached the limit. When downtown sent word to shut off enrollment, he could divert children to a school farther away, although sometimes the second school would proclaim itself maxed out as well, and the parents would appear on Hopkins's doorstep again. Yet he reacted to the uncertainties of moving large numbers of bodies with a supply sergeant's shrug.

Hopkins had his own complaints about Jefferson, however, mostly dwelling on the intractability of its problems and the failings of its faculty. Teachers rarely stayed there more than a couple of years. In his view, some members of his staff were incompetent; others were simply crazy. By and large, they were, as he put it, "a bitch-and-complain, moan-and-groan, nothing's-ever-right type of staff," and he avoided eating lunch with them.

He knew that parents invariably complained, too—about safety and cleanliness, particularly in the bathrooms, few of which were even open. Some parents groused that their children didn't read well enough. Test scores appeared annually in the paper; sometimes they went up, sometimes down; usually, they were accompanied by hand-wringing adjectives, the most popular being "dismal." Hopkins had heard the complaints, over and over. And he was troubled by things the school could not offer, such as psychological support for kids with awful home lives. He knew Jefferson was not the school it could be. But he also had explanations for the bad news. When test scores fell, he reasoned that perhaps children actually were reading better than the year before. Therefore, he argued, they were answering fewer of the test questions because they were spending time reading the passages instead of filling in the answer sheet with guesses.

Hopkins found the notion that a principal of such a vast school would be an "instructional leader"—a phrase popular among education reformers—idealistic, which in his lingo meant silly. Before he could turn the school's focus to educating, he needed to make it a safe place. That would take about three years, he figured—one to observe what was happening, one to educate the staff, and then one to start educating students. It would take longer still if he considered getting rid of any teachers, which he didn't plan to do, because they were all college-educated and had passed the teacher qualifying test, which to him meant they were fine. Anyway, Hopkins was planning to retire after the completion of this three-year plan. And as a longtime student of the administrative life cycle, Hopkins knew that no matter what he did, the person who replaced him would curse him for doing nothing; Hopkins knew it because he had said the same thing about his predecessor.

In the meantime, Hopkins did what he could. He wore a tie every day, because a study he read in 1975 said kids perform better at schools where the principal wears a tie. He devised a split shift with his assistant principal so he wouldn't have to come in until about nine. And he made sure Styrofoam lunch trays weren't mixed in with the rest of the trash, because they took up too much room in the compactor.

In truth, Hopkins did not believe that schools like his could bring grand changes in the lives of poor children. He reasoned that the uneducated masses of East Oakland should not expect to make rapid progress. "You can't jump from one level of society to another in one generation," he explained. "It takes multiple generations." And as much as he might have liked to move all these kids into the middle class, he knew they would not get high scores on the all-important standardized test. But, he said, "we're going to give 'em the test anyway, so they'll be familiar with it."

A Louisianan of Creole extraction, Hopkins sometimes identified himself as black. He did not consider himself a racist. He simply refused to adopt what he saw as politically correct fiction—that children who went to bed hungry, or who lived in homes bereft of books, would learn as fast as children whose lives were richer, literally and figuratively. So when confronted with the poor achievement at Jefferson, Hopkins was direct: he blamed "the clientele." "The children who attend this school have no background," he would say. "They haven't been read to since infancy. They haven't been read nursery rhymes—the simple things middle-class parents do. You won't find many soccer moms at Jefferson school. Why? Because the moms are cleaning other people's houses, or working in a factory, or have multiple children."

Some might have taken Hopkins's own story as evidence that the American dream is still alive—that with education and hard work, one can change one's circumstances for the better. Hopkins was one of three black children who "graduated" from his St. Louis elementary school, and one of four from his high school to enroll in college. As a black student, he belonged to an infinitesimally small minority in college, but that status only drove him harder toward success. Then, at a time when the armed services had few black officers, Hopkins attained the rank of second lieutenant in the Air Force. Now, at age fifty-nine, he lived in Lafayette, a posh East Bay suburb. Yet he didn't see his story as one of progress, but of maintaining social class and school achievement. His father, a standout, had graduated early from high school, and his mother was the first in her family to pursue education after high school, becoming a registered nurse.

If Hopkins had little patience with Horatio Alger fantasies for his indigent black and immigrant students, he likewise found little to love in the faddish school policies designed to achieve such miracles. The most recent example was called site-based management, a reform aimed at upping the involvement of parents and teachers by giving them a hand in truly important decisions, such as hiring and the apportioning of the budget. Hopkins found the idea not just useless, but actually dangerous—"a farce," he termed it, "crap, educational lingo." It was asinine, he thought, to ask parents who themselves had not been educated to render decisions about education. That was like asking someone who knew nothing of medicine to tell doctors how to do surgery. In the inner city, he figured, "parents can't take on an establishment they don't know anything about." The worst irony was that the government actually required parent decision making only in schools that enrolled many impoverished, low-performing students. Hopkins felt that was backwards. He wondered, "What do these poor unfortunate people living in subsidized housing know about education that these people in the hills don't know?"

When the OCO parents first showed up, though, their requests were fairly innocuous. Hopkins sat through numerous meetings with them, and was responsive to their requests. The parents wanted a picture of what their children should be expected to be able to do at a given age and grade. The teachers provided those standards, with Hopkins's blessing. The parents talked safety; Hopkins allowed them to meet with a police officer on campus. They talked cleanliness; soon, "school beautification" volunteer days started up, and Hopkins scheduled meetings between the parent group and the school's janitors. That was where the trouble started.

Parents left the meetings with the janitors convinced that the employees were working as hard as they could, but that three workers could not clean a multiacre school with more than a thousand occupants. Hopkins responded that the creation of an additional position was out of his hands, and referred the parents to the downtown district headquarters. There, they met with the superintendent herself, Carole Quan. But in meeting after meeting, Quan acted as if she were hearing about the issue for the first time. She sent the OCO parents back to Hopkins, who sent them back to Quan again. They went back and forth until, finally, Quan asked Hopkins directly whether the school really needed another custodian. Hopkins had been around long enough to know the correct answer, and he said no, everything was fine. For the parents, it was a first, and decisive, breach of trust.

In the meantime, other events were conspiring to spark far more serious conflict. Hammer, enjoying some quiet hours during the Thanksgiving holiday, opened a book he had long meant to read. *The Power of Their Ideas* was a concise, deeply thoughtful treatise by education visionary and MacArthur "genius award" winner Deborah Meier. The book—which wrapped together Meier's journal entries from the small school she led in Harlem with analysis of urban education—electrified Hammer. Meier gave shape and sense to the endless, daunting complaints Hammer heard from parents and teachers—the mired stolidity of the system, the inability of teachers to make changes that traveled farther than the doorway of their own classrooms.

In the book, Meier urged the creation of schools small enough that every teacher would know every child, with enough autonomy that the staff could formulate on-the-spot curriculum decisions tailored to the needs of its children. Meier herself had made the idea work in Harlem, where large schools were divided into smaller ones, still in the same big buildings, but operating independently under separate leaders. Hammer, who had begun making contacts with teachers at Jefferson, saw connections. He realized that schools like Jefferson could be awful places not just for parents and kids, but for teachers as well. Where parents complained about the lack of homework, teachers complained that they were not allowed to send books home, nor to make enough photocopies to create their own homework. In a school as large as Jefferson, there was no agreement on anything overarching—a discipline policy, a reading program. In a small school, under Meier's vision, things could be different.

By December, Hammer had bought a hundred copies of the book, and was distributing it to every parent, teacher, and principal who would read it. Lillian Lopez read it, and she, too, was intrigued. She recognized that small schools had substantial evidence on their side; a collection of studies indicated that kids aren't just safer at small schools, but learn more as well. Among the OCO parents, and to a small group of Jefferson teachers who had joined forces with them, Meier's book, and her powerful ideas, spread like a revolutionary manifesto. By the new year, the parent group's mission was about more than just simple school improvement. Now, Hammer and Lopez were approaching Hopkins and the teachers with a bold new idea, evangelizing for the gospel of a new small school.

•   •   •

Hopkins had little trouble with the idea of a small school at first, when it seemed like a minor and harmless program. That changed when he saw how ambitious the plan was. These teachers, who had never managed a school, wanted more than just a few classrooms. They wanted a serious fraction of the budget. If they enrolled a quarter of the school's kids, they would demand a quarter of the money. Hopkins knew that many of the extras his school could offer—copiers, a nurse, computers in every classroom, overhead projectors and VCRs, even a comfortable book budget—flowed from an economy of scale. As he saw it, small schools were the same as large schools, just with less stuff. "Been there," he said privately. "Done that. Don't like it." He harbored significant doubts about how the dividing would be done, too, because as he liked to put it, principals don't share. The school had one nurse—how could they have a quarter of her? How would they divide a quarter of the school's supplies? How would this tiny school do parent training? Would there be two cafeterias? "They never looked at food," he later remarked derisively.

To Hopkins, these teachers had no idea what they were doing; "they were a bunch of inexperienced people—idealists," he said. Moreover, he figured a small school would draw entirely from the type of teachers who made up the largest single group in the district: white women. Probably, the principal would be female, too. His hostility grew further when he began to suspect the small-schoolers were keeping the real dimensions of their plan—for a fully autonomous school with its own leader—secret from him and the rest of their colleagues. In his mind, Hopkins resolved not to preside over the splitting up of his school.

But the district's top administrators—some of them Meier fans—gave a cautious nod to the plan, and Hopkins publicly followed suit, hiding his doubts and saying he would support the idea. In repeated meetings, he never revealed his real opinion, and he maintained a polite distance from the details. "I don't want to know, I'm not interested in knowing, and I don't care if I don't know certain things that are going on," he decided. "Because I can't know everything."

Blissfully unaware of their principal's attitude, a core group of teachers met repeatedly, serving as architects for the new home the parents had described. A vision statement they wrote later illustrated how closely in tune they were with the parents' desires. "As the day begins," it opened, "children enter the building and walk through clean, uncluttered hallways where they are greeted by teachers that know them by name. This is a place where students know they are valued and feel a sense of belonging." The plan stated its underlying principles, which read like a direct refutation of Hopkins: "All children are capable of reaching California state standards. Parents play a significant role in the academic life of their child. Small schools allow for a sense of community and a greater accountability for all involved." The small school would have eight classrooms of its own. A teacher named Julie McPhail, who was working on a master's degree focused on school reform, would be principal. And if the plan seemed bold, that, too, was in keeping with Meier's teachings; Meier was fond of saying that her group had not been handed autonomy, but had seized it.

The first months of 1998 were a time of excitement and possibility for the teachers and parents involved in the plan, which later took the name HOPE, for Helping Oakland Provide Excellence in Education. At first, working together with colleagues seemed simply a route to survival in a dysfunctional place. Soon, however, the small-school plan evolved into something greater: a well of joy and enthusiasm about creating something fresh, rather than being beaten down by an unwieldy, sad system. The teachers were especially enthused that the idea had been brought to them by parents, who in the past had seemed distant from their struggle. Likewise, for the parents, there was an air of new promise. Even Lillian Lopez's young son Alex enjoyed accompanying her to meetings, because he could see how happy it made her.

But the group faced some delicate, potentially explosive issues. The HOPE group had announced its meetings in the school bulletin, and invited all interested to join. All the same, its members comprised a special, golden minority within Jefferson, selected partly by their willingness and desire to participate, and partly by a word-of-mouth process of choosing good prospects. And therein lay a dirty secret. There were excellent teachers at Jefferson, but there was also plenty of deadwood—the lazies and the crazies, as some put it. The group had found it easy to avoid the bad teachers, who never showed up at after-school meetings anyway, but it was hard to deny that the small-schoolers were a self-anointed group of the best and brightest. This fact didn't sit well with faculty members who weren't included. Moreover, the HOPEsters were working on something new, which presumably meant the rest were stuck with the old. And if their plan succeeded, it would give them "autonomy," which meant, among other things, control of their curriculum and their budget—a power no other Oakland teachers enjoyed. In some areas, they demanded—as a separate school—to be directly answerable to the district, rather than to Hopkins. And perhaps most dangerous of all, numerous teachers feared the scheme to remove eight classrooms from the year-round plan might make overcrowding elsewhere on the campus even worse. Clearly, the small-schoolers would have to think carefully about how, and when, to explain their idea to their colleagues.

Matt Hammer applied community organizing wisdom: it's better to approach people one-to-one, or in handfuls, than in large groups. He and the teachers also reasoned that it would be better to present a finished plan than to publicize a work in progress. Some teachers also worried that if the plan got out too soon, a few heavies among the faculty might kill the idea in its infancy. And even when they held open meetings, the old-timers didn't attend. So the small-schoolers worked quietly, consulting regularly with Hopkins and with the district's top administrators. And they tried, in the hot-house atmosphere of the elementary school, to keep the plan shrouded. It was a giant miscalculation.

•   •   •

Wednesday, April 29, 1998, was the day the HOPE teachers chose to present their plan to the rest of the Jefferson faculty. It was a perfect Bay Area afternoon, continuing a run of warm and crisply sunny spring days that marked an end to the El Niño rains. Lillian Lopez, borrowing time from Wells Fargo, arrived just in time for the two P.M. meeting. After months of work on the plan, the group felt this was the right time, now that the idea had assumed shape and form. Moreover, some uninformed talk had been circulating; teachers outside the group had been spinning rumors about the new small school. In spite of the whispers, Lopez and the teachers anticipated offering a friendly introduction to an exciting new idea created by passionate parents and teachers. With some luck, Lopez figured, it would be received in the same spirit.

One look at Matt Hammer's face told her things were not going to go that way.

Hammer had just come from meeting with Hopkins, an assistant principal, and the leader of the HOPE teachers, Julie McPhail, in the principal's office. Now, uncharacteristically nervous and angry, Hammer strode up to Lopez. Leaning into her ear, he whispered, "I think Hopkins has backed down."

Indeed, as Hammer later explained, Hopkins had been remarkably direct. Previously, McPhail and the other teachers had believed he was on board with the plan to create a small school. But in their brief discussion that afternoon, Hopkins had stated simply that it wasn't going to happen at his school. McPhail, suddenly at sea, had suggested that the decision wasn't his to make. She noted that Terry Mazany, a former General Motors executive who was now the district's number two employee and reform guru, supported the small school. Hopkins was unfazed. "Fuck Terry Mazany," he had said. "Who the fuck is Terry Mazany? He's a businessman, not an educator."

In truth, Hopkins's efforts to undercut the small-school plan had begun days earlier, in conversations with teachers. He had made it clear that he believed it was not workable, and that the teachers behind it didn't have the experience to run a school. Yet, that day, despite what he had said to Hammer and McPhail, Hopkins made no move to take the plan off the meeting agenda. The discussion would go forward, but now it seemed tainted with a sense of preordained doom.

The meeting took place in a sunny, high-ceilinged classroom. By some unspoken plan, the fifty-one teachers and dozen visitors arranged themselves by allegiance. The small-school teachers settled into student desks up front. Parents who supported the new school stood in a line along one side. At the back of the room, the teachers most vehemently opposed also stood, along with high-ranking representatives from the teachers' union and the district. As she took her seat, McPhail was visibly red-faced with anger.

Lillian Lopez had figured that Hopkins would introduce the HOPE teachers and then step back so they could explain the plan. Instead, after some everyday agenda items, Hopkins took the stage, clad in white shirt, tie, and suspenders. Although an improbable spokesman, he—and not the HOPE teachers—would explain Meier's ideas.

"The model comes from a plan back east," he said, leaning back against a wall, with one foot propped on top of a chair. "What it talks about is how you take a large school and you build a smaller school within a school, and how the smaller school is more success-ful than the larger school." He conceded it was easy to assume that such a small school would be better, just as small classes were obviously better than large ones. But then he doubled back, seem-ingly mulling the ideas afresh as he spoke. "How do you take the larger folks and say, 'You're not as good as we are because we're smaller and we're better than you'?" he wondered. "Well, you don't. Because the larger may be better than the smaller."

Hopkins argued that the only thing that mattered was the teacher-student relationship, and that, he said, wouldn't change in a small school. "When you boil right down to it, you have a little box there," he said, referring to the classroom. He clasped his hands over the dangling end of his tie. "You put a teacher in the middle, and whether you believe it or not, that's where the education comes from. It doesn't come from the Jefferson that's around it"—he made a sweeping motion—"nor the Oakland Unified School District that's around that, nor the state of California."

It was true, Hopkins admitted, that the unity the small-schoolers were trying to create would make for better education. But he made those goals sound like an impossible fantasy, like hundred-dollar bills raining from the sky. Yes, children might learn better in a school where every student had mastered the material from the pre-vious grade, where parents all brought kids to school on time every day, and where teachers used logically sequenced lessons and simi-lar methods from one grade to the next. But he doubted a small school could guarantee those changes. "I think what the misconcept is, is that if you label it something different, or put an armband on us or wave a flag over my classroom and a couple other classrooms, all of a sudden it's going to make a whale of a lot of changes and kids are going to come out a lot better than they are presently being turned out," he said.

For Lopez and the rest of the OCO group, this was death. For months, they had believed Hopkins stood behind them. Now, how-ever, he was doing publicly what he had been doing privately—in his quiet and even amicable way, slashing the Achilles tendon of their plan. The small school had been Lopez's reason to believe something might change, and now it was slipping away. In an hour, she and Hammer were supposed to board a bus to the state capital, ironically to attend a rally for the building of new public schools. But she no longer cared about anything beyond Jefferson and the small school.

Hopkins did not invite the HOPEsters to defend their idea. Instead, he opened the floor to questions. A special-education teacher wanted to know whether this plan was a done deal; Hopkins suggested it wasn't, and that he would leave that choice to the staff. There were questions about how many students would attend the small school, and whether it would make up a full track in the year-round system. When a teacher asked whether this new program would get any extra money, Hopkins, remarkably, intimated that he had asked Mazany, the associate superintendent, for funds for the small school but got turned down. "I twisted his arm," Hopkins said. "The man gives me a great smile and says no. Which I would have expected. Because the first thing I'd ask him is, who are you taking the money away from, Terry, because I'm going to call them and tell them that. If you need a principal for one thing, it's to make sure no other principal gets more than you do." It was a telling moment; followers of Deborah Meier would have offered a very different view of a principal's purpose.

Lopez and Hammer watched the small-school plan crumbling, not just in Hopkins's hands, but also under the attack of the very teachers who labored under the sad conditions the idea was meant to change. But the veteran teachers had their reasons for fighting this new idea, and they gave angry voice to their views. For many of the old-timers, this latest reform notion—especially since it had the support of suits from the district office—recalled the countless problematic initiatives attempted, and abandoned, at Jefferson in the past. Others saw it as elitist, a potent charge in a system where equity was the watchword. For Sally Brook, a fifth- and sixth-grade teacher, this represented just another attempt at a burdensome, short-term solution that didn't require investing extra funds in the school. In loud and strident tones, she declared, "I think we're putting our energy in the wrong place. This doesn't make us a smaller school. We're still going to be overcrowded, with everybody roving. I'd rather see our energy going into doing something to get rid of the four tracks, to get us all on one track, and to get us smaller, get new schools built. And this is really neat: you don't have to put any funding into this"—she was shouting now—"but you can say wow, look at what we're doing, when you're not doing a damn thing."

Other teachers wanted to know whether such a school would truly be separate, and why Jefferson's money should fund the small school. McPhail tried to explain that these were Jefferson kids, and the money followed them—in this case, to be spent as the small school chose. But Hopkins had a different view. "You've only got one person here who's in charge, and that's me," he said. "The kids are here at Jefferson because they attend Jefferson school. If they attend the school within the school, they're attending Jefferson school." Therefore, he said, the money still belonged to Jefferson—and was his to dole out.

That view, which quashed any real notion of autonomy, was too much for a teacher in the small-school group named Pam Frick. She had been waiting at length to speak; now, she couldn't restrain herself. The original hope, she explained, was to have a school that was truly autonomous, and she felt the idea rested on logic and right. Her reedy voice rising steadily toward a shout, she told her fellow teachers, "The desire was to try and form a small group, experiment, and ultimately achieve something that we are all frustrated about: a better education for our children. The desire was never, never, to take anything away from anybody." The tax money, she reasoned, belonged not to the Oakland school district, but to the children.

Hopkins tried to calm her. Speaking as if to a small child, he said he had tried to avoid budget discussions because the teachers didn't have enough background to understand it. "Everybody in here, whether you're in a school within a school, or a state within a state, you're an employee of the Oakland Unified School District," Hopkins said. "The only way you can become autonomous is to quit the Oakland Unified School District and go join a ch—"

"That is not true!" Frick cut him off.

"Chill out," someone told her.

"You chill!" Frick shot back.

On the verge of despair, and late for the Sacramento rally, Lillian Lopez stood to speak for the first time. "I have a second grader here at Jefferson," she said. "I really don't have a lot of choices. This sounds to me like something that I would like for my child." She held up both her hands plaintively. "Just put yourself in my place. This is the neighborhood and the school where my child has to attend school. If there's something that's better, I want to try it."

"Why is it better?" a few teachers in the back asked in near-unison.

Lopez gestured with her right fist, as if literally hammering the point home. "Because it's smaller," she said simply. "And smaller is always better."

Hopkins remained unmoved. "Call it whatever you're going to call it—one thing will not change," he said, speaking slowly and with finality. "The kids are still the same kids coming from the neighborhoods. They're still going to be grouped in a little box. There'll be one teacher teaching. That's it." Looking briefly at Lopez, he confessed, "I understand what you're saying. You want something better for your child. We all want something better." However, he said, "This is not an ideal situation. But it's reality. I mean, it's urban education."

•　•　•

For Lillian Lopez, the Jefferson small-school plan died that day, and she expressed her dismay vividly. "Nine months of work," she said, "and there was no climax."

In the days following that painful afternoon, Lopez and Hammer agreed with Hopkins that they would meet in his office to figure out what might be salvaged of the small-school plan. Hopkins missed the meeting. They rescheduled, and Hopkins missed that meeting, too. Lopez was despondent—worse, even, than she had been before they started talking about a new school.

Yet as they sat in the school office, humiliated by Hopkins's absence, Hammer offered a new hope. He wondered if they could open their own, truly autonomous public school—without the so-called help of Hopkins and the district. "Maybe," he said, "we should start looking at this new charter school law."

It was only days later that Hammer got a call from one of his fellow organizers. There was a company in San Diego that helped inner-city parents form charter schools, and a representative wondered whether OCO would like to schedule a meeting.

For Lillian Lopez, it was a sure sign that God's guiding hand was still with them.

Chapter 2

The Taste of Hope

Matt Hammer was an alchemist who took frustration and made fuel for the engines of change. Where others saw defeat in the Jefferson small-school fiasco, he saw opportunity. When Mike Hopkins showed the OCO parents the door, Hammer counted the setback as a battle lost in a war that could be won. He knew, though, that before the parents' anger dissipated, he must harness it.

The battle plan—the idea for revolt by way of charter—arrived in the form of a miraculously timely phone call from Scott Reed, the assistant director of OCO's parent network, the Pacific Institute of Community Organizations. One of Reed's friends, Brian Bennett, a longtime Catholic-school principal and a lawyer, had left his school to become operations chief for the School Futures Research Foundation, a young nonprofit that was starting urban charter schools.

Now, in June 1998, a month and a half after the rigged contest at Jefferson, Bennett had come to Oakland to make his pitch. Around the square Formica table in OCO's dim, dowdy conference room, fifteen parents—including Lillian Lopez—sat riveted to his presentation. For the first time, Hammer thought, someone was telling them the truth.

Bennett was a slight, energetic white man with graying hair, glasses, and a constant smile. Despite the sober nature of his subjects, he talked like a favorite uncle telling stories at a weekend barbecue. Humble and sincere, he accorded the parents honor and dignity. The effect was powerful; the parents, charmed, listened well.

Bennett offered a painfully vivid illustration of the ties among race, wealth, and education in America. He asked the parents to imagine three sets of a hundred kindergartners—one group white, one black, and one Latino. Among the hundred white children, ninety-three would complete high school, while only eighty-six of the blacks and sixty-one of the Latinos would graduate. In college, the numbers turned even starker. Of the original one hundred white children, twenty-nine would earn bachelor's degrees, compared to a scant fifteen blacks and ten Latinos. If the slicing was done by income rather than race, the picture was still more discouraging: among a hundred high-income kindergartners, forty-eight would finish college, while from a hundred low-income kids, only seven would graduate. That gap, Bennett said, had been closing until recently. In the last few years, however, the progress had stopped, and by some measures even reversed.

Poor black and brown kids performed worse in school, Bennett argued, because the system gave them less. Kids in impoverished areas like Oakland were less likely to have adequate class materials and properly trained teachers. Their schools were less likely to enroll them in challenging classes, more likely to assign fill-in-the-blank worksheets, more likely to use computers for rote "drill-and-kill" practice than for programs that demand creative thought. But when the system provided good teachers and demanding courses, Bennett said, such students thrived.

Hammer had struggled for two years to expose the inequities in the education landscape. Only after seeing the full picture, he reasoned, would the parents challenge a school system they had been taught to respect. Bennett had the numbers to prove the point. Hammer was thrilled; the lawyer from San Diego was speaking his language. Bennett's message was the kind that starts revolutions: by rationing good schooling, America was denying its poor children hope.

In the manner of a skilled salesman, Bennett had convinced the parents of the problem. Now, he offered the solution. Parents, he argued, should take control by creating their own schools—with some help from his company, the School Futures Research Foundation. School Futures would open charter schools, which, he explained, were independent public schools that ran on taxpayer dollars. Charter schools had to accept any child without charging tuition, like other public schools. They were barred from teaching religion, but could choose teachers who would provide a strong moral foundation. The school would answer to the parents who had established it, not to a distant, impersonal school board. Aside from a few basic safety regulations, it would be up to the founders to draft the charter school's rules, and to define its standards of success. "The power of it," Bennett said, "is that the community can set the vision for the school, set the educational outcomes, and control the selection of the principal and teachers." Bennett hastened to add that School Futures—unlike Edison and other for-profit charter organizations—wasn't aiming to make money. A nonprofit organization, School Futures brought funds from billionaire John Walton to develop schools, and its own expertise to operate them.

Hammer and handful of others at OCO knew about the Walton connection, and it worried them. Walton was one of four heirs to the fortune of his father, Sam Walton, who had created Wal-Mart, the biggest retailer in America. Hammer dissected political motives for a living, and the name Walton stirred no love in his heart. In the rural South, where Hammer had cut his teeth as an organizer, predatory Wal-Mart expansion had busted unions and driven local stores to ruin. Walton's conservative politics also sparked concern; Hammer carried the progressive banner proudly, if quietly. Both his parents had worked as liberal neighborhood activists, and his mother had served as mayor of San Jose. Walton championed causes that disgusted progressives. He had supported education vouchers, which some OCO activists viewed as an attempt to destroy public schooling. Walton also had pushed ballot initiatives aimed at limiting union influence. In OCO's alliances with labor and with teachers, Walton could easily prove an uncomfortable bedfellow.

On the other hand, Bennett had put on the table a fine feast for the starving: the promise of high-performance schools, up and running in mere months. Hammer had evidence that School Futures knew how to achieve such a feat. A week earlier, he had visited School Futures' only school in Northern California, and had been thoroughly impressed. The school, located in East Palo Alto—a frayed little city recently known as America's murder capital—was like nothing Hammer had seen in the Oakland flatlands. Every student appeared engaged; the campus enjoyed peace and order; vibrant teachers taught challenging lessons. The principal was energetic and smart, and teachers were unified around a coherent course of study. Hammer wanted schools like that in Oakland. Moreover, Bennett's offer matched neatly with OCO's goals. It would answer the leaders' cries for better schools. It would fulfill OCO's promise of reform through small, autonomous schools. It would vault OCO from its current weakness in education, following the Jefferson defeat, to formidable power over the district, by demonstrating that if the district didn't give the parents what they wanted, they would walk out and form their own schools. That threat was particularly potent because as each child departed for a charter school, the district would lose that much per-student funding. And Hammer reckoned that OCO could keep building new schools until the district paid attention. The decision whether to join forces with School Futures was not Hammer's to make; as an organizer, he would bow to the parents' choice. But he was very excited.

When Bennett had finished his presentation, several members of the group—notably the nonparents—fired tough questions at him. Who would control the school? How much say would the parents and community have in designing and running it? Who would choose the principal? Much of the questioning came from the activists in the crowd, who pounced immediately on the Walton connection. They asked about vouchers, casting the charter schools as a conservative conspiracy to pave the way for a voucher assault on public education. They asked about Walton's involvement in anti-union political gambits, funded by a nonunion store chain. Bennett took the questions head-on. Yes, Walton had funded campaigns for vouchers; yes, he had given millions for privately funded vouchers called opportunity scholarships. Yes, he had contributed to a California ballot initiative that limited political influence for unions. But, Bennett argued, it was tough work to get an inner-city charter school approved. If Walton's real motivation were to attack public schooling, there would have been easier ways. And as for the running of the school, Bennett promised, parents and community members would wield considerable power, through a board where OCO and School Futures would cast equal votes.

At the meeting's end, the OCO group told Bennett that they would let him know their decision soon. They wanted to discuss the matter privately.

Lillian Lopez was angry, and she wasn't the only one.

Brian Bennett was offering the thing that she, and the other parents in the room, wanted most. The grilling he'd received at the hands of OCO's nonparent leaders, about Walton and politics and such, might drive him out of town. Surely, she figured, he would find more receptive audiences elsewhere, and Oakland would lose School Futures.

During the "debrief" session following Bennett's presentation, a tense mood hung in the room. The clergy and the activist types didn't like Walton's politics, and they wondered whether Bennett could deliver on his ambitious promises. Lopez and the other parents had little patience for political niceties, and even if they weren't certain his plan would succeed, they were sure that the status quo wasn't working. Lopez felt that people were raising objections just to raise them. Finally, she spoke up.

"I come from a parent's perspective, and I don't care where this guy comes from," she said, her voice telegraphing her frustration. "I like what I heard. This sounds good to me, because I have a child that needs to be educated. I wish everybody could put this stuff aside and think about the kids." She glanced at Hammer, hoping he would support her, but he kept his silence.

Nothing was resolved when the meeting broke up, and Lopez

knew that she had irritated many of the other leaders with her bitter outburst. That night, her thoughts whirled in worry that the group's hostility had frightened Bennett away. As a sleepless night wore on, she pondered calling him and inviting him back to Oakland to pursue the charter plan, even without checking with Hammer. The OCO members had been groping for consensus, and if they continued to dither, they might lose Bennett.

The next morning, she phoned Bennett. He was still interested. Relieved, she invited him back to Oakland. Then she called Matt Hammer and announced, "Guess what I did!"

In the week that followed, OCO leaders consulted with parents at their various member churches. Despite the political and practical concerns of the activists and the clergy, the parents were hungry. Lopez was determined to create a charter school—with or without OCO. A similar determination had swept through the other parents who had heard Bennett's presentation, and who now displayed a desire for urgent action.

Their willingness to defy the system was no small matter. Many of the parents had grown up in Mexico, where they had been taught from earliest childhood that challenging the schoolmaster was just short of a sin. In America, they were further discouraged by anti-immigrant sentiment from making too much noise. But the depth and durability of the problem had reinforced Hammer's efforts. Schools like Jefferson and Castlemont served as convenient examples of the problems Bennett had highlighted so vividly—a scourge that infected poor communities, urban and rural, throughout the country. In that sense, Oakland didn't differ much from Detroit, Atlanta, Philadelphia, Washington, D.C., or dozens of other great cities whose public schools were distinctly less than great.

These inequities had fueled the hunger, the anger, of the OCO parents. Few missed the middle-fingered message sent by the physical appearance of the campuses—cracked expanses of asphalt with aging portables in the grittiest flats; cozy acres lush with grass and blossoms in the hills. Hammer had helped the parents to see that the inequities went further, encompassing academic performance. He had shown them that the performance of the hills schools dwarfed the scores at Jefferson. A survey of district-wide statistics exposed a situation that provoked still greater outrage. For instance: the longer a child attended the Oakland public schools, the further he or she slipped behind. Among Oakland's second graders, 69 percent could read at the national average. By fifth grade, that figure declined to 50 percent. By eighth, it was 29 percent. And by tenth grade, a dismal 20 percent. Algebra was required for graduation, but most of Oakland's students were failing. For African-American students, who made up 52 percent of the district, the average high school grade was a hair above D-plus. The district, which enrolled fifty-four thousand children, was handing out more than 10,000 suspensions a year, a number that included 381 suspensions of kindergartners and first and second graders. African-American children accounted for 72 percent of suspensions, and for a similar proportion of special-education classes—notorious as sidelines on which there was little hope of rigorous schooling.

Throughout America's inner cities, the troubling numbers differed only in their details. They smeared what was otherwise a fairly happy report card for American education in the twentieth century. As the OCO parents had learned from Debbie Meier's book, American education had adapted significantly to the sunset of an industrial and agricultural era, when the nation had seen little need for an advanced education for most children. Yet now, despite victories in expanding the reach of schooling, a stubborn gap separated educational haves and have-nots—a gap closely associated with race and income. And that gap did not exist by happenstance.

It was not until "just yesterday," as Meier put it, that American schools had taken on the unprecedented task of providing a competitive education to all students, regardless of race and wealth. For much of the century, Oakland, like the rest of America, had attempted nothing of the kind. Indeed, the nation's school systems had worked vigorously to cull the college-bound few from the many headed to factories and fields. Oakland's school system eagerly adopted the notion of dividing those with the capacity for an academic future from their duller classmates. Around the end of World War I, the district's research director, Virgil Dickson, administered "mental tests" to some thirty thousand children, and wrote that the tests "prove conclusively that the proportion of failures due chiefly to mental inferiority is nearer 90 percent than 50 percent."[6] The trick, Dickson added, was to "find the mental ability of the pupil and place him where he belongs," namely in one of five distinct academic tracks. (Other school systems later refined that to ten tracks or more.) Dickson wrote that removing the slower kids from "the regular classes relieves both the teacher and the class of a great weight." And his system as a whole, he argued, "is more democratic than former systems because it offers to every child a freer opportunity to use his full capacity."

In crafting such efficiency, Dickson was early into a movement that swept American school systems. The new way of thinking emanated from the nation's great universities, where experts sought to lay rational foundations for the major city school systems of the future. One of the most influential thinkers was Elwood Cubberley, an education professor at Stanford University, across the San Francisco Bay from Oakland. In his effort to devise the most "efficient" system, Cubberley brooked no illusions about what such changes meant. In 1918, he wrote that urban schools should "give up the exceedingly democratic idea that all are equal, and that our society is devoid of classes." And indeed, Oakland's scheme to cull the mentally inferior also separated the poor from the rich.[7] Oakland's school chiefs were thrilled with such division by mental testing, pronouncing it "the most important factor in effective educational administration that has been introduced in recent years."

At the time, people did not speak in terms of dropout rates, let alone equity of opportunity. Indeed, the district was admired for its efficiency in directing so many children into vocational rather than academic programs. Back then, Oakland, a bustling hub of rail, sea, and truck traffic, teemed with low-skilled and semi-skilled jobs. Later, in World War II, shipbuilding at Oakland's port attained such a frenetic pace that manufacturing magnate Henry J. Kaiser handed out rail tickets to would-be workers all over the country. Now, though, the trades that had pumped lifeblood into Oakland and so many other inner cities—automobile manufacturing, shipbuilding, and the like—were gone, the jobs obliterated by machines or cheaper labor overseas. Oakland didn't build ships anymore, and no one particularly noticed the trains. Now, a large proportion of jobs required a high school education, or better. Even the Oakland Police Department demanded four years of college for officer recruits, a sharp change in what had once been a gainful profession for high school graduates.

Yet urban education systems had not met the challenge of crafting a single track, with academic achievement for all. Indeed, the Oakland district still simultaneously operated some of California's best- and worst-performing schools. A state rating system, which scored schools on a one-to-ten scale, awarded three schools in Oakland—all in the richest, whitest hill neighborhoods—a perfect ten, even compared to other schools for the rich. Six schools, in black and Latino neighborhoods of deep poverty, scored a one, even compared to other schools for the poor. Alarmed by the gap, Delaine Eastin, the state schools superintendent, declared that the Oakland scores "raise issues of civil rights."

The current ed-school buzz phrase held that schools would educate "all the children" at high levels. The statement hinted at a yawning crevasse in American education. In the suburbs, schools were, by and large, meeting the modern needs of their students. To be sure, academics argued—rightly—that students weren't working hard enough and weren't being held to high enough standards. But still, they were able to find jobs that provided for comfortable lives, and suburbanites for the most part pronounced themselves satisfied with their schools. In the inner city, the picture was appallingly different. In New York, for example, only 7 percent of employers believed that students from the city's public schools had the skills to succeed in the workplace. In places like Oakland, likewise, the situation still bore a distressing resemblance to the days of Virgil Dickson, when so many poor children were deemed unready for the rigors of a real education.

How to correct the situation, on the small scale and on the quick, was the question that confronted Matt Hammer. Meier, in her book, condemned resorting to alliances with groups like School Futures. "Taking the existing school system and turning it over to private managers," she wrote, was a mistake for many reasons, including the poor record of competition in schooling. Hammer, however, didn't have the luxury of pondering that irony. The parents wanted to move.

On June 22, a week after the original meeting with School Futures, a large crowd of parents collected in the OCO office to talk to Brian Bennett. Once again, the crowd peppered him with tough questions, and once again, he handled them directly and easily:

> QUESTION: Whose school will this be? Will it belong to School Futures or to the community?
>
> ANSWER: It will be your school, the community's school.
>
> QUESTION: What happens if School Futures leaves?
>
> ANSWER: We won't leave. If we do, we will give your children vouchers to go to private school.
>
> QUESTION: Will you kick out problem kids?
>
> ANSWER: No.
>
> QUESTION: What happens if parents are dissatisfied with School Futures?
>
> ANSWER: You can ask us to leave and we'll leave.

This time, when the OCO group met in private, the parents would brook no more resistance. "We're satisfied," said one. "So please."

It was done. With help from the parents, Matt Hammer began to search for buildings that might house these new schools. Brian Bennett, meanwhile, met with groups of OCO parents in various parts of town, interviewing them about their hopes and visions for their children's schooling. From those conversations he would draw forth a charter, the written constitution for these brave little schools of their dreams.

•   •   •

William Stewart didn't ask all that much from a school.

Stewart had two daughters—one an adult and the other an eight-year-old third grader named Malory. He loved his young daughter tenderly, but entertained few illusions; to him, she was not brilliant, just average. What he wanted for her was simple and ordinary: a classroom with order and civility. A place where the teacher was in charge and the students listened, where third graders learned third-grade material. He had no desire and no plans, at the time, to join a schooling revolution. All he wanted for her was a decent education.

On this afternoon in late September 1998, Stewart stood silently inside her classroom, with its tiny chairs and its broad windows that faced the faraway hills. As he watched what passed for a lesson, he knew his daughter wasn't getting a decent education.

He was visiting Malory's school, Whittier Year-Round Elementary deep in the East Oakland flatlands, to check in and help out. He had always played the role of the involved parent, and all the more since his wife's death five years earlier. On disability relief following a work injury, he had plenty of time to spend at Malory's school.

Soft-spoken and generous, William Stewart was comfortable around people of ranks high and low. A beefy man with a round face and a quick smile, he hewed to a strong moral code that, in his language, sounded like plain common sense. He was not afraid to demand what he knew to be right, particularly regarding children— and especially his young daughter. Through that struggle, William Stewart ended up a foot soldier in the charter school battle.

Stewart had grown increasingly worried since the opening of school that year. More than a week into the school year, Malory's teacher, Ms. Cowan, still had not shown up. It turned out Ms. Cowan, a brand-new teacher with an "emergency credential," had not known about the year-round schedule when she planned her honeymoon. A string of substitutes stood in, but proved unable to control the class. Now, with the school year ten days old, Stewart strolled onto the blacktop playground at the end of afternoon recess. He found the class in the shaky hands of yet another young teacher who could not get the children lined up to go inside. After the teacher finally managed to usher the students to the classroom, Stewart stopped in the office to ask when the fabled Ms. Cowan would return.

"That's her," one of the secretaries said. "She's back. She just called the office for help. Maybe you can go in there and help her."

Stewart, upset, strode into the class, introduced himself to Ms. Cowan, and surveyed the room. There was garbage strewn on the floor. Ms. Cowan was trying to teach a lesson, but only a handful of children even pretended to pay attention. Some wandered about the room, chatting and taking stuff from each other. The teacher seemed focused on the noisiest ones, so for a while, Stewart helped the ones who were working. As the end of the day approached, he picked up a broom and swept up, all the while studying the class. The teacher, still struggling to win cooperation from her eight-year-old antagonists, promised pencils as a reward for good citizenship. Malory's table fell silent, folding their hands, but at the other tables, chatter continued. Stewart feared that soon, Malory would tire of trinket rewards and start to act like her classmates. He plunged deeper into despair. At day's end, he climbed onto his mountain bike for the short ride back to his house. As he rode home, he began to cry.

His tears flowed from frustration as much as from sadness. In his search for a decent education for Malory, he felt stymied. She had spent two good years—kindergarten and first grade—at a private church school, the Hope Academy, a fine, strict place with small classes. The school, which was connected to the Center of Hope Community Church, lavished on Malory the kind of attention Stewart felt she needed after the loss of her mother. But she had few friends there, and in the absence of her mother, he believed Malory ought to have more companions her age. Her cousins, who lived next door, attended Whittier, and she wanted to go with them. As long as her grades stayed high, he decided, she could enroll there.

At the beginning of her second-grade year, he transferred her to Whittier.

The move to the neighborhood public school proved a depressing mistake. Malory's second-grade teacher seemed convinced that the children's home lives rendered them useless in the classroom. When Stewart visited, the teacher would demonstrate her point by asking for a show of hands from those who had completed their homework. When few hands shot up, she would complain about the students' lousy parents. Whittier wasn't pushing Malory to learn, Stewart decided. He suspected that the teachers, too accustomed to their high-poverty neighborhood, expected little from their students. They were simply baby-sitting. But by the time second grade was over, Malory could not switch back to Hope. The school had gone bankrupt and shut down.

When Stewart was a kid, it had been possible to get a solid education in this neighborhood. Born in Baton Rouge, Louisiana, in 1957, he had come to Oakland as an infant. It was a common story for African Americans, who had moved in great waves from an impoverished South to search for opportunity in California. Oakland, which burgeoned as one of the nation's great railroad hubs in the nineteenth century, had a tiny but stable African-American population well through the early twentieth century. During World War II, though, Oakland's black population surged from less than 3 percent of the city in 1940 to more than 12 percent in 1950. Yet the following decade—the one that brought infant William Stewart—marked an even larger rise; by 1960, African Americans constituted almost a quarter of the city. Eventually, that proportion would grow to nearly half the city's inhabitants. But the combination of migration and the slowing of industry was to set the stage for the poverty that surrounded Stewart as an adult. After the war boom ended, families kept arriving for jobs that no longer existed. In 1950, the black unemployment rate in Oakland hit 19.8 percent. Three decades later, it remained above 13 percent—and that counted only the people still actively looking for work.

For William Stewart, as a child back in Baton Rouge, discipline meant a lick from a yardstick or from an automobile fan belt. The schools in Oakland where he spent most of the early grades, less than a mile from where he now lived, maintained a similar code of discipline. A young and conscientious William avoided the smack of the paddle himself, and earned respectable grades. In high school, though, he discovered with some shock that there was no one to reprimand him if he slacked off. Stewart went on to Castlemont High, in the flatlands near the eastern border of Oakland. A 99 percent black school in 1972, Castlemont had been an integrated, mostly white institution a decade earlier. White students, however, had fled in a dramatic exodus after the building of the affluent Skyline High.

At Castlemont, there was plenty to distract Stewart from his studies. He was no athlete—he had been hobbled by tumors in his knees—but he was popular, and handy with cars. As a tenth grader, though, he watched friends sleeping through class. If he wanted an education, he realized, it was up to him to pursue it. The teachers might help, but they would not force students to study. Moreover, Stewart had to ration his hours. He had moved out of the family home, and was working full-time to support himself, first at a filling station and then at a car wash. Nonetheless, he managed to graduate in 1975. Through a series of jobs that revolved around cars, he worked himself up from cleaning them at a dealership to building them at the General Motors plant in the nearby city of Fremont.

Had the course of American business proceeded differently, Stewart might have ended up as a well-salaried manager at that plant. Instead, in 1982, GM shut the factory down. The corporation offered him another job—in St. Louis. But by then, he had more to think about than just his own career.

A few years earlier, Stewart had fallen in love. Her name was Brenda Faye Mitchell. Circumstance contrived against them at first: he had fathered his daughter with another woman, and although that relationship was failing, they were still together. But love has little respect for circumstance. Stewart had first met Mitchell in high school, but he didn't spend serious time with her until years later. When he did, something felt natural and right; he left his then-girlfriend and wooed Mitchell. He had that rare combination of money and free time, thanks to the generous GM severance package. Stewart and Mitchell went skiing—a sport Stewart loved, even if he was the only black man on the slope—and dined to the strains of live jazz. She was a few years older, and he enjoyed her sophistication, her maturity, her beauty, and her generosity of spirit. He told himself he didn't mind too much that she didn't want to have a child. And when she warned him that she had a serious, chronic illness called sarcoidosis, he didn't pay much attention to that, either. If she hesitated on the ski runs to catch her breath, he was happy to wait for her. In 1983, a year after the GM shutdown, they traveled to Hawaii with another couple and celebrated a double wedding. Brenda—now Brenda Stewart—worked at the phone company, a job that paid better than his own, so there was little talk of relocating with GM. He lived on that income, and unemployment insurance, and eventually started a carpet-cleaning business, with limited success.

In 1989 he landed a job in the warehouse of Emporium Capwell, a department store in Oakland's sleepy downtown. The store sat amid monuments to what the city had once been: the ornate Paramount Theater, now usually dark; the grand Rotunda building, by then used only as a backdrop for television dramas; and the sixty-year-old Sears Roebuck store, which soon would close its doors, too. Although he liked his new job, his home life had turned sour. After a series of arguments, Brenda moved out and cut off communication. Her lawyer told Stewart that she wanted her share of the house they had bought together. Finally, in desperation, he phoned her at work. She asked if he was sitting down. The question filled him with dread, but what she said next turned his fear to joy. She was pregnant.

He persuaded her to see him, and soon they reunited. At the time he did not see a connection between her sarcoidoisis, an inflammatory disease which attacked her lungs, and her desire not to have a child. As the delivery date approached, he teased her that if the child was born during the Super Bowl, she would have to go to the hospital alone. Brenda went into labor during the pregame show, and Stewart watched the game at the hospital. Malory was born on Super Bowl Sunday, 1991.

Despite the joys of fatherhood, Stewart's time at Emporium—the only department store left in Oakland's now-sleepy downtown—soon came to resemble GM all over again. He worked harder than most, earned a promotion, impressed the top managers, was on track to become one himself. Fate's knife mangled his plans again. In 1993 he slipped in hydraulic fluid, cracked a vertebra, and tore his shoulder, an injury that required surgery. While he was out recovering, Emporium got swallowed in the decade's merger fervor. Federated Department Stores, which owned Macy's and Bloomingdale's, acquired Emporium and shut it down. By law, since Stewart's old job would no longer exist when he recovered, the company had to train him for a new one. He opted to take classes to become a real estate appraiser.

It was then that his wife's long-frail health suddenly took a turn for the worse.

Brenda's condition had been degenerating over the years, and she had been using oxygen at home for some time. On April 15, 1994—Stewart's thirty-seventh birthday—a sudden downturn sent her to the hospital. Although her doctors tried to describe to him the seriousness of her condition, Stewart vowed that she would recover. As he sat by her bed, he dimly remembered that the deadline to begin the real estate classes was passing.

A month later, his wife was dead. Stewart had no direction, no reality. He had spent more than a third of his lifetime with one woman. Fourteen years had slipped away since he fell in love with her, ten since they made their sacred promise to stand by each other, in sickness and in health. Now, jobless, hopeless, and hobbled, he fed and clothed their daughter by cashing his wife's life insurance checks. Eventually, he applied for a job with the city, reasoning that it was one business that wouldn't succumb to the vagaries of the marketplace. He took the test to become an "animal control officer"—a dogcatcher. One of 350 people applying for three jobs, he came in seventh.

By 1995, when the time came for Malory to start school, the days of educational opportunity had left the neighborhood, in Stewart's view. His alma mater, Castlemont, was just one symbol of Oakland's inability to teach its children. Yet, through this barren landscape,

Stewart persevered, seeking a good school for Malory. Dismayed by the public schools, Stewart enrolled her at the private Hope Academy. He found some solace playing the role of traditional father to neighborhood children. He piled kids into his truck and took them to Oakland A's games or fishing in the Napa Valley. After one of his trips, as he was unloading the truck in his driveway, a pair of Mormon missionaries approached him. For reasons he was never able to explain, he invited them into his home, and then into his life. Before long, he was baptized. The color returned to his world. He began dating again. After two years at Hope, he switched Malory to Whittier, and volunteered regularly there.

The experience, however, was a catalog of frustrations. Stewart attended parent meetings, which were held during the workday, a fact he considered foolish, because the timing barred anyone with a job. He accounted for about a third of the attendance. There were many complaints and lots of discussion, but nothing ever seemed to get done. Searching for a way to offer concrete contributions, Stewart tried to use his handyman's skills to fix up the small, aging campus, which somehow crammed in more than seven hundred children. A plaque still hung in the main hallway honoring the school board that had "reconstructed" Whittier in 1957. Stewart offered to patch the potholes in the blacktop playground, which turned into slippery hazards when they filled with rainwater. The bureaucracy never approved the project, which would have violated union regulations.

Then a new principal, Yolanda Carrillo, arrived, determined to clean up a school where, in her view, many teachers set their own hours and did little work. Mass defections ensued; among the thirty-four teachers at Whittier, thirteen quit when Carrillo accepted the job. For Stewart, a bad school had gotten worse: it now had a staff roster full of holes.

All his effort had not won a decent classroom for his daughter. As he rode his bicycle, and cried, Stewart tried to think of a way around the problem. The woman Stewart was dating had found space for her child at a public school in the hills, where scores were high. Perhaps, he thought, he could enroll Malory there. Another part of him, though, recoiled at the thought of driving miles into a rich part of town to find an acceptable classroom. Why, as a citizen and tax-payer, could he not have that in his neighborhood school?

He arrived home, but it wasn't long before he mounted his bicycle again.

He was headed for Yolanda Carrillo's office. He was determined that the matter would be resolved today. Now.

It was 4:30 in the afternoon when William Stewart parked his bike and walked into the office at Whittier Year-Round Elementary. He accosted the principal and wasted no time making his business known.

"Look," he said. "The kids is disruptive. The teacher does not have control of the kids in the classroom. They're not getting an education." He wanted shock treatment. He wanted the teacher to go home, call the parents of the misbehaving kids, and tell them the children would not be allowed back until the parents showed up to take some responsibility.

"All you gotta do is call these kids' parents around seven o'clock and let them know what their kids are doing," he said.

Although sympathetic, Carrillo could not answer his urgency. She had no quick fixes. None of the other third-grade classrooms were any better, she said.

The visit to the principal only magnified Stewart's frustration. He would not get anywhere, he concluded, as one man against the system.

He had been impressed, however, by OCO's achievements. The progress he had seen involved small matters—speed bumps, meetings with neighborhood cops. Nonetheless, OCO was getting results. The system paid attention to OCO.

Matt Hammer had recruited Stewart during the summer to do some work on OCO's school effort. Stewart's combination of free time and interest had made him an appealing target for Hammer's organizing efforts. Stewart liked the fact that, rather than simply complaining and protesting, OCO was pushing actual solutions. He hadn't paid much attention to the discussions of charter schools, hadn't attended those meetings. But he had noticed the way OCO had confronted the overcrowding and the hugely unpopular year-round schedule at schools like Whittier. OCO kept talking about a campaign to develop small schools, though. Stewart longed for more immediate solutions.

Indeed, Stewart wasn't thrilled with OCO's approach to school change. OCO had been talking a lot about trying to replicate a schooling scheme from New York City. The coalition was even planning a trip there to see these wonderful small schools. Stewart felt Oakland could grow its own solutions, but he didn't have a lot of other options. One way or another, he was going to get Malory out.

That passion led him, later that year, to rise up as a sudden spokesman for OCO's school effort. At an OCO press conference at Whittier, Stewart—who had intended simply to sit in the audience—stood to talk about his daughter's situation. Calmly and plaintively, but in a voice rough with emotion, he told the assembled officials and reporters that his daughter was receiving A's and B's, but he knew the grades were worthless. He had visited the class, inspected the homework. The lessons, on the sounds that letters make, for example, were painfully basic—Malory had done them two years earlier at the Hope Academy. "You're setting her up where she's in fourth grade, they're going to say she's not prepared," he said. "I'm not saying she's bright or anything—but doing the *o* sound, she's past that." The journalists pointed cameras, jotted in notebooks, asked him later for the spelling of his name.

After the press conference, a school staffer pulled Stewart aside. Whittier did have a better class for Malory after all, she said.

•   •   •

By fall OCO's scheme to perform heart defibrillation on Oakland's school was looking increasingly real. The Debbie Meier–inspired small-schools idea hadn't died at Jefferson after all. Meanwhile, the fast-track charter school offer from School Futures was generating growing excitement. Brian Bennett met with several groups of parents, and got an enthusiastic go-ahead from each. Those groups then provided ideas that Bennett would forge into the language of a written charter proposal, eventually to be presented to the school board. The district superintendent, Carole Quan, continued to offer OCO's leaders a bizarre, maddening reception when they sat with her to talk about charters and small schools, still acting as if she had never heard about their plan before. The beauty of the charter plan, though, was that they wouldn't need her anymore. The charter would go before the school board, and if it was approved, Quan could not stop them. One way or another, OCO would create some small schools, soon.

In November 1998, at the height of the excitement, OCO won a grant to travel to New York City, the mecca of the small-schools movement. It was there, in Harlem, that Meier had founded the legendary Central Park East in 1973. There, too, a host of other small, innovative schools had sprouted up from the cracks of the asphalt laid by the nation's largest education bureaucracy. Hammer planned a two-day visit, with an itinerary that included a few of New York's best small schools. Master of ceremonies was Sy Fliegel, the onetime chief of alternative schools in New York's District Four who had overseen the creation of Central Park East and a litter of lesser-known innovative small schools. (As those schools took hold, District Four climbed from the city's worst-ranked district to fifteenth out of thirty-two, and violence and truancy fell, as Fliegel detailed in his book *Miracle in East Harlem.*) Carlos Medina, who had served as District Four's superintendent, acted as tour guide. The grant, from the Donner Foundation, provided for more than a dozen people to go, including Lillian Lopez; a teacher from the Jefferson HOPE group named Chelsea Toller; and a sweet but fiercely determined grandmother named Mayola Lewis. OCO also convinced some of the Oakland school district's heavyweights to board the plane: two members of the school board, Dan Siegel and Bob Spencer; the district's curriculum chief, Yolanda Peeks; and one principal, Yolanda Carrillo. In a sign that OCO's little project was indeed a big deal,

Noel Cisneros, a talented reporter from NBC's Bay Area affiliate, agreed to tag along, accompanied by a camera crew.

November 16 was a drizzly, cool autumn day in Manhattan, and the Oaklanders bundled against temperatures that, back home, came only in the coldest parts of winter. At the Central Park East high school, articulate youngsters guided the tour. They spoke about how, rather than working for standardized test scores, they focused on projects and "portfolios" that would demonstrate their readiness to graduate. Yet the visit to this touchstone of small schools and progressive education was, for most of the Oaklanders, underwhelming. True, a couple of teachers in the group liked the school's freedom and found the classes challenging. But the parents saw chaos. They didn't need to leave Oakland to visit schools that lacked structure, where kids roamed the halls without evident purpose. In the van after the visit, Lopez argued with one of the Oakland teachers, because she felt the school was too laid-back. Dan Siegel, the school board member, might have been expected to be the most tolerant in the group, for he carried the most impressive liberal credentials. As a hippie student at Berkeley a quarter century earlier, he had shouted the legendary call to occupy People's Park. Yet even he grumbled about the teachers dressed, unprofessionally, in jeans. To judge from the hallway bedlam, he said, he might have been touring Castlemont.

But the next stop, across town on the Upper West Side, captured many of the dreams the parents had brought with them on the long plane trip. The Manhattan School for Children had been founded by neighborhood parents, and occupied the top floor of Public School 165. MSC welcomed its families with a warmth that was utterly, sadly foreign to the Oakland parents. Just past the main entrance was a comfortable sitting area where a large pot of coffee was brewing. Lillian Lopez had never been inside a school where, without asking anyone's permission, she could help herself to a cup of coffee. Neither had Mayola Lewis, who had shepherded two generations of children through the Oakland schools, and now was raising a grandson who attended Castlemont. Susan Rappaport, the principal, invited them inside. The group toured the bright, spacious classrooms, each peopled by students of a striking mix of races and income levels. That diversity was a bragging point for MSC—a public school where, unlike in Oakland, the poor and the wealthy sat side-by-side.

Lopez noticed signs of parents' care; fresh flowers graced the rest room—a painfully sharp contrast to the trashed bathrooms that so galled parents in Oakland. Such touches made it easy to understand how a public school like this, while serving many poor families, also attracted the middle class. Here, the measures of success included the impressive breadth of enrollment.

Rappaport held a Q-and-A session in the school library, remarking on the difficult times in the school's first year. The pain of the defeat at Jefferson still fresh in her mind, Lopez asked the first question. "What enabled you to make it through that? What was the factor for success? That all that resistance didn't bring you down?" Rappaport gestured with both hands to punctuate her earnest reply. "The thing that has made us successful is everything that makes our school very special," she said. Lopez listened intently, chin on hand. "It's a sense of community. For us, community quickly translates to the word *family*."

A few minutes later, Lopez looked in on a class immersed in a stimulating discussion of geometry. The teacher asked where a line segment began.

"There's no definite starting place," answered a girl named Melanie.

"It can be anywhere you want it to be?" challenged the teacher.

Melanie pondered that. "Well," she said slowly, "in anything, you have to start somewhere."

Lopez beamed. She had never seen a teacher ask a question that provoked a child to wonder, that didn't have a simple, factual answer. "They're thinking," she murmured out loud. "The teacher's not just saying, 'This is the way it is.'"

For all the warmth at the Manhattan School for Children, however, the high point of the trip didn't come until the next day. On a second foggy, drizzly morning, the Oaklanders boarded the vans and made the long rush-hour trip into the Bronx, past Yankee Stadium to a school called KIPP—the Knowledge Is Power Program.

KIPP was located at the heart of the South Bronx, an area the *New York Times* once called "the nation's most infamous symbol of urban blight." The school occupied a handful of classrooms inside a vast, brown-brick elementary- and intermediate-school building, abutting the junction of two railroad lines. The building itself was faceless; one could circle it entirely looking for the entrance and end up in the garage of the welfare department next door. Across the street, an imposing monolith of public housing towered, its peeling paint the dull gray of slush. Rubbish piled up, or lifted and tumbled on wind gusts, on vacant lots and empty side streets. The door to the school bore a sign: STUDENTS FROM P.S. 31 AND I.S. 151 ARE NOT ALLOWED IN THE BUILDING UNTIL 8:00 A.M. NO ONE IS ALLOWED TO WAIT INSIDE.

The Oakland group arrived with the opening bell, and bustled their way through the building's steel doors along with teeming streams of children. Inside the dim entrance, a uniformed security officer observed the influx, grousing audibly with a teacher about how bad the children were. Most of the building, of course, belonged not to the KIPP school, but to the elementary and intermediate schools whose signs were posted on the front of the building. (KIPP didn't have a sign.) As they trudged through the mazelike corridors, the Oaklanders were struck by the familiar dreariness, the lack of energy, the tired, banal hostility between child and adult. At one point Matt Hammer saw a young child—perhaps in third or fourth grade—being restrained by a security guard.

Crossing the imaginary threshold of KIPP was like entering a different climate, a different era. There was no sign, no doorway, nothing official to indicate that one had left the area controlled by P.S. 31 and arrived at KIPP. But to many of the visitors, it was like stepping off a shaky boat onto dry land. The change was announced not by some different color of paint or floor tile, but by the faces of the children and the teachers, which reflected a sense of respect, affection, and purpose. Even the walls advertised a mix of seriousness and celebration; every inch was covered by certificates for perfect attendance or academic achievement or admission to a competitive high school; plus photographs of the children white-water rafting and skiing; plus invocations to excel: "Work hard! Be nice!" "There are no shortcuts." "All of us will learn."

The group crowded into the office of David Levin, the school's impossibly young-looking director. Letters of congratulation to Levin adorned the wall—one from President Clinton, one from Dick Riley, the secretary of education. Levin wore a suit and tie, but the effect was more of a teenager heading to a corporate internship than of a maverick educator honored as one of the nation's most effective principals. (Once, a woman on a date with twenty-seven-year-old Levin had demanded proof of his age.) But for all his evident youth, when Levin told his story, every member of the Oakland group could identify with it. It embodied all their frustrations with their existing schools, and all their hopes for the schools they dreamed of building. This tiny upstart middle school was producing the highest scores in the Bronx. The kids toiled all day, from 7:30 in the morning until they were dismissed at 5:00 P.M., in an atmosphere that was friendly, but clearly disciplined. When the Oakland group arrived along with the children from the rest of the building, the KIPP students had been working for nearly an hour.

In the cramped office, Levin told his story. He had started teaching in Houston in 1992 as a corps member of Teach For America, a program that recruited graduates of top colleges to tough urban and rural classrooms. In a blunt and touching confession, Levin explained that he had an immediate affinity for struggling students because he himself had struggled, as a special-education student with a reading disability at a private school in Manhattan. He was a terrible teacher at first, Levin admitted, but he learned quickly. As his students' success grew, however, he became a target; his tires were slashed, and he had to store his class materials in the trunk of his car. The school named him teacher of the year, and then laid him off. Levin and his roommate, Michael Feinberg, taught fifth grade in separate schools, but agreed on a troubling fact: No matter what progress they made with their students, the kids regressed in later grades to the same low achievement, drug use, and teenage pregnancy that afflicted so many other children.

In a single marathon night of brainstorming, with a CD by the band U2 blaring unchanged, Levin and Feinberg had hatched the plan for the Knowledge Is Power Program. KIPP would recruit any student willing to make, and sign, a list of commitments: to arrive at school on time, to take responsibility for his or her own behavior, to stay for extra hours each day, and to attend for forty days on top of the regular school year. The program would demand ceaseless hard work and responsibility, from children and parents alike. No one would be forced to go there; families and teachers would choose the school. But, Feinberg and Levin felt, it would allow them to change the trajectory of a few dozen kids. After they persuaded the district to lend them a pair of classrooms, they knocked on doors to recruit students.

By 1995 the program—though it enrolled mostly low-skilled kids—was turning in enviable test scores, and perhaps too enviable. A tendency known widely by urban educators as the crabs-in-the-bucket phenomenon kicked in—an apt description of the need of the unsuccessful to bring down anyone who might achieve greater things. The district threatened to withdraw the classroom space. Faced with the demise of the program, the pair sought a new location. Levin inquired about opening a new KIPP in his hometown, New York. Sy Fliegel, the former District Four alternative-schools chief, by then had joined the conservative and influential Manhattan Institute. He heard about Levin's plan, and pried loose a pair of classrooms inside a public school in the South Bronx. Only after New York agreed to host KIPP did Houston's schools chief, Rod Paige, overrule the ouster from his district. Now faced with two offers, Feinberg remained in Houston while Levin traveled to New York alone, to open KIPP in the Bronx. Now, with 223 students in four grades, KIPP had established itself as an academic powerhouse. And along with its Houston cousin, it was garnering national attention, with profiles on *60 Minutes* and in the *New York Times*. But its impact transcended mere test scores. The comparatively tiny school had assembled a 120-piece string orchestra that rivaled any middle-school ensemble in the nation. It offered an afternoon, weekend, and summer enrichment program that included art, dance, and trips to the Grand Canyon and the White House. And its graduates won admission to Deerfield Academy and a host of other highly competitive prep schools. KIPP, Levin said without apology, sent zero of its graduates to the dismal neighborhood high school. And he explained that the school's freedom from the dictates of the bureaucracy had made such success possible. KIPP called upon teachers to work extraordinarily hard. The idea would not have succeeded if the school were compelled to accept whatever teachers the board of ed chose to send.

Levin's was an inspiring, genuine speech, even if it sounded like he had given it many, many times. What impressed the Oaklanders more, however, were the remarks of a couple of students Levin invited into the office, apparently at random. Poised and confident, they admitted their history as troublemakers. One had lost her opportunity to go on the school's summer trip because she had been in a fight. But, in a refreshing turn, she blamed no one besides herself. "I knew going into it, when I made the decision to fight," she said. "It was my responsibility."

The girls served as tour guides for the morning, and the visits to classrooms struck the Oaklanders powerfully. Although the teaching adhered to a traditional model—the teacher in front, the chairs in rows, sharply contrasting the voguish "cooperative learning" groups favored in education schools—each child was paying attention, focusing, learning. It was reminiscent of a prep school. Teachers spent four hours or more per day planning lessons, and received daily support and coaching from a "professional developer"—a sort of attention that most Oakland teachers could only imagine.

For the Oakland group, the visit to KIPP was electrifying. It proved to them that excellence by any measure was possible, even in the toughest neighborhood, in a small school of choice. The school had established order and discipline, yet without a robotic or militaristic feeling. A few in the group were uncomfortable with KIPP's narrow margins for bad behavior, but everyone else savored the sense of order. The educators in particular admired the serious engagement of the students in their classes. Chelsea Toller, the Jefferson teacher, was impressed by the logic behind the discipline policy. In Oakland, kids who committed serious infractions earned suspension—which may have been a sensible practice in some Ozzie and Harriet reverie, where Mom was home all day to glare at the offender, but which now constituted little more than an unscheduled vacation. At KIPP, the children served their suspension in school, studying. For Toller and for others, there was an evident sense of purpose and high standards at KIPP, a culture that the Oaklanders keenly wished to emulate.

For Lillian Lopez, KIPP inspired the most hope of any school she had seen. Certainly, she had admired the Manhattan School for Children and the way it welcomed parents. But here at KIPP were tough kids—many had been in trouble before they got there. Now they clearly enjoyed attending class and had turned around their school ways. It was the sort of turnaround an awful lot of children in Oakland needed to make.

On the second evening of the trip, Noel Cisneros, the television reporter, interviewed Lillian Lopez on-camera. They traveled to the other side of the East River, arriving at twilight near the base of the Brooklyn Bridge, where the camera could frame Lopez against the Manhattan skyline. Sunset had painted a stunning cloudscape of dusky violet, and across the river, the lights of the Empire State Building and the Chrysler Building presided over the city. Lopez, looking very New York in a slick black leather jacket, visibly brimmed with excitement after the visits to the schools. She couldn't stop beaming, even when Cisneros asked whether it was frustrating to have her son Alex at Jefferson.

The truth was that, this year, Alex had a caring and competent teacher. But Lopez didn't say that. She represented more than just herself now. As the videotape rolled, Lopez recited the familiar complaints—the dirty bathrooms and classrooms, the crowding. The playground at Jefferson, she said, was so shrunken after the incursion of portable classrooms, and so bereft of play equipment, that the children had invented a gladiator-style fighting game in which they would form a circle and "throw two kids in the middle and have them go at it. Whoever wins, they'd select another kid and throw him into the circle." She bit her lip.

"If the conditions are like that at your school," Cisneros asked, "what makes you think you can fix it?"

"Because I'm determined," Lopez said. "I've run away for too long. This is my third child growing up in Oakland. I have gone through private school, and I moved away from the area for a year, and I'm tired of running. I'm staying and I'm in it for the long haul. I want to make things better, and I know that we can."

Cisneros wondered whether she expected resistance.

"Yes," she said. "People don't like change, and this is a major change. But this is a crisis in Oakland."

•   •   •

At six P.M. on January 21, 1999, nine months after the anguished meeting at Jefferson, Matt Hammer dialed a cellular phone from his aging gray Honda. The charter school plan had evolved far enough to go public, OCO's leaders had decided, and public attention could speed it forward. After a few rehearsals with Lopez and Stewart, Hammer spoke to a reporter he knew at the *Oakland Tribune*. Even in the moment's heady excitement, he observed proper community organizer protocol. He would hold the conversation only "on background." For quotes, he said, the reporter would have to speak directly to two key parent leaders in the charter school effort. When pressed by the reporter, who was jittery about reaching Lopez and Stewart so close to the evening deadline, Hammer agreed to supply the basic facts. Even as he talked, though, he was surprised by the stir the school plan was causing.

Hammer gripped his bulky cell phone, its broken antenna attached with tape, one hand on the steering wheel. OCO, he explained, would work with two organizations with solid financial backing: the School Futures Research Foundation, which operated four schools in California, and University Public Schools. "These two organizations have the capacity to run six effective schools," he intoned confidently. He credited parent organizations throughout the city, through their churches, as the driving force. The main obstacle, he conceded, would be space. OCO, however, hoped for the help from Mayor Jerry Brown, who had campaigned on a call for charter schools. OCO planned to submit its own completed charters in February, Hammer said.

Then, Hammer recited phone numbers for Lopez and Stewart.

Lopez, of course, had been working on the school plan nearly from the start. Stewart had signed on just a few months earlier, but Hammer had considerable confidence in the father, who was emerging as an articulate, plainspoken, deeply motivated leader. Moreover, he had played a crucial role in the search for a building. Months earlier, during a chat with Hammer, Stewart had a brainstorm: the now-vacant Hope Academy, where Malory once went. OCO enjoyed strong relations with the Center of Hope Community Church, which owned the school building. The matchmaking, which started with a phone call from Stewart's living room, was working out well. Stewart had the makings of a persuasive and capable leader.

But now, Hammer was anxious to know how the charter school plan would play in the press. Anxious enough, in fact, that he woke up early the next day. Disappointed that his *Tribune* had not been delivered to his home yet, he hurried to the OCO office to find a copy there. He was surprised to discover the story on the front page:

OAKLAND—In a sign that frustration with the Oakland public schools has turned to outright revolution, a group of parents announced Thursday night that it plans to open six charter schools serving 1,500 students in September.

The parents, brought together by the Oakland Community Organizations, said their ambitious plan is backed by two well-financed, expert charter school groups. Organizers said Thursday that they had been driven to create schools because the district has been unable to give their children what they need.

"Our kids are not getting a good education in Oakland and we need to do something about it," said Lillian Lopez, whose son attends Jefferson Year-Round Elementary. "We feel our schools are not part of the community and the kids are not performing at grade level . . . If we can get teams of administrators and teachers and parents working together, we can improve things. We can make things better."

Hammer was thrilled. The story, which quoted both Lopez and Stewart extensively, would propel the school effort to new momentum, Hammer knew. The front-page placement confirmed that the project, so crucial to OCO, was deemed important by the outside world as well. Equally key, the story, with its positive twist on fed-up parents who finally had taken matters into their own hands, framed the conflict squarely. If the issue continued to play that way in public discussion, OCO would gain huge leverage with the district. For an organization that treated political power the way banks treat money, the implications were immediate and big.

But as any good strategist knows, newfound attention can prove a double-edged sword. It meant new momentum, yes; but it also meant new enemies.

Chapter 3

Resistance

From within the cramped offices of the Oakland teachers' union, it was as if the Redcoats were invading by land and by sea all at once.

At the dawn of 1999, the union was in a poor position to fight off well-funded charter school privateers backed by a powerful grassroots group. The union—officially called the Oakland Education Association—was nearly crippled by angry divisions among its own. The new president, Sheila Quintana, was struggling to stake out ground, and after six months the mood remained tense. Quintana, black and Oakland-born, led a new guard against a group of old-time lefties, mostly white, who had been elected as a slate years earlier. She had axed them all from their appointed posts early on, but they controlled the union's executive board, so they just appointed themselves back to their old jobs. Meanwhile, they had accused Quintana of using the ex-president's rubber stamp to sign her paychecks and the union credit card to pay for manicures. The allegations had become enshrined in the union's official documents, despite Quintana's firm denials. Quintana had some backing within the union, but arguments over her leadership divided largely along race lines. And general meetings were growing increasingly unruly, thanks to a wacky group of radical Trotskyist substitute teachers more intent on class conflict than classroom learning.

Amid all that, the union was trying to get its real business done. There was a teacher contract to negotiate, a process made harder by a rapid turnover of district superintendents. Routine grievances from teachers—the union's bread and butter—went unheard. Some called it searching for direction. Others called it chaos.

Enter the charter schools.

The first charter onslaught was engineered by the new mayor, Jerry Brown. The former governor had taken office in January, following an election slam-dunk where he won 61 percent of the vote in an eleven-way race. The landslide was especially dramatic because Brown was a white man running in a city of color. Wielding his electoral mandate like a bazooka, Brown was pushing a four-part agenda, one of whose parts was "school reform." Charter schools comprised one of Brown's chief school reform tools. To establish those schools, Brown had chosen the Edison Project, a group that sought to make a profit operating inner-city charters. The union knew well that Edison was run from New York by capitalist cowboy Chris Whittle, who had brought "educational" TV larded with junk food commercials to America's classrooms through the controversial "Channel One."

And then there was OCO's assault. The community group, which enjoyed hefty political punch, wanted to join with the School Futures Research Foundation. The union knew School Futures to be a pro-voucher group financed with Wal-Mart money. Wal-Mart, the largest retailer in the world, had built $21 billion in personal wealth for founder Sam Walton, winning him for a time the title of richest man in America. After his death, and even after the fortune was divided among his heirs, his widow surpassed the Queen of England as the richest woman in the world. All this enriching had occurred in stores that were hostile to unions, both through efforts to keep collective bargaining out of their workforce and through sales of goods produced by low-paid foreign workers. And School Futures—which was financed from the personal wealth of Walton's son—had let it be known in Oakland that it would shut down any of its schools where teachers tried to form a union.

Together, the onslaught of Edison and School Futures represented, in Quintana's mind, some of the most dangerous ideas in American education. Indeed, Quintana lumped the two together, dismissing the idea that School Futures was a nonprofit. For the union, Walton and Whittle represented a big-money, right-wing, pro-voucher juggernaut out to undermine "government schools," as some conservative extremists put it. (Walton and another billionaire, Ted Forstmann, had contributed millions to provide vouchers so poor kids could attend private schools. Forstmann was on record as saying he wouldn't mind seeing public schooling dry up and disappear altogether.) The charters would discredit public schooling, Quintana figured, by quietly selecting the best-performing students from the most stable families, and by driving out low performers, mentally handicapped students, and behavior problems. Indeed, it would happen naturally; the most involved and aware parents were the most likely to find out about and enroll in the charters.

Lillian Lopez was a perfect example: a professional involved in her child's education, and part of an intact, stable marriage. Hers was the sort of family public schools yearned to keep—the sort of family that the union feared would abandon the district and move to the charter schools. With that "cream" of the student population, the charters would produce superior test scores. That success would prepare the ground for vouchers, which would devastate public education, critics like Quintana reasoned. The most capable families would seize the vouchers and decamp for private academies, which did not have to answer to the public in their policies and use of taxpayer money. The public schools, on the other hand, would be left with the special-education students and the children who had the least support at home. Any notion of a common educational good would wither, replaced by a Darwinistic, gated-community mentality.

More immediately, this conservative charter axis struck at the heart of everything the union had worked to establish for its own members. Charters would exist outside the agreements the union had won in years of painful negotiation and strikes. As teachers joined charter schools, the unions would lose members, and the union's capacity to win decent wages and working conditions in public schools would ebb—along with the union's power and cash flow. The scale and speed of what was happening in Oakland added urgency to those fears. If all the charter schools currently planned— five from School Futures, a couple from Edison, and a few others— actually opened, it would mark the greatest expansion of charters in California history. The union suspected that charter schools would hire less-experienced and thus less-expensive teachers, and perhaps use lower pay scales and fewer trained staff. It amounted to an end run around collective bargaining.

Indeed, though charter advocates would never say it out loud, it was a poorly kept secret that many within their ranks saw unions as one of the main problems, and charters as a solution. Many in education had argued that unions blocked creative steps toward better schooling. They complained that ideas like letting principals select their own staffs, paying teachers more for excellent performance, or keeping schools open longer often got mired in discussions of seniority, transfer rights, tenure, and years-long contract negotiations. Unions, the critics said, also turned the firing of lousy teachers into a blizzard of paperwork and due process. Charter schools presented an immediate experiment with ideas that could alter the known, comfortable world that the unions had worked hard to establish. If the charter schools did score well, they would not only undermine the union's arguments and clout, but also would insult the hard-working district teachers personally.

Super-high-performance charter schools, however, were the least of the Oakland Education Association's worries. As that union was fond of pointing out, Oakland's current record with charter schools failed to impress. There already were three charter schools in Oakland serving a few hundred school-age children. Unlike the OCO-School Futures and Brown-Edison charters, these schools had been started by parents and teachers, not well-funded companies. None of them could claim impressive test scores, and all three had battled for financial survival.

All of that, however, had not kept Jerry Brown and OCO from falling in love with charters. And if Brown's political power and Edison's money lent their joint venture muscle, OCO had caused even bigger headaches in the union offices. At least Edison's representatives fought in the style the union was used to dealing with—the corporate style. They knocked at the front door, as the union put it: talking to well-heeled executives and political chiefs, relying on others for the connection to local families. In a blue-collar, pro-union city like Oakland, Edison probably could be driven off. But OCO, thanks to its street-level connection to thousands of families, presented a tougher fight—and one that wouldn't win the union many friends. Who, after all, would argue with working-class mothers and fathers who wanted better schools for their children?

The union, however, had to find a way. In a matter of weeks, OCO would deliver its School Futures charters to the Oakland Board of Education, whose vote would decide whether these schools would actually come into existence. The union would have to try to win a majority of *no* votes on those charters.

With that understanding, thirteen members of the union's executive board sat down shortly before five P.M. on January 28 in their office boardroom to forge a battle plan. The group's executive director delivered a briefing on the for-profit and School Futures charter schools. Then a high school counselor named David Turner introduced a motion: "Whereas the Oakland Education Association is currently under fire from the proponents of Charter School [sic] and the various for profit entities," the resolution said, the parent union—the California Teachers Association—should provide money, resources, and a full-time staffer to combat charter schools in Oakland. In addition, the CTA should pay teachers to take time away from their classrooms to oppose charters. There was little discussion, and the motion passed unanimously.

The union had officially declared war.

It was true, of course, that opposing the charters put the union in the uncomfortable position of defending the status quo in a famously low-performing district. Telephoned by a reporter about the anticharter policy, Quintana argued that "there hasn't been any data that shows an increase in student outcomes" in privately managed charters, and she criticized the move as "an experiment." As an alternative, she suggested that teachers continue with a district reform plan called site-based management, which awarded more power to parents and teachers at individual schools. The union later blocked that policy, walking out of negotiations in a dispute over teacher and administrator representation. Quintana, however, continued to argue that the district was on the verge of greatness. In comments to the press, she played an emotional card, citing the name of a beloved Oakland superintendent of a generation earlier who was assassinated by the Symbionese Liberation Army, the terrorist group that had abducted and brainwashed Patty Hearst. "We're on the cutting edge of real systemic reform for the first time in thirty years," she said. "Marcus Foster was planning to make these changes," she said, "but he was, of course, killed. That ended the fearlessness he had in pursuing these reforms."

After the union approved its anticharter policy, the state union dispatched a staffer to fight the charters, along with a war chest of about $50,000. The OEA ramped up its opposition campaign. Even before the policy, OEA had distributed fliers to every teacher in the district warning that "signing a charter school petition could be dangerous" and explaining what to do "if you hear Edison knocking at the door." Now, OEA gathered information—newspaper articles, newsletters, fliers, policy statements, brochures—on charters, especially the for-profit kind, and the people behind them. They quickly filled two thick binders. OEA officers also began a campaign of lobbying local politicos—mostly Jerry Brown and the school board members—to fend off the charters.

In truth, OEA had been throwing bricks at OCO's charter effort long before the official policy. Although the two groups had once been strong partners, their bond had frayed in a bitter teacher strike in 1996. Then, OCO's backing of the small-school "HOPE" push at Jefferson had further alienated the union. Quintana and others had found OCO's role insulting. These noneducators, even as they claimed expertise about improving education, had chosen younger, less skilled teachers for their little school. (It had never been much of a secret that the young bucks saw some of their senior colleagues as "lazies and crazies.") Worse, the school the HOPE group proposed would have lived by its own hiring rules, ignoring seniority and other protections crucial to the union contract. So when the charter school idea popped up a few months later, the newly elected Quintana had her knife ready. In her notes, she wrote that charters were gaining support "due to some community organizers' personal agendas." Explaining OCO's motivation, she wrote simply, "Wants political clout." As early as June 1998, when OCO had been negotiating with School Futures for less than a month, Quintana grew furious over Matt Hammer's efforts to talk to teachers about charters. She left him a phone message warning him to stop his one-on-one talks with them. If he didn't, she told his voice mail, she might seek a court order to keep him from "harassing" the teachers. It was odd that she believed he could get arrested for exercising his free-speech rights, considering that she had taught honors-level civics classes. But the shrill attack proved a good prediction of what was to come.

With the union set in battle mode, Quintana lobbed charges at School Futures in the press and in public forums. Some of those attacks took the form of bizarre statements from which the union later had to retreat. Once, Quintana suggested to the newspaper that the schools were a business strategy to force students to buy supplies at Wal-Mart—"that's how they make their profit," she said. In a panel discussion, she linked School Futures to clothing produced by slave labor and sold at Wal-Mart, which she described as the "parent company" of School Futures. Before the Oakland school board, she branded Walton a "devil" who would "destroy collective bargaining as we know it," and argued that the School Futures agreement would mean "five and a half million dollars leaving this district and going to privatizers and pro-voucher and nonunion groups where they pay children five cents an hour to make Kathie Lee jeans for Wal-Mart that doesn't believe in unions and beat those children when they do not do it correctly in Bangladesh." While few took such declarations at face value, Quintana's statements signaled that the union would stop at nothing in its struggle to defeat the charter schools.

•   •   •

With a three-thousand-member union training its biggest guns on the charter schools, and with the other district unions falling in line behind the teachers, Matt Hammer knew he had a nasty fight ahead. He and the OCO leaders planned a war for charter schools on several fronts at once. The primary targets were the seven members of the Oakland school board, whose vote would decide whether these schools would actually open or would merely remain pretty ideas on paper. The superintendent's willful cluelessness on OCO's efforts made that lobbying all the more important. To Hammer's mind, the superintendent's attitude suggested that the district's professional staff would roughen the road for the charters. So in meetings with the school board members, parents and ministers brandished OCO's populist might as both carrot and stick. Few on the board were anxious for a fight with the unions just as the wounds from the nasty, month-long 1996 strike were beginning to heal. But OCO's numbers could sway elections. In their talks in the board offices, OCO members found themselves answering the same troubling questions they themselves had posed: Were these charter schools a stalking-horse for vouchers? Were they an attack on unions? School board member Jean Quan (no relation to Superintendent Carole Quan), a former labor organizer, suggested that the charter campaign had adopted the same tactics as some voucher efforts: recruiting inner-city community activists as spokespersons for a conservative idea. OCO strived to reassure her and the other board members: these would be public schools.

Despite OCO's progress with the board of education, another political nut just wouldn't crack: the new mayor. Jerry Brown's arrival had coincided with a sweeping ouster of old-time politicos, an overhaul that electrified the entire scene. Indeed, shocks to the system had abounded that year. The previous mayor, a darling of the powerful democratic machine, had lost a seemingly assured state assembly seat to a nearly unknown Green Party member from the wealthy hamlet of Piedmont. In the most African-American electoral district in Oakland, voters had eliminated black and Latino candidates to hold a run-off between two whites, upsetting any traditional understanding of race politics. In this moment of political volatility, the likeliest move was the one that would bring the most radical changes. OCO, like Brown, wanted to challenge the district through charter schools.

Yet OCO couldn't get through the mayor's door—quite literally. After weeks of unanswered phone calls, OCO leaders gathered on a Saturday morning and marched on his live-work-loft-commune in the trendy port district. A sleepy-eyed staffer in a sweatshirt opened the door, and the OCO people could see Brown inside, but the mayor—apparently reluctant to declare allegiances—wouldn't let them in. Later, Brown's education adviser met with them, but kept them at arm's length. The mayor's staff showed up at a press conference for the charters, but Brown himself didn't. He promised OCO limited support: some help in locating buildings; safe passage through the zoning machinery. It was, for the moment, a platonic sort of romance.

In the face of such setbacks, the strategy-minded Hammer needed to stoke the fire of the faithful with new inspiration. So he escorted the OCO parents to East Palo, to see School Futures' sole Northern California campus.

The very journey to the school served as a reminder of the contrast between rich and poor. A sociological argument holds that poverty is relative—that it is not just the misery of doing without, but the misery of doing without while watching others bask in the far reaches of plenty. In Oakland, mere minutes separated redwood forests from homes built atop toxic former industrial sites; depending on the neighborhood, community meetings might dwell on backyard forest-brush clearing or on unexplained spikes in cancer and asthma rates. Similar contrasts were on display on the drive into East Palo Alto, the tiny and violent neighbor of wealthy Palo Alto.

Hammer and the parents traveled across the Dumbarton Bridge and past the campus of computer-maker Sun Microsystems—"the dot in dot-com." Mirror-windowed office parks hinted at the Emerald City glitter of the Internet boom, then still at its peak. The road led toward Silicon Valley, toward posh suburbs like Atherton (median home price: $3.8 million), toward the grassy plazas of Stanford University. But the visitors turned off that boulevard, just beyond the headquarters of the East Palo Alto police, who at one point were so overloaded with murder investigations that they had to bring in the Highway Patrol for backup. The OCO group headed down a road the dot-commers would never see, past the strip-mall burrito joints. Here, someone had forgotten to build a sidewalk; the rutted asphalt was bordered by dirt. There was a public housing complex, behind a metal gate. Hammer was struck by the similarities to Oakland.

Then, when it seemed the road would dead-end in a field near the bay, the East Palo Alto Charter School appeared. A low-slung compound of bungalows and covered walkways, the place was quiet and pleasant; isolated near the bay waters, it abutted a sleepy airfield. Well-kept and freshly painted, it felt safe. A mountain bike leaned against a wall, unlocked.

The OCO parents were ushered into the school library, which was crowded with new computers. Donald Evans, the principal, welcomed them enthusiastically. Slim, tall, high-voiced, and energetic, he was instantly likeable. Evans introduced Danny Thompson, a father at the school who oversaw technology there. Together, they told the story of their school and School Futures, and delivered some stern warnings.

Thompson explained that he and other parents had searched for an option outside the disastrously low-performing district schools. Through lengthy battles, they had won spots for their kids in the schools of rich nearby suburbs, but that proved a continuing fight. Deciding they needed a school of their own, they had joined forces with School Futures. To Hammer, it sounded like a repeat of the Oakland parents' experience.

Evans picked up the story. It had not been easy, he said, when he moved from San Diego to start the school; racial tensions had made his start tricky. Yet eventually, parents pitched in to repair a decrepit campus, paint and plant it and render it both functional and beautiful. In the time since, thanks in part to good support from the district, the school had garnered a reputation for academic success with quite low-skilled children. But copying this model, he said, would not be easy. "It's very, very hard to start a charter school and make it last," he warned. "Parents were expecting to have this beautiful school overnight. You can't start a school and have everything run smoothly the first year. It takes time."

But now, Thompson said, they had a wonderful school where not only Spanish speakers learned English, but all the English speakers learned Spanish, because the parents wanted that. "That's the difference between a public school and a charter school: we could have the input that we needed," he said.

Evans offered a preview of the hardest fights to come: competing with districts for good teachers—innovative ones who wouldn't mind putting in extra hours. Yes, the extra hours and longer year were important, he said, but the key was the teachers. Then he walked the group around the school.

For Hammer, peeking into classrooms and talking to teachers reinforced his sense that School Futures could fulfill its ambitious promises. The children all seemed engaged in their lessons. The teachers were committed to continually improving their craft, much like the teachers at KIPP. They worked together, rather than griping. The attention to performance was intense; test scores from each class were posted on the wall of the school office. The curriculum held together logically. Principal Evans took a deep interest in the culture of his school, and in teaching his teachers to teach better. (At one point during the tour, he pulled out a stopwatch to monitor how much time a teacher spent on discipline.) To Hammer's way of thinking, this school functioned far more effectively than the ones he knew in Oakland.

East Palo Alto Charter demonstrated what was possible at a small school, reinforcing the lessons of OCO's New York tour. Here, as in

New York, the school was small enough that teachers could discuss individual students by name at meetings of the whole faculty. At such schools, principals controlled their full budgets, and had power over hiring, which allowed them to assemble a staff that agreed on teaching philosophy and actually wanted to be there. These small schools also took great care and time recruiting teachers. They were comfortable, welcoming places with visionary leaders and strong teachers who worked very, very hard.

But if East Palo Alto proved the power of a small school based on a vision, it also represented a new wave in education: a charter school run by a private company. In the minds of many, charter schools comprised a new generation of alternative schools, started by teachers and parents, like the group that had formed at Jefferson. School Futures' way typified a very different—and increasingly popular—birth process. It was one of a growing number of "EMOs"— education maintenance organizations, modeled on HMOs—through which corporations created and ran charter schools. Many were for-profit; some were nonprofit; but all were private groups seeking to start and manage schools. In many cases, parent involvement in the design of the school was sharply limited. School Futures, for instance, had asked families about their wishes and then adapted a more-or-less stock charter. These EMO apples may have fallen far from the original charter tree, but some experts saw strengths in such organizations. Many parent groups complained of being over-whelmed by the complexity and effort of running a new school. Some experts believed stable, financially secure companies like School Futures, which brought expertise and experience, had a bet-ter shot.

Yet it took considerably more than a charter to make an effective school. If asked, East Palo Alto's Donald Evans would cheerily ex-plain that there was no magic inherent in the words *charter school.* Rather, he said, the key was people with a clear idea of what to do with the freedom the charter gave them and the energy to work very hard.

The same lesson had played out at the school that so inspired the

OCO group, New York's KIPP. Not long after the OCO group visited, KIPP converted into a charter school. The reasons read like an indictment of mindless bureaucracy. Despite his success, David Levin was scrambling amid a hundred-hour-a-week workload to take enough education-school classes to hold on to the credential that allowed him to keep that position. The school increasingly had to choose between buying supplies off the books and buying them at inflated prices through a district purchasing system. The musical instruments that had so impressed the Oakland group had been purchased in secret, too, through funds the school had raised but never reported. And in the perpetually tense relationship with other schools in the building, Levin feared having to surrender classrooms if political winds in the district shifted. Going charter meant an end to all that—no more credential fears, no more worries about space, no more lying about money.

Even so, the charter, in itself, was no silver bullet. Had anyone from Oakland pressed the point, principal Evans would have confessed that School Futures hadn't done much besides the financing of the building. East Palo Alto Charter owed its academic record less to School Futures than to the hard work of Evans and his staff. And the charter did not guarantee success; it simply provided the freedom to do something new and different. But none of the Oakland parents asked what role School Futures and the charter had played, which was a shame. Months later, they would probably wish they had.

● ● ●

Jerry Brown could not slow down. Not when he speed-walked around Lake Merritt at six A.M. Not when he was talking and someone was trying to take notes. And certainly not when he was forging policy. But his charter plan had stalled. He had some work to do.

Brown had liked the charter school idea since well before his election. As a child, Brown had attended seminary school, so perhaps it wasn't surprising that he brought an unusual perspective to education discussions. In other areas, Brown had abandoned the left-fringe politics that earned him the famous nickname "Governor Moon-beam." His key policies as mayor of Oakland—a police crackdown on crime, a prodevelopment and probusiness approach to the city's economy—would have rolled easily off the tongue of a Republican. But in education, he remained that wacky maverick who, as governor, decided to forgo a limousine in favor of his old station wagon. In matters of education, Brown took his schooling from Ivan Illich, whom he called not only a friend but "one of the most important thinkers of the late twentieth century." Brown had carefully read Illich's *Deschooling Society*, a slim 1970 book which argued that requirements for schooling should be discarded, in part because time spent in school has little to do with actual learning. The book blamed the current education system for "physical pollution, social polarization, and psychological impotence." It recommended "the constitutional disestablishment of the monopoly of the school," supported by a bill of rights that decreed, "The State shall make no law with respect to the establishment of education." (This was far from Illich's most eccentric proposal; he once suggested banning cars in Manhattan and zipping children via giant pneumatic tubes to a sort of cultural carnival in Central Park.) In the book, Illich praised a proposal "to put educational 'entitlements' or tuition grants into the hands of parents and students for expenditure in the schools of their choice"—a proposal that sounded very much like today's vouchers. Illich liked the idea of choice, but dismissed the plan in question because the vouchers "would have to be spent on schooling."

Brown was impressed enough that he felt compelled, just after his election, to write a review of the book on the Amazon.com Web site, under the headline "*Deschooling* blasts the contemporary idolatry of 'education' ":

> This is a heartfelt series of essays that illuminate the nature of learning and the perverse consequences of professionally imposed schooling requirements. Far from the assumed engine of equality, modern schooling promotes inequality and social stratification. It's [sic] powerful and graded liturgy convinces the majority of people

that their inferior status derives from a failure to consume sufficient quantities of expensive educational services . . . This is a book about aliveness.

Brown wouldn't have minded wiping out the Oakland school district wholesale, but didn't see that as a politically feasible concept. The man who wrote Brown's platform favored dissolving the district power structure and putting the schools largely under the control of the union, but Brown had dismissed that idea. The district was far too unwieldy, its problems too deep and long-standing, for him to make changes in it directly. As for ideas that would break the district's Illichian monopoly on public education, however—Brown was all in favor of those. Before an audience of black ministers, Brown accused the district of "farming the students" for the state funds they brought, and quoted Martin Luther King Jr., saying the district had fallen under the influence of "the tranquilizing drug of gradualism." In his frequent public diatribes, Brown made the district seem a sleeping drunkard that needed to be shaken, wakened, and shown the error of its ways.

The more Brown criticized, the more the district produced pathetic defenses of its record and promises that the situation would improve soon. "The Oakland Public Schools are NOT academically bankrupt," Superintendent Carole Quan declared in a prepared statement that month. "We are NOT in the bottom two hundred schools in the state." She backed this statement with a careful selection of test results intended to highlight increases, and odd statistics such as the high turnover rate in principals, intended to show that Quan wasn't afraid to make changes. The silly everything's-under-control reports filled reams of paper with pretty graphics, check marks, and arrows swooshing upwards. At one point, the district released a flowchart headed "Cause and Effect Analysis of Textbook Shortage," in which each of the ten reasons began with the letter *P.*

It all just made Brown more intent. "This has to be a crisis response," he was fond of saying. "Someone has to shake up the system."

The mayor had surveyed the charter scene, and selected Edison as the charter outfit with the best chance of success. It had the track record and the bank account. (Brown reportedly had a girlfriend who was an executive at The Gap, whose founder had funded Edison's entry into California to the tune of $25 million, but Brown maintained that had nothing to do with it.) School Futures, however, presented a problem. Brown had met with Brian Bennett a couple of times, but School Futures operated only a few schools. To Brown's mind, they had not proved themselves. It was an inconvenient fact that OCO was seeking his support for its School Futures partnership. He certainly didn't want to alienate that coalition's impressive power base, and didn't want to oppose their charter ideas. At the same time, though, he wanted to be loyal to his burgeoning partnership with Edison, and he didn't want to be blamed if OCO's big, hurried plans came to disaster. So he had kept OCO at a distance.

By February, however, the landscape had changed. Edison simply couldn't get traction in Oakland. To convert an existing school to Edison management, the law required the signatures of half the teachers. The union had poisoned that ground. Even more frustrating were Brown's attempts to drum up support among parents. The mayor had figured that with the Oakland schools' record, parents would welcome Edison like a liberating army. No such luck. Brown's advisers soon decided that the only way to build a powerful movement was through a grassroots network like OCO's. And Brown was not about to transform his office into a neighborhood-organizing headquarters; he didn't have the staff or the time for it. Moreover, he had grander plans: a strategy to topple Superintendent Carole Quan by threatening a state takeover that would put Brown in charge of the district. (In California, as in much of the country, mayors usually have no direct power over the school system in their cities.) But when it came to fulfilling his promises on charter schools, Brown worried that OCO would beat him to the punch. Moreover, he respected the coalition's organizing prowess, and liked some of the OCO leaders personally. Reluctantly, he decided to throw his full support to the OCO charter push. On February 8, two days before OCO was to deliver its charters to the Oakland school board, Brown received Hammer, Lopez, and a group of other OCO leaders in his office. They asked whether he would show up at the school board meeting, to join them in a press conference and in delivering the charters.

Brown didn't have many other choices. He said yes.

•   •   •

Both OCO and the union had tried to win the other over to its side, but this reunion of estranged allies was not to be. The evening of February 4, a sizeable delegation from each side met at the OEA's overheated upstairs offices. Although each side wanted to bring the other around, the conversation only widened their schism.

OCO was seeking the union's support for the charter schools' longer work day and year, which would have violated the basic tenets of the contract the union had thrashed out during the painful strike. It was out of the question. Hammer trotted out the success record of School Futures and of the schools OCO had visited in New York. Quintana offered some views of her own about School Futures—the source of its money, the child labor, the conservative axis behind it. One of the OCO leaders cajoled, saying OCO would let the world know the union was on the cutting edge of school change if it backed the charters. It wasn't much of an offer. So he tried a new tack, talking about how OCO had pushed for an end to the strike and smaller classes. The teachers in the room, who had spent twenty-six days on a picket line fighting for those changes, chafed.

As the discussion escalated, Quintana declared angrily, "When you're dealing with Wal-Mart, you're making a deal with the devil!" That was too much for Gordon Humphrey Jr., the pastor of Olivet Institutional Missionary Baptist Church, which was to house one of OCO's charter schools. "Whenever you take state money," he said, "you've already made a deal with the devil!"

The meeting ended in stalemate. The teachers left confirmed in their plan to fight their former allies. For their part, the OCO members hoped the fuss might convince the union to give some ground on OCO's other education effort: small schools inside the district.

The OCO members left ready to continue the charter push, but knowing that their plan would face sniper fire from the union when it went before the school board.

The afternoon of February 10, Lillian Lopez's emotions were whirling in a frenzy. OCO would be delivering its five completed charters to the school board that evening, before an audience packed with OCO members—and perhaps with opponents. The board meeting, which rotated from one school to another, would be held that evening at the birthplace of her frustrations—Jefferson— almost a year after the showdown there with principal Hopkins. But what had torqued her emotions so tight was her keen sense of want. She could not think of another time in her entire life when she had wanted anything so much as she craved this better school for Alex. Shortly after five, she called her friend Priscilla to ask her to accompany her to the meeting so she would have someone to talk to about other things, someone to keep her grounded.

Truth to be told, she was about ready to wring a *yes* vote bodily from all the board members. "Vote *yes* on this charter," this mother of three wanted to shout, "or I'll kill you."

Priscilla soon arrived at Lopez's house, and the two of them walked together toward Jefferson. Theirs was a friendship based on weird coincidences, and they were to add another tonight. Former neighbors, they had met because their oldest sons had played together as five-year-olds. Later, Lillian and Priscilla discovered that they had attended the same high school in Albuquerque. Their husbands hailed from the same tiny town in Mexico. But while they had been fast friends as neighbors, Priscilla had moved away after her apartment was burglarized. The thief, she felt sure, was the landlord's son Robert, a petty criminal and drug addict.

Lillian and Priscilla had walked less than two blocks when out of the semidarkness they heard a child sobbing. Lopez recognized the child on the other side of the street as Mark, Robert's little boy; he stuck out as the only fair-haired child in the neighborhood. Lopez asked him what was wrong.

"Some little boys tried to lynch me," he sobbed.

"Come here," Lopez said.

"No," he cried. "I'm going home."

"No, come here," she insisted. "Show me." He revealed ugly red marks on his neck.

Priscilla spoke up. "What are you going to do? I don't want to see his parents." She was insistent. "Let it go," she said adamantly. "Don't get involved."

Lopez dismissed her. "He's hurt," she said. "I have to do something." But bowing to her friend's fears, she agreed not to take him home. They would bring him along to Jefferson.

Jefferson was buzzing when Lopez arrived, especially with the Jerry Brown name to attract the media. On top of the fine photo opportunity of Jerry Brown with a crowd of poor folks, word had leaked out in that morning's paper that Brown was preparing a bid to assume control of the entire school system. Despite the national distractions— it was the height of President Clinton's impeachment—the big white TV-news vans with their telescoping microwave towers were parked outside. Ready with a strategy, Hammer called, "Lillian, Lillian! Come here!" But for the moment, she had a more pressing problem: Mark. As they walked the corridors, a teacher recognized Mark. Lopez explained the situation, and the teacher said he would watch over the boy. One problem solved. But now, more than ever after Mark's trauma, she was nearly sick with excitement and tension.

Brown and OCO had set up a press conference before the board meeting, in a classroom. It was a brief affair. A couple of parents spoke first, about overcrowding, but it was Brown all the reporters wanted to hear. He didn't say much about his takeover plan, but he combined newfound encouragement for OCO with his usual scorn for the district. "Turn up the pressure," he said, talking fast in a perpetually hoarse voice. "People in Oakland are tired of the shilly-shallying. Too many students are failing." He demanded, "Where people want to start a school, why shouldn't they?" He vowed that charter schools would be "like a prairie fire across the city as more and more parents realize, 'We're in control—nobody else.' " And he suggested that families could spend their average daily attendance money, known as ADA, where they chose. "This is not the Soviet Union," he said. "The children do not belong to the school system, to be exploited for their ADA." Fiery and intent, he wanted action now. "We can't wait for Godot," he said. "We can't wait for the next millennium."

The real action, however, would unfold in the school auditorium, where some 150 OCO members already waited in the audience. Before them, the seven members of the Oakland school board were taking seats at a long table covered with blue cloth. This group, everyone in the room knew, would exercise a life-or-death vote on the thick sheaves of paper called charters.

The sheaves of paper were identical, except for the names of the schools. But the five schools differed markedly. Each was backed by parents from one or more churches, and three were planned to occupy buildings owned by churches. Those five separate identities were influenced strongly by the congregations of those churches, some African American and some Latino.

A certain degree of racial separation would not have been unprecedented. Indeed, in Oakland, some of the existing charters were largely segregated by their chosen targets. One, the American Indian Public Charter School, announced its intended population in its name. Another, the Oakland Charter Academy, had been established to help Spanish-speaking students who were not faring well in regular middle schools. On the other hand, a third charter, New Village, had opened for the express purpose of serving a diverse group, which hypothetically would include children who were black, Latino, Asian, white, Native American, gay, lesbian, straight, and so forth. Nationally, too, charter schools enrolled a higher proportion of black and Latino children than regular public schools did, putting to rest early fears that they would enroll mainly the white and the rich. Most charters, in fact, had race breakdowns similar to the districts surrounding them.

The schools that OCO had proposed spanned the miles of Oakland's flatlands, from west to east. Each of the five charters promised "a child-centered community learning environment" that would deliver "world-class education" through instruction fine-tuned by constant measurement of children's skills. The schools, as described in the charter Bennett had written, would be villages of dedicated learning, open from 6:30 A.M. until 7:00 P.M., with a 210-day school year—nearly 40 more days than the regular schools. The curriculum included "four areas of literacy"—language, technology, life sciences, and life skills—plus health, nutritious meals, fine arts, community service, environmental learning, counseling, and conflict resolution. The school would recruit "the best teachers," who would communicate with parents weekly. Within five years, the charter promised, students would gain "reading, writing, verbal, and math skills that meet or exceed those expected of students at the world's top K–12 schools."

OCO had chosen to present the charters at a school board meeting—rather than just dropping them off at the district offices—as a tactical move. A bit of a publicity stunt, it would bring Brown and the press together. Plus, the OCO leaders figured that with little time to waste, the move would leave no doubt about when they had filed the charters. Legally, the board had sixty days to act once it had received the charters. And OCO needed to move quickly. It was April, and the schools were set to open in September—if they won approval tonight.

After an amazingly long presentation of awards for student "conflict managers," the board secretary called for the OCO presentation.

Lillian Lopez, the lead speaker, had pored over the speech that Matt Hammer and Ron Snyder—OCO's senior staffer—had drafted for her. Considering how anxious she already was, the speech was the last thing she needed. She would have only three minutes before the board, but the speech ran more than five pages. Worse yet, it was dull as deadwood. She realized that it had been a giant error not to go over the address ahead of time, but now, there was no time to make changes.

The board secretary called her name. Holding a wireless microphone in one hand and the impossible speech in the other, she plunged in, talking fast. She recounted her own battle at Jefferson, OCO's efforts to improve the public schools, its travels to schools in New York and elsewhere, and then started into a detailed recitation of the need for small schools, charter schools, new schools, autonomous schools, site-based management, and accountability. She had a few good lines: "We can wait no longer for what other children already enjoy," she said at one point. But mostly, she knew she was getting automatic applause from a house packed with supporters. She trudged dutifully through the address, occasionally stumbling over awkward turns of phrase. She was barely halfway when the board president, Noel Gallo, announced that her three minutes were up. She ignored him as long as she could. "Ms. Lopez—Ms. Lopez—if you could please wrap up," he insisted. "Thank you, Ms. Lopez, it's time—" Finally, she hurried to close, flipping one page and then another, skipping to the final threats.

"Timing is everything right now," she said. "We expect the charters to be back here for approval in two weeks. The community will be extremely disappointed and very slow to forgive should this board do anything to prevent the community from taking advantage of this opportunity." She surrendered the microphone.

True to OCO's style, though, it was not words written by professional organizers that carried the emotion of the night, but rather the unscripted comments of the people who followed. Jesus Rodriguez, a cook on disability relief who lived deep in the East Oakland flatlands, had children at Castlemont and at a giant elementary school called E. Morris Cox. Introducing himself in broken English, Rodriguez yielded immediately to a torrent of emotion. "I have been waiting longest and crying out for better education for my children," he said in a high, forced voice, near tears. "I am broke in my heart when I see my son in that school, asking for resolution from the principal, asking for better academic levels, looking for safety in the site. I went asking for help, everywhere. Today is a great opportunity. We can have a choice where we put our children." He apologized for choking up, and as he started to cry in earnest, he concluded, forcing out his words like shots: "I ask you, help us. Help us parents. We cannot stay longer when there is something happening for the future of our children."

A woman named Maria Paez took the stand. Her children attended Webster Elementary, which had the distinction of some of the lowest test scores in California. She brandished the previous day's *Tribune*, and read a quotation from Sylvester Hodges, a former school board member. Hodges, an enthusiastic defender of the existing system, had argued that the board had "a responsibility . . . as people who know something about the quality of education, to make sure people are not experimenting with our children." Bitterly, Paez said, "I'm asking, if you know the quality of education, where is that quality in Webster?" The situation, she said, justified gambling on a charter school: "If someone comes and tells me, 'Buy a ticket because you have a fifty percent chance to win the lottery,' I'll buy the ticket."

William Stewart was signed up to speak, too. He carried the 1,500 signatures legally required to prove support for the school. As he thrust the big yellow envelope into Gallo's hands, he offered a few no-nonsense remarks. "You get paid to know what our kids need," he said. "We pay our taxes. We do what you ask. Do what we want now. We want our kids to get an education." He described Malory's plight, and added, "It's so hard to get a school built here, but as soon as she gets to be an adult, they'll build a jail so easy to put her in." The line received the strongest applause of the night.

The sole speaker in opposition to the charters was Sheila Quintana of the Oakland Education Association. In high dander and nearly shouting, Quintana claimed that the union would never oppose a homegrown charter, but did oppose "outsiders . . . telling the parents what's best for them." She singled out School Futures, connecting it once again to its founder's father's business. "John Walton of Wal-Mart is on record hurting people of color," Quintana said. "As we speak right now, there are places in Saipan that are paid less money for labor than anyplace else. All of a sudden this man is going to come into Oakland and work with people of color? We have some issues about that." Instead, she argued the school board should funnel more "resources" into the classroom. "We are the education professionals," she said. "We know what the kids need."

Then the school board members spoke. Their comments previewed the coming struggle, leaving little doubt that OCO would have some more maneuvering to do. Dan Siegel, an OCO supporter who had gone on the New York trip, set the tone. He complained that five charters sounded like an awful lot for a company that had established so few, and had no local presence. "To ask us in the course of two weeks to approve five schools proposed by people we don't know and haven't worked with and haven't had an opportunity to meet and converse with seems a little much," he said. "I frankly don't think it will happen." And he warned that the charter schools would help the rest of Oakland only if they could offer models of "new innovative creative teaching philosophies."

Jean Quan, the board's most frequent charter critic, talked about a report from UCLA that questioned whether charter schools really ignored race and disability in enrolling children. And Lucella Harrison, the board's most consistent apologist for its own record, wished the OCO parents would have been a bit more polite in talking about Oakland's public school system. "All of the charter schools that have come before us before have not found it necessary to trash the district," she said. She argued that people excited by this "quick fix" for "an exclusive group of two thousand children" ought to consider the tens of thousands of children in Oakland who would not attend charter schools. "We have some excellent programs going on in Oakland's schools," she said.

In voices laced with contempt, several parents answered back: "Where?"

•   •   •

OCO's fight for approval of its charter schools turned out to be less a hot war than a battle of attrition. The chief enemy, the teachers' union, had put a full-timer on the case, but he ended up sinking into the mire of the union's internal battles, and eventually left. The union delivered fliers to its members and attempted to lobby the school board, but largely frittered away its energy. Certainly, it could not match the persuasive power of OCO's teams of parents, who were prepared to inflict their stories of woeful schooling on the board members until they won agreement. More to the point, the school board was occupied at the time with concerns about its own future. Jerry Brown and a powerful state senator were threatening to declare "academic bankruptcy" in the district and to appoint a trustee to oversee the system. The move would usurp the board's chief duty—selecting the superintendent. Yet the threat might vanish if the board dumped the current chief, Carole Quan. District unions defended her with signs and shouts and threats. The resulting battles consumed the board.

OCO's real struggle, as it turned out, was with the district staff, not their elected overseers on the school board. Perhaps this should not have been surprising; OCO and School Futures had picked a fight when they announced that they planned to do what the system could not. Some administrators found School Futures' educational plans thin and unoriginal; others merely appeared to be waiting for direction from above. A few were markedly unhelpful in their work on the charters. Dozens of last-minute questions emanated from the superintendent's office, pushing the process not only past the two weeks OCO had asked for, but past the sixty days allowed by law. Later, the administration simply forgot to put the OCO charters on a board agenda, extending the process another several days, and the ensuing drama played out in the press.

Meanwhile, though the district might have complicated life for the charter applicants, the mere existence of the proposals gave parents a new voice before the district. One evening in March, the superintendent's special assistant, Steve Stevens, was dispatched to a meeting in a church basement in one of several attempts to check that real parents lay behind the signatures on the charter petitions. Perhaps five dozen parents showed up, and the meeting's purpose was pretty well accomplished when everyone had arrived. But with a high-ranking official on their turf, the parents wanted some complaints heard. One mother said her son was robbed at school, only to be told in the office that he "needs to grow up." Stevens promised "to look into it further." Another complained that her two children at Cox Elementary had no books in their class. "All the schools have been given money to order books," Stevens shrugged. "I don't see any reason why they shouldn't have them." The mother, speaking through an interpreter, wasn't satisfied. "I would like you to go to Cox," she said. A father said he had seen kids smoking marijuana in class at his child's high school. Stevens frowned, and wrote that down in his notebook.

The evening had showcased what the parents in the toughest neighborhoods had come to expect: weak excuses, meaningless promises of investigations. But the parents didn't have to sit and listen anymore.

On April 8, before an audience packed with OCO members, the Oakland Board of Education prepared for a final vote on the five OCO–School Futures charters. The air that evening carried a sense of festivity and expectation. Television cameras again had taken up positions near the stage. With a fresh haircut and a white collar, Matt Hammer looked nearly pastoral. As the meeting time drew near, Lillian Lopez and others passed out OCO stickers for the supporters to wear. Yet the maneuvering went on until the very moment of the vote. Before the public discussion began, Superintendent Quan pulled Brian Bennett aside to ask whether School Futures really could pull off five schools in so little time. Then, before the cameras, a man from one of the district unions spoke against charter schools. In the aisles, Sylvester Hodges—the former board member who had warned the board against "experimenting with our children"—was circulating a petition opposing the Jerry Brown–backed state takeover of the district.

Brian Bennett took the stand, and board members fired questions at him about whether the school would accept special-education students; he offered picky, twisted answers that left the board unsure of what he was saying. He also dodged questions about whether the schools would close if teachers sought to join a union. But on other matters, Bennett made some crucial and unambiguous promises. Under intense questioning, he promised that School Futures would indeed open all five schools, with principals in place well in advance of opening. He promised to have books in every classroom on the first day of school, and not to resegregate the public school system in Oakland. And he promised that where tensions arose, School Futures would respect the will of OCO and the community.

Evidently, few on the school board felt at ease with the decision before them. They talked at length; the tension and restlessness in the OCO-dominated audience grew. Matt Hammer chewed a piece of gum as if he wanted to hurt it, and rubbed his eyes behind small, wire-rimmed glasses.

In the end, though, the board had no stomach for telling a group of parents from lousy schools that they couldn't try something new. "This was at first a somewhat difficult decision for me to make," board member Dan Siegel told the massed parents, "because of the disagreements that have arisen between the teachers' association and OCO." But, he explained, his dilemma disappeared when he asked himself his real purpose. He said, "The only acceptable thing for me to be doing here as a board member is to support the efforts of parents in the city of Oakland to get the best education for their children." Those who felt otherwise should not try to crush the charters, he said. "The people who disagree have a simple job, and that's to do it better."

The board secretary called the vote. There was a *yes*, then another, and another. Matt Hammer leaned forward in his chair, smiling, his gum-chewing abruptly halted. Each of the five charter schools won a unanimous *yes* vote. Cheers rose from the crowd. "Think about it," Lillian Lopez breathed to her neighbor. "Three months ago we didn't have hardly any support. Now it's unanimous."

The victory was thorough, complete, thrilling. Yet now, School

Futures and OCO faced a task that many doubted they could achieve: creating five schools in the five months that remained before September.

Yes, they had five approved charters. What that meant, in practical fact, was that they had permission to attempt the nearly impossible.

One Hundred and Fifty-one Days

Building a school from scratch is no small thing. The complexities begin with renovations, a potential nightmare of contractors, codes, and cost overruns. There's the matter of finding a principal with the courage of Napoleon, the teaching power of Jesus, and the warmth of a kindly grandmother. In an era of teacher shortages and emergency credentials, a cadre of skilled and thoughtful educators must be dug up, created, or stolen. Meanwhile, the principal has a few things to figure out: food service, transportation, curriculum, testing, a field trip policy, custodial services, security, handicapped access, a plan to serve the disabled, phone service, Internet access, recruiting of students, a homework policy, financial agreements, legal agreements, employment contracts, fire codes, fire drills, fire sprinklers, water fountains, textbooks, supplies, discipline policies, after-school care, trash collection, tutoring for kids who struggle, enrichment for the gifted, what to do if parents don't pick up their kids, what to do if someone brings a gun to school, recess supervision, lunch supervision, pick-up and drop-off arrangements, parking, fund-raising, hall passes, and a policy on whether kids can use the bathroom during class time. All that before one thinks about doing something innovative and superior—something that other schools aren't already doing. It can take a year, two, three, sometimes even more.

School Futures and the OCO parents didn't have that kind of time. The parents wanted better schools, fast, and School Futures' executives had promised they could deliver by fall. And they wanted to start five schools.

The charters had passed on April 8. School was scheduled to open on September 7. That left exactly 151 days to negotiate lease agreements for five dusty, disused buildings, tear them apart, rebuild them, and populate them with teachers and children. That time would decide the shape and character of the schools, from their buildings to the nature of the families and teachers who would impart a soul to the institutions. And it all had to happen at a time when the landscape of schooling in Oakland was shuddering with change. Six days after the charters had passed, Carole Quan, the superintendent, had ended her tortuous dance on the precipice and resigned. She would leave office two months later, and no one knew who would replace her.

In this volatile climate, OCO and School Futures had proffered bold assurances to the press, to politicians, and to parents who so desperately wanted good, safe schools. The stakes were high for both organizations. After such publicity, OCO's credibility rode on opening five schools, as promised. School Futures was even more exposed, with millions of dollars and its own fledgling reputation on the line. It could not afford to have one school fail. In its five-year existence, School Futures had established five schools; in Oakland, the company wanted to open five more in five months. Now, even some of OCO's most dependable supporters were asking whether it could all be done, on that scale, that fast.

That question was costing Laura Denise Armstrong a good bit of sleep. Dr. Armstrong was a devout member of the Center of Hope congregation and a teacher with a dozen years' experience, including a year at the Hope Academy, the now-defunct private school at the church. Pastor Ernestine Cleveland Reems had chosen Armstrong to be principal of the charter school. For Dr. Armstrong, as she was nearly universally known, that honor was no less than the fulfillment of the Lord's plan for her life.

For years, Armstrong had devoted herself to the pastor in the way that the faithful in Rome are devoted to the pope. That commitment was born one Sunday in October of 1986 at church in Arizona. Armstrong had grown up a Baptist of casual faith, a black girl living, literally, on the wrong side of the tracks in Phoenix, forced to go to church by her mother. After college, she worked at entry-level jobs in electronic chip production for Motorola and Intel. Through gritted teeth, she said she loved her hometown; "It's racist, segregated, but they'll give you a job," she would say, smiling bitterly. Her mother was a teacher of sorts, having spent her career at Head Start. In Armstrong's words, her brother and sister served the state—her sister as a legal secretary in the attorney general's office, her brother an inmate in state prison, after "drugs were found in his home," as Armstrong tactfully put it. Her father had abandoned the family when she was a young child, remarried, and died of pneumonia when she was nine.

In the 1980s, around the time she turned thirty, Armstrong began hearing a voice telling her to become a teacher. She tried to ignore it, but it persisted, and she went back to school, earned a credential, and started teaching fourth grade. She even entered a doctoral program in education, through the University of Southern Mississippi in Hattiesburg. Although she was still revising her dissertation, she talked as if she had completed her degree. Indeed, she often attached the term "doctor" to her name, even using "DocArm" as her e-mail address.

In Phoenix, Armstrong regularly attended a Church of God in Christ congregation that was headed by Ernestine Reems's uncle. Reems, on one of her national tours, visited her uncle's church to preach a guest sermon. For Armstrong, who had never lived away from her hometown, that day left no part of her life the same. She felt immediately drawn to the visitor from California. Reems had been named one of *Ebony* magazine's top fifteen women pastors, but she didn't put on airs. On the contrary, Armstrong could see that the slender, elegant preacher—who had tirelessly ministered to prostitutes and drug addicts—would speak to anyone, and in ladylike language at that. Armstrong believed those were the actions of a true person of God.

That evening, Armstrong returned for a second service, also led by Ernestine Reems. There, Armstrong had the most important spiritual experience of her life.

Pastor Reems preached with the sort of power and charisma that could only be described as a gift. In private, she sometimes described herself as tired and aging, but she went through a metamorphosis in the pulpit. In Oakland she led two Sunday services and many evening and early-morning weekday prayer sessions, in addition to guest appearances during her frequent travels. At her Center of Hope Church, she drew worshippers in with fervent sermonizing that could reach remarkable crescendos of passion. Sometimes she would shed her elegant heels to move through the pews as she preached, calling and exalting, until she ran out of breath. Her services inevitably ended with the faithful thronging forward to be touched by Reems's healing hands. Often, under the tender force of that touch, as the choir and the organ and the saxophone belted out the gospel, the worshipper would fall to the floor in holy ecstasy, to be caught by a waiting usher and gently covered in blue cloth.

In her sermons, Reems ranged in lithe movements from the sacred to the earthy and often quite funny. She would compare intimacy with the Almighty to intimacy between married couples, and carry off into a flirtatious riff on marital relations. Yet even when her tone was light, her words carried a resonant message: that black people were every bit as good as anyone else, and that living in a downtrodden corner of Oakland brought no shame. That message—of self-confidence and self-worth—sneaked even into what seemed mere humorous asides. "Take yourself a bubble bath," she advised the women of the congregation one day. "Put some smell-good in there. And when you get out, fix your hair. Put on your best clothes. Quit talking about 'I just wear this on Sunday.' Dress yourself up like you're going out with Mr. Six-Foot-Two. Look good for *you*. Take your last ten dollars and go to the best restaurant you can afford, and sit there and look important. I ain't preaching nothing but some good therapy, because you have to know how to encourage yourself."

Yet when she invoked the name of the Lord, Reems could be utterly, persuasively serious. During the service at Armstrong's church in Arizona, Reems told the congregation that anyone who wanted to receive the Holy Spirit should stand in the center aisle of the church, and Armstrong obeyed. The music stopped. Reems told the faithful to praise the Lord. For the first time in her life, Armstrong found herself in the transforming presence of the Almighty. She dropped to her knees, and then fell prone on the ground, overwhelmed and still. She felt as if she were fainting and remaining awake all at once. She was fully aware of what was going on around her, but her eyes were closed. To Armstrong, that rapture was like falling in love.

Armstrong had never seen Oakland. But that day, she decided to move there, so she could join Reems's congregation at the Center of Hope Community Church. Reluctantly leaving her Phoenix students a month into the school year, she took a job at the Hope Academy. She left that school after a year because she couldn't live on the meager pay, and taught instead in San Francisco. But the experience had not dulled her ardor to do Reems's will. She embraced her calling, and waited for the chance to use her skills in the service of the woman known simply as *Pastor*.

Now, a dozen years after she left Arizona, Pastor had rewarded her with the head position at the new school, telling her that it was God's will for her to do so. True, the formal selection of principals had not even begun. But Armstrong's appointment had been decided at the highest levels. Pastor Reems had made her wishes known in private conversation with Eugene Ruffin, the chief executive officer of School Futures. For the two of them, the union of School Futures and Laura Armstrong was a marriage of mutual convenience. Ruffin, a onetime Xerox executive turned entrepreneur, had entertained doubts; Armstrong had no experience as a leader. But Ruffin was anxious to do the bidding of the black pastors who played host to so many of his schools, viewing them as cornerstones to the company's expansion. Pastor Reems had told him that Armstrong was her favorite to lead the school. So, despite Ruffin's reservations, School Futures gave Armstrong the job.

By agreeing to shepherd the school, Armstrong was accepting a grand responsibility in a formidable institution. True, the school wasn't an impressive sight—an extra arm of the boxy, faceless church building, set back from broad MacArthur Boulevard by a small parking lot. Plywood panels divided the structure's interior into more than two dozen tiny classrooms, their aging desk chairs ready to be turned into kindling sticks. The building, which had three stories including the basement, was separated from the Castlemont High School campus by a shallow creek, which doubled as a haven for pot-smoking truants and a ring for fistfights. Together, though, the church and Castlemont represented an island of life on a moribund boulevard, whose storefronts hosted a string of liquor shops, missionary churches, social service outlets, and vacant buildings. And the Center of Hope lived up to its name. Like other powerful churches in ghetto neighborhoods across the country, it offered this hardscrabble corner what government and private enterprise had failed to provide: housing for the elderly and the poor, clothing and sometimes food, and now, perhaps, a good school.

For the pastor, reopening the school would fulfill a personal dream, which she had begun talking about months before. Reems was accustomed to setting grand goals and mapping her own confident course. Decades earlier, as a woman pastor in the male-dominated Church of God in Christ, she had defied family and convention to minister from the back of a flatbed truck at the age of twenty-three. Later, she established her own church on this benighted corner of MacArthur Boulevard. The Center of Hope Community Church—a nondenominational congregation with leanings toward the charismatic movement—now counted about 1,500 members. These days, when the pastor announced a plan, no one doubted her seriousness.

Indeed, the Center of Hope had been the first to act on the idea of a School Futures charter school, thanks to a collection of happy coincidences. Although Center of Hope was no power player at OCO, William Stewart's recollection of the available space at the old church school had provoked Matt Hammer to call. For the church, the promise of a quick-start school and renovation money seemed, quite literally, like an answer to Pastor Reems's prayers. School Futures' Ruffin had hired a dear friend and former colleague who lived in the area, a portly, fancy-dressing man named Jeff Harris, to oversee construction in Oakland. Already, the contractors were drawing up plans to gut the tired old school and rebuild it with new interior walls, new floors, suspended ceilings, fire sprinklers, the works. It would also bear a new name: the Ernestine C. Reems Academy of Technology and Art.

But even with time running short, the other four schools were progressing at an almost leisurely pace. Harris's architects had started work on a few of the other schools, but only two other leases appeared certain, both in the Fruitvale–San Antonio area where Lillian Lopez lived. The larger, in San Antonio, would occupy a warehouse and storefront that belonged to Volunteers of America; the smaller, in Fruitvale, would occupy a small, vacant school building that resembled a cheaply built apartment house. Both required substantial renovation. Elsewhere, lease agreements remained open questions.

By June Matt Hammer was understandably nervous. The leases should have been signed three months earlier. School Futures, finally, had set up a phone number in Oakland, but it wasn't getting much use. So far, there were just six applicants for four principal positions. (Five charters had been approved, but the Fruitvale and San Antonio schools were to share a principal.) Hammer knew that the success of these schools would depend largely on the people chosen to lead them. Throughout America, educators faced few challenges more crucial and difficult than the recruiting of visionary, energetic, charismatic school leaders. In Oakland, the burden of creating a good school would rest almost entirely upon the principals. Indeed, School Futures' whole design revolved around the power and responsibility of the principals—the people who would select the teachers, design the curriculum, win bonuses if the school performed well, take the blame if it didn't.

Finally, nearly two months after the charters passed, School Futures scheduled interviews with the six principal candidates. The hour-long interviews were held on June 2, less than one hundred days before school was to open, in OCO's drab conference room. True to School Futures' promises, parents and OCO leaders composed most of the panel. A couple of their small children wandered through the room. A father interpreted quietly for a Spanish-speaking mother. Yet the final say in hiring belonged to School Futures, which was represented by its two newest employees: the personnel chief, a disgruntled ex-psychologist named Tim Wolf, and the new operations head, Don Gill, who had reached the level of assistant superintendent for instruction in the Bakersfield, California, school system before defecting to the charter school movement. Together with Bennett, Ruffin, and a budget officer, they comprised the entire full-time professional staff of School Futures—an improbably small crew to start five schools in five months.

The would-be principals ranged in talent and qualifications, and if Hammer was entertaining fantasies of culling four good ones from the six, he was in for a disappointment. First up was a former principal of a private special-education school who also had served as an assistant superintendent in San Francisco's Catholic diocese school system. Her five-page résumé impressed, but after the interview, Hammer voiced his concern that she would employ teachers who were friendly rather than smart. The second was a teacher and psychotherapist who entertained the parents, but who, Hammer knew, had recently quit midyear at another charter school after a fight with its governing board. The bright spot of the day appeared, however, with the arrival of a woman named Felicitas Coates.

In white blouse and print jacket, Coates conveyed a matronly warmth that enchanted nearly everyone. A vice principal at Oakland's Garfield Year-Round Elementary, she bustled in five minutes late, out of breath, explaining that she had been trying to reunite a Hmong-speaking mother and child who had lost track of each other at the sprawling school. She answered questions in English and Spanish with nearly equal ease, explaining cheerily that she believed in "management by walking around" and "just having the communications open" with teachers. She said that she spoke sign language in addition to Spanish and English, and could communicate with other ethnic groups as well, even if she didn't speak the language. Visibly nervous to the end, she walked out still holding her Styrofoam cup of water.

As an administrator in an Oakland school, Coates, for better or worse, already had a reputation. One parent mentioned a rumor that Coates had "showed the students her middle finger" at Garfield. But everyone else was charmed—by her warmth, her sweetness, her multilingual multiculturalism, her talk of raising standards. She hadn't deviated much from reciting education buzzwords, but the group quickly agreed that she would make a fine choice for the Fruitvale–San Antonio school, in the same Spanish-speaking neighborhood where Coates had already established herself. "We ought to sign her up yesterday," said Tim Wolf, the personnel man. Hammer agreed. "I'm serious," he said. "Before she goes somewhere else."

The four P.M. interview arrived—an elementary teacher who also had trained as a lawyer. A few minutes into the interview, Hammer ducked out of the room and into the dimly lit foyer of the OCO office. Gene Ruffin and his pal Jeff Harris had arrived there with a distressing update on the building situation. One church was asking an exorbitant lease price; another was mired in an internal political debate on whether to do business with School Futures. As Hammer listened with growing frustration, Harris coldly laid out a few facts. "Everybody who started out in this process may not get a school right now," he said. Ruffin suggested a new possibility: opening one of the schools in January. "There's nothing magic about August," he said.

Hammer, alarmed, noted that it would be hard to enroll children in the middle of the school year, and to recruit teachers and a principal. Ruffin disagreed. Then he played his ace. There wasn't anything magic about five schools, either. "The fact is, we feel real comfortable with three," he intoned.

It was growing painfully clear to Hammer that he could no longer take anything for granted—particularly his onetime assumption that School Futures knew exactly what it was doing. A cut in the number of schools would mean disappointing dozens, perhaps hundreds of OCO members. As he grappled for strategies, actions, to manage the situation, he left before the last interview, at six P.M., with Laura Armstrong.

Armstrong showed up, which may have been the high point of the interview. The slender, quiet woman with cornrow braids apparently knew she had the job, and struck the panelists as angry at the prospect of wasting her time before them. Although the interview made for a tense hour, Armstrong's answers to the questions were fine. She had the credentials, the résumé, the passion, and literally the blessing of the right people.

No matter the tension the panel had felt with Armstrong. No matter the stray rumor about Coates's flipping the bird to schoolchildren. The Oaklanders had found two acceptable principals. And there were only ninety-six days left.

•   •   •

Studies prove what every parent intuitively knows: the quality of a child's teachers matters immensely. A string of three good teachers can set a child on a course for success, while three lousy teachers in a row can be devastating. And as Brian Bennett had told the OCO parents, schools in areas of deep poverty simply don't get their share of well-trained, experienced teachers.

If any challenge ranked with hiring qualified principals, then, it was recruiting good teachers. As with the principal search, however, School Futures' initial approach was leisurely enough to stir alarm within OCO. If all five schools were to open, they would require fifty or more teachers. Yet responses to the Internet announcements of teaching jobs outside the district bureaucracy had arrived in a mere trickle. Back in April, School Futures had talked of having all the teachers hired by mid-June. Now, Bennett breezily promised that the teachers would be on board by August 1. Uncertainties hung in the air—over whether to hire for schools whose leases were not complete, or which still lacked principals, who themselves should have been doing the hiring for their schools.

With the outlook for teacher hiring growing dark, Laura Armstrong maintained an even, tough front. Her school expected an enrollment of nearly three hundred children, in kindergarten through grade five or six, which meant she had a good baker's dozen of teachers to hire. She knew she could turn to newspaper ads if School Futures' recruiting scheme didn't provide enough teachers. It was fortunate she had a backup plan.

The first round of interviews, on July 10, showcased not just the Herculean difficulty of staffing two schools months later than most others, but also the rising hostility between the Oakland School Futures principals and their San Diego bosses, an antagonism that would have major implications in the months to come.

The teacher interviews were held in a frigidly air-conditioned, glass-walled room at the public library near OCO. A quick scan of the résumés for the day indicated that, even more than with the principals, the teacher candidates spanned a dazzling range. Among the eighteen who had applied were a Turkish-born drummer who spoke eight languages and had played a gig at the United Nations; a Mexican former university professor who barely spoke English; a dancer; an AIDS researcher; a handful of student teachers, substitute teachers, and teaching assistants; a couple of experienced teachers; and a forty-six-year-old man who oversaw NASA grants for the San Francisco State University Extrasolar Planetary Search Team without ever having earned a bachelor's degree, even after eight years of college. Tim Wolf handed out a list of nine questions and a rating sheet to a panel that included a few OCO parents, Hammer, and Armstrong. (Coates did not attend because her hiring was not yet final.)

Soon Wolf and Armstrong were sharply at odds in their opinion of the candidates. Wolf was vocal about his disappointment with most of them, labeling them inexperienced and inexpert. Armstrong saw many of them as willing to learn, not yet stuck with bad habits. Wolf also did most of the talking, jumping in to answer teachers who asked about union representation at the new schools. "You do not have any union rights under the charter law," he told one applicant, brusquely and not entirely accurately. "We think the current union bargaining agreements in districts inhibit the sense of flexibility we need to do effective education." He aggravated the growing tension by offering jobs on the spot to a couple of teachers without consulting Armstrong, their potential future boss.

Never was the contrast in views clearer, however, than in the case of a young man named Valentín Del Rio. Wolf was dismayed before Del Rio even entered the room. Del Rio's résumé listed his jobs in the three years since he graduated from college with a degree in criminal justice administration. Del Rio had worked as a substitute teacher, and as manager of two food stores, and saw fit to include faxing among his technical skills. Wolf puzzled over a phrase in Del Rio's explanation of his duties in his current job as a substitute teacher in nearby San Leandro. "What does 'Teach lesson plans left to do' mean?" Wolf wondered with contempt. "Obviously not an English major." He lamented the number of people who apply to charters out of uncertainty that they will get jobs in regular districts, and even suggested checking whether any of the candidates appeared on a "no-hire" list from a previous district. On that note, Del Rio was invited into the room.

The man behind the much-maligned résumé was ruddy, bearish, Mexican-American, and young, probably in his mid-twenties. He wore a dark blue dress shirt with a Polo logo, khakis, and no tie. The first question concerned how to generate student success. Del Rio said he would "try to make it a friendly environment for the kids." In addition to being well organized, he said, he would "tell them it's OK to say whatever they want." He promised to communicate with parents and to seek advice from colleagues; he used the word *multicultural* frequently. He was barely out the door before a few on the panel pounced.

"He doesn't speak English correctly," said a mother named Rosalía Mendoza. "He'd make a great teacher, but I think it's very important that he be able to articulate and be able to speak effectively."

Another mom, Xochitl Garcia, noted that Del Rio spoke fluent Spanish, and suggested he could fit well into the Fruitvale school. Mendoza didn't waver; she had liked him, but she viewed speakers of ungrammatical English as one of the district's problems.

Wolf piled on. "He really stumbled through the questions," he said.

Armstrong chose to be the contrarian. "I think he would be great with kids," she said. "He is willing to learn and to be mentored."

Mendoza, torn, conceded that with good mentoring, Del Rio could be an outstanding teacher. But she said, "I personally wouldn't want my sons to learn English incorrectly."

Wolf had the last word, for the moment. Del Rio, he declared, was fit to be a teacher's assistant. Worried, he turned to Armstrong. "Either we find a lot more qualified candidates," he said, "or you principals are going to have a task on your hands."

By the end of the first day of interviews, the panel had seen eleven applicants. Two had made the cut, and two, including Del Rio, were maybes. Any one of them might opt to accept a job elsewhere before school opened.

Eighty-eight days remained until the opening of school.

At six that evening, after the marathon of discouraging interviews, Armstrong and Hammer gathered a group of parents from Center of Hope and OCO to lay plans for assembling a student body. After some talk of discipline, required "volunteer" hours for parents, and uniforms, the group agreed to hold its first recruiting meeting on June 30.

Few there saw their task as anything more than filling a few hundred seats, and thus bringing in the per-student dollars that would allow the school to exist. The process appeared simple; they would get the word out, through posters, newsletters, community meetings, and word of mouth. If there were more applications than spaces, the school would give preference to church members, and compile a waiting list. No one discussed the implications of how the choices were made. For instance, they might have pondered the crucial question of whether the charters would skim off the well-organized parents, leaving the regular schools with an even tougher job. Or, on the other hand, whether the charter school's job would be harder because it would draw malcontents and kids who had not learned in regular schools. Or whether extending favored placement to church members broke the church-state barrier. Or whether, as the law required, special-education students would have a fair shot at enrolling.

All these questions receded in the face of a surprising fact: E. C. Reems and the Fruitvale school were struggling to enroll enough children. Given the dismal condition of education in their neighborhoods, one imagined parents ready to grab at any alternative. But the June 30 recruiting session at Center of Hope was sparsely attended. Even some of OCO's faithful were hesitant to enroll. Some wondered whether the school really would open; others, mostly Latino, fretted over how their children would fare in an overwhelmingly black school. And the district provided little help with the mechanics of the actual enrollment process. Armstrong, however, was typically direct. "The schools," she told parents, "will open in September."

As June meandered into July, many of the faithful did enroll. William Stewart signed up without hesitation at E. C. Reems—he was delighted to see his efforts pay off at a school that would be smaller and, he figured, more disciplined than the regular schools. Now, he spoke not for one child, but for four. His girlfriend of several months, Jasmine McGehee, a teacher's aide at Whittier Elementary, had moved in. She had three children—baby Jasmine, and Asia and Ronrico, who were preparing for fourth and fifth grade respectively. Like Stewart's daughter Malory, Asia and Ronrico had been attending Whittier, and their mother, Jasmine, wanted a change.

Lillian Lopez, despite her anxiety to see the charters approved, had delayed enrolling; she liked Alex's current teacher, and had been pondering remaining in the district so she could speak with authority on the small-schools effort. But the morning of July 29, she appeared at Felicitas Coates's recruiting table at Jefferson, angry. Mike Hopkins, the principal, had suspended her son for the crime of cursing on school grounds. The suspension was rescinded after she threw a fit, but the pettiness of the punishment forced her decision. For his part, Hopkins was content to see the charter crew signing up students in his own hallways. He wanted the lower enrollment at his famously crowded school.

The charter schools had the opposite problem. Their enrollment was still disturbingly low. And only sixty-nine days remained until they were to open.

•   •   •

By August, the charter school project was in trouble in every important area. School Futures had hired no new principals and had leased no additional buildings. Armstrong and Coates were lagging in their search for teachers. Armstrong had largely dispensed with School Futures' hiring process and had implemented her own, using the free weekly newspapers and the social network at her beautician's shop. With fourteen positions to fill, she had hired ten teachers, including Valentín Del Rio—the one she saw as a teachable man with a big heart. Coates, with two schools to staff—San Antonio and Fruitvale—had signed only one teacher. As that crisis escalated, Coates pursued teachers who had enthusiasm and smarts, but were so bereft of formal credentials that the district rebuffed them. One was Brian Cohen, who arrived from the Midwest with ten weeks of teaching experience and a heavy satchel stuffed with plans and lesson ideas. He talked his way into an interview with the district, despite clear statements he would not get a job. An officer in the personnel department explained that since he had not taken even the basic skills test for teachers, he was untouchable. Cohen couldn't understand why he, with "a portfolio the size of Manhattan," wouldn't be hired over a teacher with a credential. He argued that "schools in the USA are in a state of crisis," and told the interviewer, "I see kids going into these schools, and their souls are dying." The district remained unmoved. At the Fruitvale charter, however, Coates offered him a job.

Meanwhile, the opening date for San Antonio slid later and later, as Jeff Harris, the construction czar, awaited city permits that never came. The lack of buildings compounded the hiring problems. Amid the continuing uncertainty, School Futures hesitated to make formal employment offers to would-be teachers. In a time of teacher shortage, the applicants had no reason to bide their time; many accepted jobs elsewhere. Meanwhile, at San Antonio, students were signing enrollment forms for a school that might never exist.

As the sense of unease grew, communication among the two principals, School Futures, and OCO deteriorated. Many in Oakland were annoyed with School Futures, ensconced in faraway San Diego and frequently unreachable. Jeff Harris missed meetings and didn't return phone calls. What finally triggered a full-fledged crisis, though, was an obscure study of the heating and ventilation system at E. C. Reems.

The saga began when building contractors told Harris that code required them to install a bigger ventilation fan than they had originally expected. The size of the fresh-air ventilation system, they explained, was determined not by the planned occupancy, but by a "load analysis" of the actual maximum number of occupants the building could hold. The school was designed for 272 students, but according to the load analysis, it could hold 403. When Harris heard that number, it gave him an idea. All along, his aim had been to minimize costs and bring in the most revenue possible for his old friend Ruffin. Plus, the project had already shot well over budget—more like $800,000 than the original $400,000. So he asked the architects to redraw the plan with more classrooms in the same space to enable the building to house more students. True, the classrooms would be smaller. But the project would be cost-effective, he reasoned, because more students meant more money. Dr. Armstrong, out of town at the time, never heard a thing about it. Then, Harris decided to make similar alterations to the Fruitvale school, even adding a diagonal wall so as to squeeze in a maximum number of classrooms. Without consulting anyone, he slashed a computer room from the plans, saving additional money by forgoing the electrical outlets the computers would have required. He canceled plans for data lines that would provide high-speed Internet access. The "staff lounge" was moved to a tiny hallway that lacked room for even a couple of chairs.

Upon discovering the changes, Armstrong grew livid, and she let the contractors know it. The morning of August 4, however, Harris dropped by in his immaculate white Lincoln Mark VIII and talked to the entire crew. He brooked no doubt: the new building design would stay.

"The principal here is very angry about some of the changes that have been made," Harris said, standing in a classroom strewn with sawdust and tools. "It's a dramatically different school than it was before we made these changes, by about 180 students, which means about half a million dollars in revenue to School Futures."

The building contractor suggested a meeting with Armstrong, and an architect agreed, "The library's getting hacked down. We'll have to explain that." It all just set Harris off again.

"You all need to understand something," he said in a don't-you-question-me drawl. "Everybody has a function. My function is to produce a facility that can provide a quality education. I don't think we have compromised that." If Armstrong didn't understand, he said, that was not their problem. He addressed the group—construction workers, architects, foreman, contractor. "This is a profit center. Do you understand? This is a profit center!"

The contractor didn't entirely understand. "Are you saying you don't want us to explain this to her?" she asked.

"That's *exactly* what I'm saying," Harris growled.

Then Harris dropped by OCO, where the scene was grim. Matt Hammer, Ron Snyder, Tim Wolf, Felicitas Coates, Don Gill, and Laura Armstrong had gathered for teacher interviews. But of the eight applicants scheduled, every single one had canceled; they'd already accepted jobs in other districts. Just before Harris arrived, Wolf explained that he was still not allowed to make formal employment offers because of the uncertain construction schedule. Nearly everyone at the table had a complaint about Harris. On that note, Harris strode in, bearing more bad news about the San Antonio school.

"I just told you October-November," Harris said, his arms folded.

"It may be December." The opening dates for Fruitvale and E. C. Reems also had been delayed two days, to September 9.

Hammer and Snyder questioned him over failing to communicate about such crucial changes. Coates chimed in. "I have a concern that my phone calls are not being returned," she said. The meeting ended on an ugly note for all concerned, and Harris stepped into a back room for a private shouting match with Armstrong.

That afternoon, a giant Dumpster-hauling truck backed into the grand, ancient oak in front of Center of Hope, felling the tree and sending it crashing into the school. (The building somehow escaped serious damage.) And the ugliness between Oakland and San Diego kept growing. In the week that followed, Armstrong confronted Ruffin on the phone about the changes. She then returned to her teacher hiring efforts. Coates, however, was paralyzed. Swearing that she would not "run a sweatshop type of school by packing kids in there," she embarked on a path to fury that would run her afoul of her San Diego bosses. On August 10, with building and communication concerns a full-fledged crisis, the principals and OCO held summit-level peace talks with Ruffin and his lieutenants.

Ruffin and Harris arrived together, carrying a chart on an easel. Harris explained how twelve classrooms at E. C. Reems had become sixteen. "That facility is going to be incredible," Harris offered. And if they had doubled their cost projections there, they had tripled them at Fruitvale, spending $300,000 instead of $90,000. No one seemed very impressed. Hammer wanted to know how large the classrooms were. Harris estimated between four hundred and six hundred square feet. "Four hundred is pretty, actually real, small," Hammer said.

"OK," Harris said. "That's what the code says."*

Ruffin had more news. With the San Antonio date still uncertain, no students should enroll there, he said. Hammer, who knew that children already were signing up, bit his lip for a good while.

---

* It wasn't entirely clear what code Harris meant. The state education code recommends at least 960 square feet per classroom, but charter schools are exempt from that code.

But by the meeting's end, Ruffin made clear that he understood the communication problem, and he promised to work on it. There was, for a moment, a sense that the Oakland–San Diego rift might ease. But the time for all that was desperately short. It was now less than a month until the first day of school.

For Laura Armstrong, the building changes were facts in lumber and plaster now, and she didn't waste time on further battles. What she needed was a student body. What she and the church produced was a recruiting drive that the peacetime army might have envied.

In mid-August the school was about halfway to its target of 270 children. (Just because the school was now built for 400 students, Armstrong figured, didn't mean she had to fill it.) Ratcheting up the recruiting machine, the Center of Hope Church threw a community fair on August 14, complete with hot links on the barbecue, a moon bounce, booming gospel music, and outreach booths from the fire and police departments, the county infant health program, and the slavery reparations movement. It was the first warm, sunny day in a long time, and the place was packed. Armstrong and her new teachers signed up parents all afternoon. Then, with help from parent volunteers, they scoured the neighborhoods, knocking on doors and dropping off pink fliers that promised, "Outstanding faculty . . . Excellent facility . . . Beat the Rush!! . . . Enroll Now."

Armstrong described the academy as "a public private school" in her chats with prospective parents. The less well informed volunteers went further. A sweet-tempered mother named Lisa Fobbs spread the word on Eighty-second Avenue that week, her son trailing behind on a dirt bike. Mostly she stuffed fliers into chicken-wire fences, but occasionally she accosted residents. "Before, it used to cost, because it's a Christian school," she told one mother. "But now it's free." Elsewhere, she promised that the "wonderful curriculum" meant that children in the first grade would be doing second-grade work by the middle of the year. The school would also offer tutoring and after-school programs "where they really care about the kids," she assured. Many parents seemed interested. One, sitting in her car, clearly wasn't. "Oh, no, no, no," she said. "I have a ten-year-old and a twelve-year-old, and he goes to Spectrum." That was a special-education school for children with behavioral problems. Fobbs moved on.

In some places, it would have been hard to imagine choosing a school on the basis of a pink flier and a cheery sales pitch. On Eighty-second Avenue in Oakland, it worked fine. By week's end, the E. C. Reems Academy of Technology and Art was fully enrolled and was building a waiting list.

Many of the parents who enrolled were markedly less involved in schooling than William Stewart and Lillian Lopez. Among those who signed up was the family of a ten-year-old named Nazim Casey Jr. Nazim was being raised largely by his grandfather, because his parents had effectively departed from the scene—his father in prison, his mother on the streets, strung out on crack. The grandfather, Askia Casey, did not savor the idea of spending extra time to handle Nazim's schooling. Even so, he thought the charter school sounded like a better place than the regular public schools when he heard about it from Nazim's aunt, Monique Adanadus. She, in turn, had heard about it from her own aunt, who attended the Center of Hope Church. To Adanadus, it was a church school, no matter the public label. And indeed, the wide community of the church led the school to recruit many families in tough circumstances. Before moving in with his grandfather, Nazim had lived at the E. C. Reems Gardens apartments, a low-income housing complex built by the church, on a street the city had named E. C. Reems Court. Many of his classmates were to come from there, too—children of single parents, many of them surviving on government assistance checks, and many with little time or inclination to help out at school. Most of the children came from single-parent, low-income families, and many were being raised by formidable grandparents who had taken on five or six children at once.

Yet for all the tough cases, some children weren't so warmly invited. The school had hired a secretary, a young man named Lawrence Tottress, who was Dr. Armstrong's first cousin. Tottress had developed a habit of asking parents who were planning to enroll whether their children needed special education. If they did, he suggested they look elsewhere, because the charter school would not have a special-education class. The practice of turning away the disabled was illegal and highly risky; if it had been discovered, it would have been grounds for shutting the school down. Indeed, one of the powerful criticisms of charter schools across the country was that they didn't enroll their share of special-needs students. Armstrong privately acknowledged that her cousin was acting on her instructions, and she knew the school was legally required to provide special-education services. Yet she chalked the problem up to the lack of a formal agreement with the district, and, oddly, did not see her policy as screening out special-education students. Ultimately, though, no one in officialdom ever did find out.

Meanwhile, as uncertainty about how many schools would open persisted into mid-August, the tension between the new operations chief, Don Gill, and the two principals in Oakland heightened. A meeting on August 17 at OCO devolved into a round of accusations. Armstrong and Coates had questions about problems with furniture and materials' deliveries from San Diego. Then Armstrong addressed the continuing problem with communication with Ruffin and the rest of School Futures' headquarters. "Gene promised answers today; he's not here, it's not done," Armstrong growled. "You may hear a little bit of frustration in my voice." She also hadn't been able to reach the School Futures controller, which meant she couldn't spend money for materials she needed. "It's not working for me," she said. "I'm getting a little bit pressured here." Gill, meanwhile, didn't like having the discussion in front of an OCO audience, and he wondered out loud about the meeting's purpose. "A phone call takes care of this stuff," he snapped.

Abruptly, Armstrong walked out, trailed by her senior teacher, Carol Fields. Gill called out, "Does she have a minute?"

Armstrong heard him. "No," she told her boss brusquely. "Call me."

Gill, perturbed, asked, "Is that the meeting, then?"

It wasn't. Quietly, Ron Snyder asked where things stood with construction. A School Futures consultant gently asked what would happen if the San Antonio deadline were missed.

Matt Hammer answered in a calm but forceful voice. They had already asked children to enroll there, he said. If the deadline didn't hold, he said, "we're up a creek."

There were twenty-three days to go.

Laura Armstrong might have been a less than skilled diplomat, but she took her responsibility to assemble a school profoundly seriously. In truth, she didn't devote much thought to the matter of her relationship with Gill. As a teacher, independent in her classroom, she had never worked directly under any boss, and certainly not a white one, a situation she viewed with particular annoyance. She focused instead on the countless tasks that would give her school its character and soul. Already, she had recruited nearly all the teachers she needed, with little help from San Diego. Now, thanks to responses from the newspaper ads and the recommendations from her beauty shop social network, she had only a few jobs left to fill. She turned to developing a curriculum for the school, along with the rules, policies, and schedules that would shape a child's daily experience there.

In that effort, Armstrong benefited from plenty of dedication but very little time. Other charter schools in Oakland had devoted two years or more to advance design efforts with close attention to vision and mission. Such planning mattered, because the school's culture would affect students. Whether intentionally or not, the way teachers treated students, the way disputes were settled and people were talked to, would both shape the school and teach crucial lessons to children. And ominously, some charters had discovered that when such matters weren't decided ahead of time, teachers often fell back on what they already knew. That might have been called the opposite of innovation. Dr. Armstrong, however, didn't have years to plan and to work with her staff. In the few weeks she had, she strove to forge an identity for her school.

There were fourteen teachers in all. In keeping with Armstrong's vision of teachable teachers, classroom virgins outnumbered veterans two to one. A handful had taught before: Alan Foss, a refugee from a chaotic San Francisco charter school; an eccentric South American Spanish teacher named Gabriel Fumero; Troy Brookins, a friendly but tough-edged man who had taught in the rural California foothills; the lead teacher, Carol Fields; and Theresa Bade, a sweet, always smiling kindergarten teacher who had worked in Wisconsin for two years, and then spent a heartbreaking year teaching autistic children in the Oakland district with virtually no training or materials. The rest had recently graduated from college. Valentín Del Rio was among that group, as were Emily Deringer and Michelle Kalka, a couple of last-minute hires from Teach For America, a corps that recruits graduates of prestigious colleges to teach in tough schools. Yasmine Alwan, the other fourth-grade teacher, was the daughter of two teachers, but had never taught before. Also new to teaching was Roland Anderson, a bearish man of six-foot-several with a shaved head who was to teach, of all things, kindergarten. Likewise Cherlon Simms, whose name Armstrong heard at her beauty shop. As a group, the E. C. Reems faculty was strikingly young, idealistic, and free of whatever baggage came with teaching experience, because most of them had none.

The second morning of the staff-training week, Armstrong invited a professor from San Francisco State University to instruct the teachers about prejudice and ways of treating children. In one of the early exercises, the professor asked the staff to stand in groups by race and sexual preference. Four teachers among the fourteen came out as gay. Not everyone on the staff appreciated such forced self-revelation, though for the gay teachers, it was a moment of unity and support. Through the formative week, though, Armstrong—who sidestepped that particular event—was forming a relationship with her staff. Although reserved and sardonic, she was solid, a leader, in charge, and many of her staffers enjoyed her sarcastic banter.

At the same time, Armstrong was laying the foundations for what is called, in ed-school circles, the charter's "governance," which in plain English means who's in charge. Under the charter, a governing board of five people, including one each from OCO and School Futures, held the reins of the school. Ultimately, that body would have final say over major decisions. Indeed, in legal terms, that board *was* the school, in the same way that a corporation is indistinguishable from its board of directors. School Futures, according to the charter, was merely a contractor, with a renewable one-year agreement to manage the school, overseeing hiring, finances, and curriculum. Yet there was little talk of establishing that five-member board. Armstrong was focused on composing another group, with less power than the main board, called a "school site council." It was composed of the earliest, most involved parents and a handful of teachers. And parents had a real voice at the school, even voting on what math curriculum the newborn academy would use.

But for all Armstrong's good works at the school, the tension between her and San Diego had not diminished. Everyone had noticed her walking out on Gill at OCO. Gill had phoned her to discuss the matter, and Armstrong torqued up the confrontation, claiming that she did not work for him and hadn't called him back because they had nothing to talk about. With Coates, if anything, relations were even more hostile. She remained outraged over the school's redesign and seethed over the choices of paint and tile color. Those concerns, in fact, appeared to obsess her, eclipsing the need to hire teachers. "I'm not going to start the school with this bullshit," she told Gill on the phone, and she threatened to resign.

By the end of August, the tensions had reached the point where CEO Ruffin decided to intervene. He met with Pastor Reems, who shared his concerns over Armstrong's rudeness, and then visited OCO, where he discovered even more reasons to worry. Lillian Lopez complained that Coates seemed to be keeping the number of teachers she had hired a secret. (Best guesses suggested that she had hired about four; for Fruitvale alone, she needed seven.) Matt Hammer praised Armstrong's staff training, but said, "I'm just worried that none of this has gone on at Fruitvale." Stunned, Ruffin asked, "You mean the person who's never been a principal is more organized than the person who is?"

Across the OCO conference table, he told Gill cheerily, "You need to fire somebody." He seemed to have a preference about where the ax should fall. He mused, "I think we're going to be able to save Laura."

Ruffin and Gill then took both principals to lunch. The meeting was intended as a warning, but the two principals didn't seem to hear it. Coates, however, did make one remarkable statement: that she had hired all the teachers she needed for the Fruitvale school. To anyone familiar with the situation on the ground, it was a surprising claim; as of a day earlier, she still needed at least two more. With two weeks to go, one could only hope she was telling the truth.

• • •

In the world of Eugene Ruffin, things were not supposed to work this way. The cheekiness of his two Oakland principals—the first women to serve School Futures in that position—bewildered him. Ruffin himself had learned his relationship with authority inside giant institutions with clear lines of command: the Marines, IBM, and Xerox. To him, anyone who spoke in the way that Armstrong did to Gill "had kind of a death wish, or wanted to be fired."

In truth, the whole situation in Oakland mystified Ruffin. He couldn't understand why employees insisted on airing their internal complaints about "communication" in community meetings at OCO with parents—the customers—present. He didn't understand why there were so many gripes about the buildings. Nowhere had he seen evidence that a school couldn't achieve world-class results without forty square feet of classroom space per child. School Futures' Nubia Academy, in San Diego, had raised scores from the nineteenth percentile to the seventy-first, and it didn't even have phones in every room. Moreover, the fact of a rich backer didn't mean School Futures could spend money willy-nilly. Perhaps worst of all, he was deeply troubled by the ugly *them* versus *us* division between School Futures' San Diego headquarters and its Oakland principals.

Ruffin's vision of how things were supposed to work was on

display a couple of days later back in Southern California, home to all but one of the School Futures campuses. The evening of September 2, aboard a yacht rented by a conservative foundation, School Futures took its San Diego teachers out for a dinner cruise. It wasn't just a celebration; it was the night awards, and bonus checks, were to be presented. The scenery in the purple-hued San Diego sunset was lovely, as the craft cruised at five knots past Harbor Island, Shelter Island, and Coronado. But few on board seemed to notice; the teachers were avidly discussing bonuses. Who had earned the $350 pay supplement for not missing a single day of school? From memory, they offered page references in the employee handbook for calculating the cash awards. Such conversations were well-nigh impossible in the regular public schools, where union contracts had, by and large, wiped out notions like merit pay and bonuses. Ruffin was stirred to strong words by the scene. "It's like finding a cure for cancer," he told the teachers in his dinnertime speech. "Except in this case the cure is known. It's just a question of overcoming the barriers."

School Futures' "cure" depended on three basic concepts: solid, packaged curriculum; constant adjustment of teaching through frequent testing; and absolute accountability for principals and teachers based on the structures of business, not of school districts. Districts and unions gave teachers tenure and job security. School Futures believed teachers should earn their jobs every year. If their students learned and performed well on tests, teachers and principals received bonuses; if they failed, they got fired. And anyway, Ruffin reasoned, there was no need for unions, because School Futures treated its employees well.

It was a curious position for a man who himself had played a part in a labor movement of sorts. At Xerox in the 1970s, Ruffin had participated in a bold action by black salesmen to smash a glass ceiling keeping them out of the executive ranks. Ultimately, Ruffin rose to the position of vice president, overseeing the office-products division, and his good friend Harris became his director of strategic planning. In his fight for equal chances for black employees, Ruffin persuaded the man who then managed the national sales force—David Kearns, who was later to become CEO—of the rightness of his cause. Ruffin also filed legal actions against the company, ultimately achieving considerable success. Yet he now regarded collective bargaining as a holdover from some Stone Age of American industry. Although necessary in the past, unions were obsolete and annoying, an inflamed appendix.

The man whose money and vision built School Futures, the elusive John Walton, was on the boat that evening, too. Despite his shyness, he delivered a speech from talking points Gill and Ruffin had written for him, congratulating the successful teachers and doing his best to get his mouth around phrases like "You base your school on the teachings of Kwanzaa." But it seemed to come from the heart when he said, "This is the most rewarding experience I've ever been a part of."

Walton guarded his privacy remarkably closely for a billionaire seeking to influence national policy. The plainspoken and plainer-dressing man rarely spoke to the press. Yet in a world of hidden agendas, Walton seemed genuine about his reasons for getting involved in school choice. Indeed, when people asked him about it, he would stare, puzzled and a bit annoyed, as if he had been asked the color of the sky on a clear day. "This is the single most important issue we face as a country, because it affects all the other issues," he said with characteristic simplicity. "Those with education are eligible for high-pay jobs. Those without are not." If you can't offer kids a decent education, he said, you might as well lock them up at age six.

Walton, raised on the notion of free enterprise, remarked on the yacht that night that he was disappointed that the school-choice battle couldn't be waged with the districts in an air of friendly competition, like best friends competing on the Little League ball field. Someone wondered aloud whether his actions resembled traveling to a competitor's ball field just to show off one's own talent. Walton's eyes flashed fury for an instant, but then he controlled himself, paused, and chose his words: "It's not their ball field."

Walton, the son of a multibillionaire, had his reasons for playing in the school-choice game. Ruffin, conceived out of wedlock by an eighteen-year-old girl in Birmingham, Alabama, had his own. From searing personal experience, he knew the changes a solid education could bring to the life of a poor African-American boy. His mother was a tenth grader when she got pregnant with him, but even at that spring age, she took it upon herself to hide the pregnancy so the father-to-be would stay in school. The young man, then a high school senior, was on track to become one of the first blacks in town to attend college, and she decided to keep the secret rather than divert his course in life.

Ruffin's mother moved to the South Side of Chicago and opened a beauty salon. They lived in the back rooms. A devout Catholic, she converted to Baptism when Ruffin's Catholic school kicked him out for racial reasons. He enrolled at Hyde Park High School, where he was one of twelve black students. Like his father, he enrolled in college, majoring in philosophy and psychology at DePauw. Then, after one stint in the Marines and another at IBM, he did a term at the University of San Francisco Law School until money ran out, and he joined Xerox.

Ruffin had come to education rather accidentally, when he did a bit of market research on private schools for an Atlanta investment group. Later, John Walton—who, like Ruffin, lived near San Diego—invited Ruffin to chat about building a company that would pave the way for vouchers in California and elsewhere. Ruffin never suspected that Walton meant to appoint him chief of that company, which took the name School Futures Research Foundation. Once there, Ruffin went to work on the voucher idea and quickly came to see it as an idea ahead of its time; California, and the rest of the country, had little appetite in the late 1990s for what many saw as an assault on public schooling. Looking for a new reason to exist, tiny School Futures set about creating charter schools in the inner city, in part to give some credibility to the idea of school choice and education outside the big system.

Now, Ruffin was determined to bring poor black children quality education, and in the process to further Walton's political aims, embodied in School Futures' business plan: "To demonstrate and put pressure on the current monopolistic system to change." Like many EMOs, School Futures brought the language of business to schooling, talking of "market development and penetration" in the $384 billion "potential market base for quality education nationally." "In brief," the document concluded, "our marketing plan is to outperform our competition, acquire recognition as the best, and build a profitable national organization that cares about children." In the five-year plan were three objectives. They not only indicated the remarkable scale of the plan, but also almost accidentally let readers in on Ruffin's real ambitions—despite the fetters of a nonprofit corporation. Within five years, the document said, School Futures would manage and operate one hundred schools, increase student performance 20 percent per year, and make an 8 percent profit.

•   •   •

In Oakland, where September had arrived like an unwanted houseguest, few were talking of business plans, bonuses, or fancy curriculum strands. If people had read School Futures' pledges to place "a heavy emphasis on science and math with technology used as both a subject and a tool," along with "language arts, music, leadership principles, public service, and ethics," they had either ignored or forgotten it. With barely a week until the opening of school, Armstrong and Coates were hurrying to assemble at least a bare-bones structure for their schools. Teachers had spent some time on lesson plans and rules at E. C. Reems, but were spending as much time moving desks and chairs into a building where floors were still being laid and electric wiring installed.

The one piece of good news was that Coates had been telling the truth when she told Ruffin all her teachers were hired. Somewhat miraculously, Fruitvale—which had only five teachers signed up that morning—had rounded out its roster with three more genuinely good hires that day. The change marked a stunning rescue for Coates, who had been reduced to trying to use her contacts to poach bilingual teachers headed for district classrooms.

Only the Fruitvale school—now renamed Dolores Huerta Learning Academy, in honor of Cesar Chavez's legendary partner—and E. C. Reems were prepared to open. Construction at San Antonio remained dormant. The other schools looked even more uncertain. Confusion reigned over what to do with the kids already enrolled for San Antonio. Reems's opening got pushed back two days, and then two more, because of construction problems. Each time, the teachers had to call the entire parent body and explain. Valentín Del Rio, sitting at a picnic table in his grassy backyard in San Leandro, handled most of the Spanish speakers. After the delays and uncertainty, a handful of families bailed out and returned to the district schools. Construction work ran past two A.M. some nights, through seemingly endless crises—a drunken electrician, a lack of Dumpsters to haul away the mounting debris. The scenes were sometimes comical; a construction worker looked hopeful when a delivery truck arrived, asking the nearby Armstrong, "Are those doors?" "No," Armstrong said, "these are books."

The excitement lasted well into the late hours of Sunday, September 12, the night before the true opening day. Even then, as teachers hurriedly decorated their classrooms, workmen were still finishing hallway floors. The rooms themselves were awash in randomly placed furniture, as if the gravity had been switched off for a while, allowing the chairs and tables and desks to drift. Sewage had flooded the basement Friday, and it stayed flooded through the weekend. "I'm going to start swearing," said one of the few veterans, Troy Brookins.

Amid all the chaos, though, the E. C. Reems staff was coming together to form a team. They met daily, and the veterans helped walk the newbies through matters both trivial and great. The final teachers were hired, thanks to Teach For America. No one within the school knew about the recent threats to Armstrong's job, but Pastor Reems certainly did. And with less than a week until opening day, on September 7, she appeared at a meeting of the teachers to stress that Armstrong still had her crucial support. She told the teachers that she knew there were candidates with more experience, but she said, "I really, really believe that Laura's teachable and that she's willing to walk through this schooling for children who really, really need it." She blessed the teachers for being there, in the inner city, and reminded them that "all you see here is by faith. We bought the building by faith. We feed the hungry. We house the homeless." She asked the staff to pray with her, and they bowed their heads.

"I give you all the glory. I give you all the honor. I give you all the praise," Reems extolled. "We want to deposit all the good we can into these children. We believe that some of them are going to be governors, doctors, lawyers." Sweeping her view over the teachers, she said, "I praise you for these people who are willing to come into our community. I thank you for all of it and I ask all of these blessings."

Valentín Del Rio, who had been assigned to teach fourth grade, wasn't quite sure what to make of all the prayer and such. Religion was a private thing to him, and it didn't belong in a teachers' meeting at a public school, he figured. But he was more focused on preparing for the first day. He liked his second-floor classroom, with its windows overlooking the little creek and Castlemont. He didn't mind that it was a bit small, even if he had to rearrange it several times to get all the desks to fit; now, he just wanted to decorate the walls. Del Rio, a man who washed his car and had his hair cut every two weeks, cared about the appearance of things, and he wanted his room to look good. He picked up a few things at the teacher supply store—an alphabet illustrated with pictures; a sign that said LEARNING IS FUN; a hand-me-down map of "Afrika," circa 1976. On the night before school, he placed a seventy-sheet wide-ruled notebook on every desk, and an ancient boom box at the front of the room, and wrote on the dry-erase board:

Sept. 13, 1999
Mr. Del Rio
Room 304
Good morning!!
  1. Please come in quietly.

2. Find a comfortable seat and get organized.

3. Put your name on your journal and then start writing.

What do I want to learn this year?

The question was directed at the children, who would show up in the room a scant twelve hours later. But it could as easily have been posed to their teacher. Del Rio figured he belonged at Dolores Huerta or San Antonio, not here at this school in an African-American church. He wanted to work with Mexican Americans like himself. He also thought he'd had a terrible interview, and wondered why he had been hired—maybe because they wanted a male teacher? But for all his doubts, Del Rio was an optimist, and he was excited by this adventure. He was also more than a little humbled by it. He hadn't done much since graduating from college—bummed around at some minor jobs, earned some pocket cash as a substitute teacher. This was his first significant step into adulthood. He knew how important teaching was, and he wanted to be good at it.

Del Rio left the school around eight that night, with construction still fully underway. He picked up a banana at the store, and some cream for his morning coffee. His roommate had friends over to watch a video, but he retired by 11:15, serious about being ready for the next day. But before he slept, he prayed. Del Rio always talked to God, and tonight he needed that conversation especially. He prayed to God to help him choose the right path. *If this is what you want me to do,* Del Rio prayed, *help me make it go smoothly.*

As consciousness slipped into slumber, Del Rio's mind drifted. He thought for a few moments about rising on time in the morning. And then Valentín Del Rio, the new teacher, fell asleep.

PART II
A School

Beginnings

Shortly before midnight on Tuesday, September 12, some eight hours before classes were to begin, the last of the construction workers and cleaners trudged out of the E. C. Reems Academy. As the clock swept slowly into Wednesday, silence settled over the school.

Just a handful of hours later, while most of MacArthur Boulevard bathed in six A.M. slumber, the Center of Hope Community Church started its day. Elsewhere on the street, few lights shone in the chilly predawn mist. But brightness beamed out from the heavy glass doors of the church, where eighteen people had gathered for the early-morning service. Arrayed in attire from the fashionably professional to the casually athletic, they took seats in a small chapel. It fell to a lanky man known as Brother Brumfield—the term "Brother" signified that he was "saved," or born again—to open the service. Seated on the stage in a sweatsuit, Brumfield interspersed prayers with his own observations, warning the worshippers to be careful in their daily lives because "so many people are unsaved."

A quarter of an hour into the service, Pastor Reems arrived, to the gentle applause of the worshippers. Shedding a flowing overcoat, she revealed an elegant pinstriped suit. Reems, who had a gift for melding the earthy and the divine, sometimes referred to praying as "making love to Jesus." Today found her in an especially celebratory mood. "The Lord has been good to us," she told the faithful early risers. "We're going to open our school today."

She called for a reading from Exodus that follows the parting of the Red Sea and the drowning of the Egyptians: "I will sing unto the Lord, for he hath triumphed gloriously: the horse and his rider hath he thrown into the sea. The Lord is my strength and song, and he is become my salvation. . . . The Lord is a man of war."

Pastor Reems told her flock that the opening of the little charter school stood as a triumph for the church, over gangs, over bureaucracy in the city and the education system. "Nobody but the Lord would understand the enemy," she said. "I just kept praying and believing in God, and God brought it to pass."

As the congregants read, Laura Armstrong slipped silently through a side door and into a pew on the edge of the sanctuary. She wore a strong front; no one would have known she was nervous and afraid, sleepless and jazzed, and humbled by the realization that she, alone, would lead the school. Indeed, she faced down an anxiety that knew no parallel in her adult life. Today marked the peak in a journey of destiny, her path mapped by the Lord himself. Today, all would look to her. She prayed for guidance to make the right decisions. And she took great comfort in joining with her fellow congregants in worship.

"Let this be a day of just praying and rejoicing and thanking the Lord," the pastor said. "Not only has he done great things, but you expect great things." Then, with stunning early-morning vigor, the congregants launched into song: "My Soul Loves Jesus, Bless His Name." Laura Armstrong, lost in her thoughts, closed her eyes and sang gently.

It was not yet dawn.

•   •   •

Valentín Del Rio was ahead of schedule. He had set the alarm for 5:27—an odd number he arrived at by pressing the "fast" button on his digital clock—but he woke at 5:05. He rose without delay, ironed his white Polo dress shirt and his navy slacks, showered, dressed, and made coffee, which he drank as he darted around the house and climbed into the car. He had planned to leave home at 7:15, but as he turned the ignition key in his Honda, the dashboard clock read 6:35. He laughed at himself, amazed that a bunch of nine-year-olds could cause him such anxiety.

Less than ten minutes later, he walked up the short flight of steps at the entrance to the school, and marveled. The space was immaculate, the floors a mirror of freshly laid wax. It was like entering a church, he thought. He walked to his room and swung back the heavy door, making a mental note to find a doorstop. Then, for a moment, he panicked, thinking that he had forgotten to bring the copied handouts, but he discovered them in his bag. An hour remained before the children arrived. Searching for things to do, he decided to fix up the interior decorating.

He had discovered little that appealed to him at the downtown teacher supply store, and perhaps as a consequence, the decoration of his room had a slightly random quality. On phosphorescent paper, posted at intervals around the L-shaped classroom, were large-print words in English and their translations in Spanish. They hung on the wall, though they apparently were meant to be cut out and pasted to the items they described: "Table/Mesa; Door/Puerta." The cardboard-mounted 1976 "Afrika" map had sprung loose from its sticky-gummy moorings and lay on the floor.

Del Rio picked up Afrika, rearranged the stickum, and reversed continental drift, murmuring, "It's going to keep falling and falling and falling." His nervousness and excessive preparation came with the territory of a first day in teaching, as surely as the blank grade-book and the freshly sharpened pencils. Del Rio wondered whether he would be able to handle his charges—whether, through some bizarre miracle, a couple of dozen willful, whimsical children would do what one adult asked. If he was anything like most other teachers, he would never forget this first day, or the names and faces of the children in that first class, no matter how long he stayed in the profession. And, like many new teachers, Del Rio combated his nervousness through what's known in education-speak as overplanning—devising far more activities than could possibly be accomplished in one day. He knew he had overplanned; he had seven activities scheduled for just the first two hours of class, and hadn't left time for the all-school assembly. But he had other worries. After glancing over his roster, he ran down to the office to check the spelling of a child's name that was printed unclearly. Then, back in the solitude of his classroom again, he wrote instructions on a portable dry-erase board to explain how the kids should fill out their emergency information cards. It was 7:45—high time, Del Rio felt, for the bell to ring.

The truth was, Del Rio was ready—as ready as a first-year teacher could be. The room was arranged, the handouts in neat stacks, the journal assignment on the board. Del Rio himself looked ready— neatly shaven, his red tie and crisp shirt lending him a sharp, professional air. For all his preparations, though, it had slipped his mind that the teachers were supposed to gather on the yard at 7:40—five minutes ago—to pick up their kids. (The school didn't have a bell.) Alone inside the building, he might never have remembered if not for Donald Evans, visiting the school on its first day, who strolled down the hall on a mission of mercy and poked his head into Del Rio's room. "You ready?" Evans asked. Del Rio offered an unconvincing affirmation. Gently, Evans delivered the news. "I think they're downstairs meeting the kids," he said.

With a groan of remembrance that sounded like he had been shot, Del Rio dashed out the door and speed-walked to the yard. It was cool outside; a dreary gray sky hung over the onetime construction site at 8411 MacArthur, now neat and clean. Only a few signs of the renovation frenzy remained: a cherry picker and a Dumpster, fenced off with orange plastic, and the building's temporary nameplate, a scrap of wood spray painted with *8411*. The teachers were lined up, looking like police academy graduates in their blue pants or skirts and white shirts. Every Monday, they would wear the same uniform as the kids.

The tiny island hummed with the frenetic energy of two hundred children on their first day in a new school—and of eight newly minted teachers among a staff of fourteen. A year ago this school had been an idea not even committed to paper. Three months ago it was a dusty, empty building. A week ago it was a crew of twenty-somethings in shorts and T-shirts, dreaming up curriculum. A day ago it was a dusty, cluttered mess. Now, it was a school. A swarm of children swirled around as mothers, aunts, sisters, grandmothers, and occasional fathers worked quietly but intently to connect child with teacher, and then to form a line in front of each teacher. Overseeing the surprisingly orderly process was Principal Armstrong, aware that all eyes—the kids', the teachers', the parents', and the pastor's—rested on her. She smiled at the sight of so many children from this gritty, forgotten neighborhood wearing the uniform of their new school, eager to learn. She held the microphone of a portable public-address system, scouring her memory for the opening remarks she had written the week before. Armstrong sometimes had to listen to her own voice to gauge her anxiety level. Now, she instructed the children to repeat after her: "Good morning, Principal Armstrong." As she said her own name, her voice cracked like a teenager's.

* * *

Some of the seasoned teachers had arranged their students into meticulously straight columns before ushering them into the building. Valentín Del Río's students, numbering ten so far, were not in anything resembling a neat line. They were in a clump. Del Río, however, beamed at the simple miracle of the children's expectant presence, at the class that was finally his, at the threshold of his grand new venture. He led his students—*his students!*—to the classroom and directed each child to an assigned seat. Many read the instructions on the board and opened the journal notebooks he had put on their desks. Some didn't. One chose not to sit down at all, but instead ambled to the window and peered out.

"Are you guys able to read what it says on the board?" asked Del Río, speaking in a game-show-host voice whose pitch had risen two octaves in boyish, hopeful enthusiasm. The class murmured general assent, then turned to the morning's journal topic, on what they wanted to learn this year. Del Río followed with a round of good-mornings and encouragements and instructions and upbeat questions: "Are you guys ready for school?" Four more students trickled in, two accompanied by their mothers and two by their fathers. Most of the children stayed silent. Some toiled torturously slowly in their journals, while others wrote nothing at all. Del Rio called the roll. There were now fourteen children, two Latino, the rest black.

Del Rio circulated through the room, glancing at pages, and found many of them sparse. "Whoever writes the most gets a prize!" he announced. One child asked what to write about. Squatting in front of the boy's desk, Del Rio looked imploringly at him, suggesting starting places: things he had seen on television, or facts about athletes or the president. None drew a reaction. "There's nothing that you want to learn about?" Del Rio asked. "No." Daunted, Del Rio bailed out. "Well, just do your best," he said.

Now, a boy in the first row complained that he couldn't concentrate on his writing because Jonathan—the boy who had gone to the window earlier—was talking. "OK, shhh," Del Rio said unconcernedly as he passed Jonathan's desk. But the complainer, who had decorated his notebook with the Arabic-sounding name Nazim, seemed to be having troubles. When Del Rio asked whether the class was finished with the writing assignment, Nazim begged for two more minutes to work. He stood over his desk, scribbling with violent strokes, hoping to attain the largely theoretical Prize for the Journal Entry of Greatest Length. "I think we're ready, right?" Del Rio asked once, and then again a minute later, but each time, Nazim cried out, "No!" Finally, Del Rio cut off the writing period, which had stretched far past the five or ten minutes he had planned. "Who's going to be first?" he asked.

"Me!" Nazim volunteered, nearly shouting, a look of life-or-death urgency in his eyes. "Can I go?" he called. Del Rio agreed, and the boy marched to the front of the room.

"My name is Nazim." The handsome student had microscopically close-cropped hair and a smile that recalled Denzel Washington. Del Rio's class listened raptly to this first student performance of the year, as Nazim read in a halting voice. "I want to learn about the school and how to spell. I want to learn to read. I want to learn about the kids." Del Rio encouraged him to continue, not knowing that was all Nazim had written. So the boy improvised, pretending he had written more. "I want to learn about the teacher. I want to learn about math. I want to learn about reading. I want to learn about science and social studies." At Del Rio's prompting, the class applauded. Nazim sat, but he was not done talking. Dismayed at the lack of other volunteers, he announced, "C'mon! I said mines. Y'all won't get a treat though, dawg." His street slang provoked laughter. A girl read her journal entry, and Nazim played cheerleader. "Dang, give her applause! Dang!" Del Rio was growing impatient. "Did you see anybody else doing that when you were up here?" Nazim shook his head no, and shut down his act, for the moment.

Already, though, Del Rio knew which child would present his greatest challenge. And even in these first minutes of the year, it was painfully clear that Del Rio needed to establish control of his class. Indeed, Nazim's calm proved only momentary. He did listen spellbound to the next reader, Asia McGehee, whose pretty face and first-day-of-school braids immediately tickled Nazim's fancy. "I want to learn about division, reading, spelling, and making friends," she read in a clear, confident voice. "And I want to learn about my planet, my city, and the world, about plants, chemicals, lava, gas, and other things, too."

Nazim seemed more interested in her name than in her academic pursuits, and wondered aloud whether Asia was from Asia. Del Rio asked why he thought so, and Nazim said she sounded like it. Del Rio, unfortunately, took the bait. "What do people from Asia sound like?" he asked. Aided by a couple of other boys, Nazim immediately launched into a jabbering mimicry of Chinese. Flustered, Del Rio demanded an apology from Nazim. "Sorry," the boy said. Del Rio squatted in front of Nazim's seat, telling him that from now on he must raise his hand to speak, and that he was not to turn to talk to classmates behind him. But a minute later, Del Rio saw Nazim turn to a boy behind him. "How many times do I have to tell you not to turn around?" Del Rio asked, now angry. Nazim dealt another card from his formidable deck of excuses: the I-was-helping-you line. "I was just telling him to read," he said. Moments later, Nazim carried his disruptions a step further; now he was plugging his ears and singing as another boy tried to read to the class.

Del Rio tried to reason with Nazim. "He was quiet when you were reading," Del Rio said. "No he wasn't," Nazim shot back.

The more the energy in the room built, the more overwhelmed Nazim became by the teeming streams of information his eyes and ears dispatched to his brain. At one point, glancing at the paper of the girl behind him, he called out in alarm, "Mr. D! Do you have to indent? Because she didn't!"

Meanwhile, as the reading of the essays went on, the signs of trouble mounted. Jonathan had compiled a lengthy list of interests, ranging from shapes and food to history and electricity, but he read only two sentences. The rest "is personal," he said. "It's classified." Del Rio coaxed and cajoled his more reluctant students to read, telling those who had written nothing at all that they could make it up out loud, assuring them it was easy. Nazim, meanwhile, wanted to reclaim the center of attention. "Can I say my poem now?" he asked.

As the interruptions increased, Del Rio didn't know what to do. He liked the way the rest of the class was behaving, and felt relieved that the students liked him, too. But little Nazim left him angry and uncertain. The boy was clearly smart, but he continually talked out of turn, riling his classmates. And much to Del Rio's consternation, none of what he had tried so far was having much effect, except maybe for shouting. So he did something that a more experienced teacher might have considered a dangerous mistake: he started bargaining.

"You need to behave," he said. "If you behave, I'll let you do anything you want." Nazim skipped the poetry recitation and left his seat to go to the window instead. "Hey, come on," Del Rio said.

With journal time over, and exactly one hour gone, Del Rio asked the children to fill out cards with emergency contact information for their parents. Del Rio couldn't have anticipated the immediate question: What if you don't know how to spell your parents' names?

After puzzling that one out, Del Rio decided to lay out class rules. He opened with a reasonable gambit: "There's rules in this class like there's rules at home, right?"

With eyebrows arched, Nazim flashed the class a thousand-candlepower smile and announced, "No, I get to do anything."

Del Rio figured that was probably true.

Del Rio worked to elicit a code of conduct from the kids, and he targeted his chief annoyance. "Nazim, you're going to be in trouble all year if you don't pay attention," he said. "I need you to be good." He then offered a lengthy explanation of why obedience was important, committing what many teachers would regard as another cardinal mistake: he told them he wanted not just their compliance, but their affection, and that he would regulate his own affection according to their behavior.

"My job is to make you guys want to be here, to make you guys wake up and say, 'I want to go to Mr. Del Rio's class and see what he's going to teach us today. I had fun yesterday. He's a really nice guy.' And that's what I want to say about each and every one of you."

Nazim interrupted, and Del Rio turned on him, the flow of his address broken.

"Nazim, that's exactly what I'm talking about. Right there."

Then Del Rio resumed his speech, detailing what would happen to rule breakers—calls home, after-school detention.

As usual, Nazim had a question.

"Are you mean?"

•   •   •

Looking out over the parking lot that served as the school's playground on that first day, one discovered a lovely scene, resembling one of those cheery movies where the good people of the community unite to improve the lives of ghetto children. Kindergarten girls in navy jumpers and white blouses hopscotched in opposite directions, miraculously avoiding collisions in the middle square. Older children drew on the asphalt with colored chalk or skipped rope in complex double-Dutch choreography or blew massive soap bubbles. Brother Brumfield from the church directed workers repairing the fence.

Inside, however, the scene was less inspiring. Del Rio actively questioned the ability of his students. Their writing confirmed his fears. He asked them to compose a letter to him about themselves. He wasn't sure exactly how fourth graders should write, but he was pretty sure these examples did not meet the standard. "To day is the fist day of shcool," one girl's letter opened. "I am 9 yeas old and was born in Oakland Californa I Afircan-American I went to shcool at lakevie."

Nazim erased and revised industriously until he had the school's name spelled correctly. He wrote, like almost all the other students, in block print rather than cursive.

> Dear Mr. d My name is nazim My favirate school is Ernestine Cleveland reems Academy. Mr. d I like this school a lot Mr. d you a nice to. When I am bad make me wirte.

Some of the kids themselves seemed aware of the reasons for choosing a new type of school. "i was bor i california and im mexican america," one boy wrote. "My old shcool name was Lockwod wasan ril good."

For all the mechanical errors, though, the children's letters betrayed a charm and hope undimmed by difficult circumstance. "I Love to explore, figerout, and most of all I Love to invent," wrote a boy named Jason. "When Im all grown up i want a Baskitball Star."

No one, however, wrote in sunnier tones than Asia, who clearly had heard Del Rio's plea for affection. Covering a whole page with her generous, bold print, she wrote,

> Dear Mr. Del rio,
> Welcome to your first few days of a great shcool year. My name is Asia McGehee. I am 9 years old I was born in san francisco. I am

African ameircian. I don't speak African. I went to shcool at Witther elamentry shcool. I hope you like very much.
  Sincerely, Asia McGehee

She decorated her signature with a heart with a smile inside, and then added:

P.S. You sure are a nice techer

As the first afternoon drew to a close, though, Valentín Del Rio wasn't feeling like a nice teacher. His initial pleasure at a friendly, quiet class had evaporated as the kids interrupted him over and over. He fought to maintain his composure, and pondered his options—could he send kids to the office for misbehaving? Worse yet, he wondered whether things would be this way all year. His concerns went beyond behavior: after seeing the kids' stunted, grammatically troubled letters, he suspected many were way below grade level. And he was uncomfortable. His classroom, on the sunny side of the building, had turned stuffy in the afternoon heat, and Del Rio sweltered in his tie and long-sleeved shirt. His sweaty nervousness stoked his irritability.

With minutes left in the school day, he assigned homework: an essay on good behavior. The kids' response dramatically indicated what had—and had not—been happening in their previous classrooms. First, the word *essay* produced blank looks. So Del Rio settled for demanding twenty lines of writing, which sent Nazim into a fit of sobbing which, at first, Del Rio could not tell was faked. Other students were trying to figure out the assignment. "Now I get it," Asia told the class helpfully. "You're supposed to write how you're supposed to act in school, twenty times." Battling exasperation, Del Rio wrote some suggested openings for an essay on the board, and told the class to copy them down. The volume in the room was growing. "I can't concentrate," complained Nazim, the chief distractor. Del Rio just glared.

Then Afrika fell off the wall again. As Del Rio went to pick it up, Asia went to deposit a piece of trash in the can at the front of the room. Seeing his opportunity, Nazim whispered a nasty remark out of the teacher's earshot. Asia kicked him, and Nazim leapt from his seat, all righteous indignation. "Why did you do that?" he bellowed at a volume calculated to get Del Rio's attention.

Del Rio called for silence and addressed the class, explaining that the excess talking had used up the time that would have been spent on math and science. "I have been interrupted too much today," Del Rio said.

That was the moment Nazim chose to belch.

Del Rio was outraged. "You don't burp in front of your mom," he challenged.

"Yes I do," Nazim shot back.

The noise swelled again, and Del Rio attempted to match it, nearly shouting. Once again, he was bargaining—this time with his entire class.

"Let me talk and then you guys can talk all you want, I promise you," he begged. "I'll even let you go home."

•   •   •

At 3:30, half an hour after school let out, Armstrong gathered the faculty to ask how the day had gone. Everyone seemed worn, but few complained, save for a few remarks about broken bathroom locks and confusing schedules. "I had a good day," Del Rio said simply.

He meant it, in the sense that he had survived and now knew what to expect—the fear of the unknown had dissipated. Moreover, except for Nazim, he felt he had a great class. The kids had sided with him in his quickly developing disciplinary battle with Nazim, and many said they liked the teacher. Even Nazim, for all the trouble he caused, was smart—he just had to harness that intelligence. Nonetheless, Del Rio knew he needed some instruction in how to discipline his kids. He was unhappy at having wasted nearly the entire day on rules and behavior, and it angered him that one child could inflict such damage. If the problems lasted the week, he figured, he would try another approach.

Shortly before five P.M., Del Rio climbed into his car with two thoughts in his mind: He hoped that his kids' behavior would improve tomorrow. And after a full day of standing, his feet hurt.

The profile of Del Rio's class revealed much about the population of the school. In income and living conditions, his students spanned a surprisingly wide range, representing not just the immediate neighborhood but also a larger community throughout the city. The Center of Hope Community Church counted members all over Oakland, many of whom brought their children to the school. Each class had a few educated professional parents, identifiable not only by their carefully phrased, politely challenging questions about their children's education, but also by their shiny cars and their tastefully coordinated clothes.

Most of the families that constituted Del Rio's class, however, hailed from the working class. Some, especially the recent immigrants, did housecleaning, repair work, or gardening, sometimes mixed with bouts of unemployment. A good number, though, worked in educated and stable professions such as teaching and nursing. At least a few of the children, like Nazim, lived with grandparents, a common situation in that part of town, and one or two resided with foster parents. Some lived in true poverty, subsisting on government relief checks, the bulk of their time spent behind vandal-proof metal doors. In apartments filled with television noise and cigarette smoke, those parents struggled each morning to put clothes on their children that would not embarrass them. Indeed, few families enjoyed comfortable incomes: among the school's 250-odd students, nearly 4 out of 5 qualified for a free or reduced-price lunch, a rate that placed Reems among the highest school poverty rates in the city.

Yet, for what the comparison was worth, E. C. Reems's families did enjoy a notch more stability than those at the district school down the street. At Webster Elementary a few blocks away, with frequent shifts in population, a typical class might, at any given moment, include two or more homeless children, who perhaps would carry their tattered Xeroxed handouts back to school after a night at a shelter. Certainly, plenty of families at E. C. Reems had it tough, but not many homeless parents had heard about the enrollment fair.

•   •   •

On the second day, they behaved. Del Rio gave the students copied handouts to complete, and they set to work directly, industrious and nearly silent. Thrilled, Del Rio suspected the homework—on class rules—had made an impact. And the homework pleased him for another reason. Of the fourteen thus far enrolled, twelve returned with completed assignments, which by the standards of neighboring schools, especially on the first day, was astonishing. Their proposed rules, however, conveyed more about their past schools than their current one. "Go straight to the bathroom, and come straight back," Alicia ordered in strikingly neat handwriting. Reyna advised, "Don't talk in line . . . Don't put our hand in the plant . . . Don't hit the teacher."

Del Rio had particular reason to be relieved by the newfound calm. Other teachers had warned that he would be tested in the early days, and he hoped the current cease-fire would hold. One of the great truisms of schooling is that the first few days indicate how the rest of the year will unfold. By that measure, as the first day rolled into the second and third, years delightful and difficult were shaping up in the dozen classrooms of the E. C. Reems Academy. Carol Fields, the most gifted and experienced teacher, worked with the assurance of a master weaver, anchoring strands on the first days that would develop, without her fifth graders ever noticing, into grand themes and ideas. Even snack time became a lesson; she would ask, for instance, how to feed sixteen students evenly from her fourteen-slice bread loaf. And she carried the magic of the confident longtime teacher—that spooky unspoken spell that, through a moment's glance or shift in voice, causes children to act right. A visitor to her class might have thought her children had been shipped from a different supplier than Del Rio's on that rough first day.

That same confidence, that unflappable calm of a traffic cop who has already heard every excuse, undergirded the comparative serenity of the other veterans' classes. Theresa Bade was forging bonds with her kindergartners, but she brooked little nonsense. It was the same for Alan Foss with his first graders. But for many of the virgin teachers, the beginning days of school revealed frightening, vertigo-inducing visions of the next 175 days. Emily Deringer and Michelle Kalka, the two last-minute recruits from Teach For America, faced the greatest chaos, but even the giant Roland Anderson in the Lilliput of kindergarten had trouble establishing the rule of law. One morning that first week, during recess, Kalka surveyed a wall where she had ordered four of her students to stand motionless as punishment for misbehavior. "I don't like punishing kids," she worried to another teacher. "I still have to learn exactly what that means—to be strict."

• • •

In his first week at Reems, Del Rio set himself the reasonable task of assessing the children's skills. He did not expect that the challenge would derail his classroom's tentative calm. One morning, he handed his nine-year-olds a Xeroxed sheet with fifty math problems, all of them simple subtraction of a one-digit number from a two-digit number: twenty-seven minus eight, for example. A few seemed insulted by how easy the problems were; one, a meticulously coiffed and dressed girl named Alicia, asserted later, "We cannot do first-grade work. We're fourth graders." But several students immediately griped that the work was too difficult; some asked for help. Apologetically, Del Rio explained that this was a test, and that he couldn't help them. Predictably, Nazim was the most upset. "This is too hard," he growled, bouncing in his chair. Finally, he ran the eraser end of his pencil all over the page in frustration, which crumpled up the paper. "How come this is so hard?" he moaned again. Fearing a blowup, Del Rio relented and showed him how to do the subtraction problems on his fingers.

It wasn't enough. Nazim, well schooled in the art of provoking diversionary scenes when the work got too hard, now perceived amusement in the classroom at his agitation. "It's not funny—I can't do this," he snarled, and fished for a ticket out of the room. "I gotta fart." That gambit failed, so he slammed his hand down on the desk of the child behind him. "Don't hit this chair," he warned after some real or imagined bump, "because I'm going to sock you." When this plan failed, too, Nazim tried another problem, subtracting three from eleven, and got it right. Then he developed a brilliant strategy to conquer the math problems. He was accustomed to using a number chart—simply a list of the numbers in order, on which he could count backwards as he would on his fingers to do subtraction problems. Del Rio had said the students couldn't use a number chart for the test, but he had allowed them to calculate on scratch paper. So Nazim wondered: could he draw a number chart on the scratch paper? Del Rio smiled, but told him no, he would have to rely on his fingers instead. Deflated, Nazim grumbled, "I ain't got no twenty fingers."

For Del Rio, the children's troubling academic performance could not compete in urgency with their decaying behavior. Had he been assigned a mentor, she might have foreseen this; often, the behavior of the first day is the best the teacher will see all year, while any mischief from the early days tends to grow roots and vines, becoming ever harder to eradicate. As the first week went on, the noise and chaos hurled itself into Del Rio's face each morning. Invariably, Nazim led the pack. Sometimes he put on a dramatic and entertaining show, saying the oddest and most intriguing things. The boy, who had never left California, remarked one day, "I go to Hawaii every holiday—not this Halloween, though." At times it seemed he was not the captain of his own ship. He reacted to every word he heard and every deed he watched with a tight-jawed immediacy, but sometimes, a threatening, enraged look would melt into a smile with volcanic suddenness. The class rapidly reached consensus that Nazim was the spoiler in the crowd. "You better watch out," Alicia warned a visitor who sat down next to Nazim. "He's a *very* bad kid."

Del Rio had never learned the basic techniques of "classroom management," as teachers euphemistically call it. He had to discover it for himself, at significant loss of time and angry energy. He had never learned some of the key strategies—a consistent demand for hand-raising, paying attention to small infractions. What was more, Del Rio wanted the children's affection, as well as their respect, and took their misbehavior as a personal insult. Yet the behavior challenge was also entirely predictable; children everywhere challenge their teachers, and in neighborhoods where classroom chaos is common, the challenge is bound to be tougher. The real test for any school was not whether such challenges occurred, but how well the school had prepared, and how much help it could offer the teachers who needed it.

For the moment, though, most of the new teachers weren't asking for help. A few went privately to the veterans, asking for tips and advice; Kalka had a mentor assigned by Teach For America, a talented third-year teacher at nearby Webster. But for the most part, if they had problems, they kept quiet, as if it were some private embarrassment. Armstrong had visited the classrooms only briefly, but she had a clear sense of where chaos was brewing. She knew several teachers were trying to sell her a prettied-up version of what was happening. But she was counting on Carol Fields, the official master teacher, to provide mentoring. As for dispensing her own advice, she reasoned that her faculty would be most teachable when they realized they needed the help. Moreover, she felt that if she arrived uninvited, she would make her teachers uneasy. They would do best if they maintained their own dignity and sense of control and independence, she figured. And they would learn better by doing, rather than with her in the classroom, intimidating them. As she put it, "I'm not doing anything until they ask."

Perhaps more to the point, as the principal of a new school, she had plenty of things to worry about besides the classroom demeanor of prepubescent miscreants. She was consumed by the urgent problems that accompany running a new school in an old building. Toilets jammed with wads of paper or failed to flush. The sewers backed up several times, flooding the basement with fetid water. The bathrooms themselves sometimes locked kids out or, worse still, locked them in. Armstrong faced these problems without much of a support network, even as she undertook, under budget pressure, to recruit students anew. The enrollment hovered around 250— short of the magical 272 figure at which the school could pay its bills—though it inched up daily with a steady trickle of new arrivals. Some parents seemed to view the school like a new restaurant, waiting to hear the first reviews before going there themselves. Other late arrivals involved grandparents who were raising children, but needed the parents' permission to enroll them. Yet even with the enrollment pressure, the school was still turning away special-education students. Also, the student body was not nearly as integrated as Armstrong had hoped; 85 percent of the students were black, and all the rest were Latino. The imbalance heightened tensions when Armstrong had to ration spaces in a full class. Armstrong could not bring herself to deny admission to a well-connected African-American member of the Center of Hope congregation—even after she had rebuffed a Latino family that had volunteered in developing the school, but had not registered on time.

There were other tensions, too. Armstrong had put in requisitions to School Futures for the books she wanted, but some had not arrived, and some had been delivered to the wrong classrooms. A set of workbooks that School Futures sent had been used already, the answer blanks filled in, sparking a sense of insult for students who had thought they were through with second-class treatment in school. And as if to test the brittleness of everyone's nerves, an eruption of injuries hit during the first week—not just the inevitable playground variety of bloodied knees and elbows, but true medical emergencies. The first day of school, after a nighttime meeting, teacher Alan Foss suffered abdominal pains that left him writhing on the floor until an ambulance arrived. The diagnosis: a gallstone attack. Then, during a morning recess, a student in Del Rio's class named Cesar dashed full-tilt into the iron fence, gashing his forehead and leaving him shrieking but conscious, blood surging down his face. The ambulance crew was learning too well the route to 8411 MacArthur, but Cesar's injuries proved minor, and like Foss he was quickly released from the hospital. As Armstrong celebrated her forty-second birthday on the last day of that first week, with a low-key staff potluck, she might have been forgiven for feeling that she was being tested.

•　　•　　•

At E. C. Reems, one teacher after another probed the students' abilities as Del Rio had, and discovered a complex challenge. First—no revelation in this blighted corner of the city—large numbers of kids were so achingly behind that they might have been runners wandering at the starting blocks long after the race had begun. One seven-year-old had never been to school. There were second graders who could not recognize, let alone give the sounds of, all the letters. There were fourth and fifth graders who, when they wrote at all, scribbled garble barely recognizable as English. One sixth grader arrived at Reems when his district school said it was planning to hold him back in fifth grade. Many of the new teachers' classrooms were descending into bedlam, and immediate solutions eluded them; Yasmine Alwan phoned the assigned guardian of a particularly difficult boy, only to be told that if he caused too much trouble, the guardian—a foster mother—might "give him back."

Furthermore, many teachers were also waging a battle on two fronts: not just low skills, but a wide range of skills as well. One or two students in each class—some veterans of private school and some who had been shepherded with great care through public schools—were performing at or above grade level. A blessing, certainly, but also a hefty burden for teachers seeking ways to push the more advanced while rescuing those badly behind. For the most experienced and able teachers, that was a rugged climb. For the majority—neophytes like Del Rio—it was like handing a violin student an instrument for the first time and asking him to play a concerto.

For Del Rio, an additional annoyance of working, untrained, in a new school was that he lacked a clear idea of exactly what children entering fourth grade were supposed to be able to do. He was pretty sure, though, that their skills should have surpassed two-digit subtraction problems. Had a copy of the state standards existed in the school, or if the school had had access to the Internet, or if Del Rio had owned a home computer, he would have found he was right: California expects students exiting third grade to be able to add and subtract *five*-digit numbers, to manipulate simple fractions, to understand some basic concepts from algebra. Most of his kids were nowhere close to that.

Likewise, in English, he would have discovered standards that reflect the nearly universal agreement that third grade is a crucial year for reading and writing fluently. According to the state standards, third graders should "extend their writing strategies," producing paragraphs with topic sentences and supporting details, using reference books, and "revising drafts" as part of "the writing process." A handful of Del Rio's students could write a paragraph. But several—especially those who had written little or nothing the first day—fell disastrously short of the official standard. Some, in fact, wrote almost undecipherable prose, when they wrote at all. A girl named Wilneka submitted this as her first journal entry, a week into the school year, in answer to the question of what grade she had liked best: "17 Why Becaue I what to B in wrell life in I wat to Dive in do what I what to Do. in got me a agrsh to go to Calioga, Irin a lot. Dive a lot." Paul had this to say on the same subject: "I like kindagarde. Beacuse I do hafeto breing MI homework home. Yeay I wat to go to kidigarden en. Becase I bo not wan't to bring MI homework I bo not like fourthgrade becase I bo not want to go Ba k to kindgarden."

Del Rio was anxious to see the results of the standardized tests he would administer in October, to confirm his suspicions that his kids had arrived already way behind.

As for the pressing matter of Nazim's behavior, Del Rio took action almost immediately. By the end of the first week of school, he had met with Nazim's grandfather and discussed the problems in detail. But if he entertained any notion that a call and a conference would solve the problem, it quickly dissolved. Del Rio appreciated the grandfather's willingness to meet with him, but found him not much help, and imagined he wasn't strict enough at home. Without other options, Del Rio hovered over Nazim's desk during class, ready to snap his fingers whenever Nazim started fooling around. The class, meanwhile, had accorded Nazim the status of chief troublemaker, their irritation with him occasionally betraying a bit of envy. As sometimes happens with mischief makers, Nazim also was becoming part mascot, part commandant. The first Friday, when Del Rio divided the class into teams for a game aimed at learning the four food groups, Nazim was elected captain of his side. "Today he the leader," reasoned one girl. "If he be bad, tomorrow he's not the leader."

The truth was, Nazim's problems were bigger, and more frightening, than mere mischief. In one of the first paragraphs he wrote for class, he invented a world in which his father and sister still lived with him:

> I my dad like wach foot Ball and I do. My litle sister like to play whith dall I do to if I don't she will cire . . . My dad lik to sit around the house and drink Beer I dont I like to drink coladed

That cozy vision represented a wistful sort of fiction. Nazim's sister—by a different mother—lived in Chicago. His father resided in a prison. Nazim himself lived with his demons.

Nazim tended to make things up—not just domestic scenes that he might have wished for, but also dramatic events that he feared.

In vivid detail, at home and in school, he reported men with guns chasing him, or deaths in the family, or people breaking into the tiny apartment he shared with his grandfather. Once, an innocent seventeen-year-old had gone to jail because Nazim claimed the boy had menaced him with a gun.

Something needed to change for Nazim—for his own sake, and for the good of the class. It wasn't that he lacked gifts, by any stretch. His undeniable intelligence caught the attention of adults, and he had charm to burn. His fabulous smile and his big, deep eyes completed a charismatic package. Back at Parker Elementary, the adoring girls in his class had shared him as their "boyfriend." When Nazim got angry, though, he had a quarter-inch fuse. Often, in his early years at school, his teachers had to restrain him, his little chest heaving inside an unwashed shirt, as he swore, "That boy's messing with me! I'm gonna hurt him!" Even on good days, he had to move, had to talk, had to react. He raised his hand to answer questions he had no answer for—sometimes before the teacher had even finished asking the question. And while his "relationships" with girls were entirely innocent, Nazim talked about sex with a disturbing level of detail, even as a young child.

Del Rio was slowly piecing together the picture of Nazim's life. He knew that Nazim's parents were absent, but didn't really know why. He didn't know much about the boy's home life or upbringing. Del Rio had few tools at his disposal for dealing with a child as complex as Nazim. Every school in a neighborhood like the one surrounding Reems enrolls children like Nazim—brilliant, beautiful children with woeful histories and loads of troubles. How well the E. C. Reems Academy handled Nazim and a handful of children like him would stand as a crucial test of the school.

In truth, though, the rest of Del Rio's class was boisterous and squirrelly, too. He had announced rules against getting up without permission or talking without raising a hand, but he had little experience with what it meant to enforce the rules. He wanted his classroom to be a pleasant, welcoming place for children; he didn't want to make them cry, or to criticize them at every turn. So he stopped somewhere short of meticulous refereeing, enforcing the rules strictly only when his patience was exhausted, demanding the raising of hands and then slacking off again. He had never had occasion to learn the arts that make for a peaceful classroom: the smooth, seemingly instant transitions from one lesson to another; the wisdom of catching even the tiniest infraction and drawing the line there; the magical talent of writing at the board and watching the class at the same time. And sometimes, when an answer was solid and on-point, it seemed hardly sporting to punish the speaker for not raising a hand. Who, after all, would have reprimanded Nazim for leaping out of his seat to explain the genesis of a pickle: "A cucumber! They put it in some kind of vinegar, and that make it taste like a pickle!"

•   •   •

Before the school year was ten days old, Del Rio was reaching distressing levels of frustration and anxiety. His students' lack of skills was, in many cases, heartbreaking. Their behavior produced even more alarm. A day earlier, one of his girls had fled the classroom following a round of verbal torture by Nazim. In a frightening, humiliating chase through the school halls, she outran Del Rio, forcing him to choose between supervising the rest of the class and tracking her down. In the end, he had to face Armstrong and report the girl lost. But the problems went beyond the kids' behavior. The school's late start, and missing curriculum materials for math and social studies, had angered him. He still harbored doubts about why he was hired, wondering whether it was the mere fact that he was Mexican American and male—rather than some actual talent or ability on his part—that had landed him the job. Moreover, he had applied in hopes of teaching at Dolores Huerta, where he could use his fluent Spanish to benefit Latino children, rather than at an almost entirely black school. He felt cheated and occasionally considered refusing to speak Spanish at all at school. Now, the lengthy days, and the consequent exhaustion, were exacting a price. Gone was Del Rio's daily exercise regimen; it had been three weeks since he had visited the gym or mounted his bike. Now, in unsettlingly vivid evidence of his stress level, a blood vessel in his left eye had burst. Although not dangerous, it tinted his entire eye an angry red. He looked like he was losing a boxing match.

Del Rio had been looking forward to back-to-school night as an opportunity to confront the trends that were angering and worrying him—the missing homework, the tardiness, the sleepiness. He prepared a sheaf of papers for the parents, complete with brightly hopeful tidbits of advice ("Make sure your child eats something in the morning") and gentle nagging ("It is important that you ask your child about their homework"). He included the class rules ("Disruptions will not be tolerated"), but even they hinted at the painful negotiations surrounding behavior: "This plan was devised from a class discussion based on the fact that the teacher has a right to teach and the student has a right to learn." After an internal debate, Del Rio had decided to leave on the board the names of the five children who had not turned in assignments that day. As with the kids' writing, he wanted the parents to see where the children stood. Now, after some uplifting, well-attended ribbon-cutting festivities, he prepared to address the handful of parents who had drifted into his room. Unfortunately, those in attendance turned out to be the same ones who already brought their children on time and checked their homework. Before the faithful parents, Del Rio didn't hesitate to reveal the troubles he faced. "My main concern is, I need everybody's support, because it's tough," he told them. "It's tough."

Brenda Roy, mother to the sweet-tempered Alicia, had a pretty good guess what he was talking about. "Do you have problems getting them settled down and doing their work?" she asked gently. "Yes," he confessed, relieved that someone had raised the subject of behavior. "That's probably the hardest part." As usual, he carried the troubles on his own shoulders. "This is my first year," he said. He lamented, "My day doesn't start off too well when I have seven kids not doing their homework. It hurts my feelings."

Celestine Henderson, grandmother of LaShay, one of the top students in the class, politely deepened the inquest into the behavior problems. "How's the discipline been?" she asked. "Because I know she's been concerned about some of the kids acting up in class."

"I was a little too lenient at first," Del Rio confessed. Still in easy, unthreatening tones, Brenda Roy agreed. "That's about the most I've heard, too, is not being able to concentrate on her work."

"I'm working on it," Del Rio said, struggling. "I've been talking to other teachers."

Del Rio chatted individually with the parents, who wandered in and out of the room. And despite the concentration of "better" parents, he did have a sidebar with the mother of a girl who was reading at second-grade level. He showed her the girl's work; the mother seemed shocked. Del Rio wondered: had she never seen her daughter's writing before?

By evening's end, his sign-in sheet had nine names on it—half the class. In that neighborhood, at a regular public school, many teachers would have considered that a healthy turnout. The experienced teachers, such as Carol Fields and Troy Brookins, had even better numbers. All but a couple of their students' parents showed up—a testament, at least for the moment, to the power of parental choice, and perhaps a newfound sense of ownership in a school. In Christine Landry's classroom, fifteen parents came; at her previous school, she could count the parents in attendance on one hand. Del Rio, however, was frustrated; the person he most wanted to talk to hadn't been there. He shot a look at Nazim's clutter-stuffed desk, as if that would make the boy's grandfather appear. To himself, in angry tones, Del Rio murmured, "He didn't come."

Nazim Casey Jr. didn't have the kind of family that volunteers at school, chaperones field trips, and participates in school committees. He did have a father and mother, in the biological sense. But neither, at that moment, was playing a role most people associate with true parenting. The events of the previous decade had well-nigh destroyed that possibility.

Nazim's mother, whose name was Candace, had once appeared a

promising mother-to-be—despite her own difficulties. In the view of her relatives, she had always been slow. Her narrow-set eyes suggested she had suffered alcohol poisoning in her mother's womb. Monique Adanadus, who was her niece, although they were the same age, had looked out for her in childhood, sometimes even showing Candace how to put her clothes on. In school, when Candace wasn't in special-education class, Monique would sit next to her to help her.

Candace was seventeen and a student at Castlemont when she met Nazim, the tall, skinny boy who was to become Nazim Jr.'s father. He was sixteen and was enrolled at Castlemont himself, though he didn't attend regularly. Trouble was literally written on him, in the form of a tattoo proclaiming his nickname, Big Nock 700. "Nock" testified to his prowess at fighting—it meant knockout— and the 700 boasted of a run of city blocks where he sold drugs. Certainly, the nickname fit better than his given name, Nazim, which in Arabic—a nod to his father's Black Muslim leanings— meant "discipline." Candace was fascinated by his car, a souped-up Chevy Nova with fat tires in the back and a big 350 engine. Nazim used Candace's place as a safe house where he could hide from the cops when his drug-dealing adventures got hot. The escapes didn't always succeed; Nazim loved fast cars and guns, and had been arrested for the first time around the time he became eligible for a driver's license. He racked up ten arrests before turning eighteen, starting with robbery and moving on to drug possession, auto theft, and an assortment of other crimes. By that time, he was a father.

Even when he first met Candace, he knew there would be a Little Nock to follow Big Nock. After they started their romance, it seemed like no time at all before she was pregnant. It wasn't her first pregnancy—she reached that milestone at fourteen—but it was the first she would carry to term. For a while, it appeared that Candace and Nazim, though only teenagers, would take parenthood seriously. But Nazim was snorting cocaine and smoking what he called "an extreme amount of marijuana." Then he started romancing other women during Candace's pregnancy, and Candace got even. She found diversions in crack cocaine and the men who gave her the drug. By the dawn of the 1990s, crack already was well established as probably the most addictive drug ever to hit the ghetto streets, a cheap rock so compelling that the need for a fix could trump every maternal urge. She went into labor in the midst of a rocketing crack and marijuana high, and was so beset with venereal diseases that doctors opted for a caesarean delivery to protect the baby from perilous exposure in the birth canal. Little Nock—Nazim Casey Jr.— was born on New Year's Day, 1990, addicted to the cocaine in his mother's bloodstream. The hospital notified the authorities, who ultimately declined to press charges against Candace. Nazim Jr., meanwhile, spent his first weeks of life shrieking and shaking in withdrawal.

Candace wasn't there to see it. She moved in with Richie, her dealer. Their "home" was a garage with no electricity. Richie quickly tired of giving her rock and smack for free, and Candace started turning tricks on the corner. Richie pimped her. He didn't have a car, so he operated from a bicycle. "A tore-down pimp, too, on his ten-speed," was how Monique summed up the scene. Sometimes, little Nazim was in the house when she brought the johns home. Before long, Nazim Sr. tired of seeing his baby living in such filth—not that he was a model housekeeper himself—and took the baby. But Nazim Sr. was still selling pot for a living; sometimes he brought his son with him on his business jaunts, on days when he didn't feel like paying a baby-sitter.

When Nazim Jr. was six months old, Nazim Sr.—who was developing a heroin habit of his own—got locked up again. Little Nazim went to live with his father's father, Askia, who didn't particularly want him, but didn't see many other options. This pattern was to last through the first seven years of the boy's life: bouncing from one inconstant caretaker to another. When Nazim Sr. wasn't locked up, he usually kept his son. But poverty and drug addiction fouled the toddler's world. Nazim Sr.'s home—Candace's, too, when she claimed it—stank of urine and unchanged diapers. The filth in the carpets was so deep that baby Nazim's little feet stayed soil-black all the time. Relatives suspected that the boy didn't eat regularly. Nazim Jr.

was in the house when his father injected heroin and his mother turned tricks. Sometimes, grandfather Askia would take Nazim Jr. away just to make sure he got fed.

When Nazim Jr. was three, Nazim Sr. married another woman. For a while, they lived in the E. C. Reems Gardens low-income housing complex, across the street from the Center of Hope Community Church. Candace, though, remained on the margins of the picture. Eventually, when Nazim Jr. was five, Nazim Sr. and Candace started smoking crack together. Nazim Sr.'s wife, LaTanya, by that time had discovered heroin, and developed a habit of her own. Meanwhile, Candace gave birth to three more babies fathered by other men, and abandoned them the same way she did Nazim Jr. (One child she never even took home from the hospital.) She kept turning tricks. Nazim Jr., meanwhile, was demonstrating the hallmarks of a "crack baby": the short attention span, the irritability and rage, the inability to connect cause to consequence, including and especially in his own behavior.

Then Nazim Jr. reached school age. Some days, Nazim Sr. sent him to school; on others, he didn't bother. Sometimes the boy was absent from school for long stretches. Nazim Sr. and his new wife would occasionally show up for parent conferences, eyes glazed, promising to talk to the boy about his behavior. Once, Nazim Sr. and his wife brawled outside the classroom as the boy and his schoolmates watched. Nazim Sr. made occasional gestures toward helping; they took pathetic form, such as promising himself he would do no drugs on the morning of a day when he would be meeting with a teacher. Most of the time, by his own frank admission, Nazim Sr. did little to support his son's education. He had a street life, a drug addiction, and his new wife's children to worry about. He was also unemployed; he had been working for his mother at a San Francisco linen service, but had been too high to work well. Ultimately, Nazim Sr. was fired by his own mother. Nazim Jr., meanwhile, had earned that nasty label of *problem child*—acting aggressively, talking back. A trial for his teachers, he constantly moved about the classroom, talked out of turn. But they saw the situation and took pity.

In July 1997, when Nazim Jr. was seven, a string of painful events combined to end his nomadic travels from home to home. It began when Nazim Sr.'s mother died of cancer. Even in her last days, she was aware enough of her son's addiction that she willed him no money directly. She left her modest savings to another son, who wisely offered the elder Nazim only enough for rent and for the children's clothes and food. But her death threw Nazim Sr. into a deep depression. As usual, he medicated his sadness with heroin. He resorted to violence to feed his habit—stupid, mean, occasionally dramatic stickups, ill planned and vicious. The last came shortly after nightfall the evening of October 29.

Nazim Casey Sr. and five fellow junkies armed themselves with guns and climbed into a van, searching for a victim. (One of the men, Clemon High, better known as "Manny," had been staying occasionally in Nazim Jr.'s room.) They drove across the Oakland border to San Leandro, but couldn't find anyone to rob, so they looped back to Oakland. Around 7:25 P.M., they chose as their target a Vietnamese-owned meat and fish shop on a busy corner of International Boulevard.

The robbery bore the marks of drugged desperation: great risk of arrest in exchange for paltry prizes. The men walked down the sidewalk and strode into the store with stocking caps over their faces. Manny carried a shotgun inside his long winter jacket; Casey and another man, known as "Twin," brandished pistols. On their way in, they saw a woman pick up a pay phone on the street. They knew she was calling the police, but in their drug-deluded state, they believed that they would get the job done before the cops arrived. In truth, the robbery was an inefficient, stumbling affair, prompting several 911 calls, including one from the meat shop's owner, who heard the commotion from the back office. Out front, Casey's buddy, Clemon High, demanded that one of the workers open the cash register. The worker didn't know how. Angry, Manny smashed him in the face several times with the butt of the shotgun. The manager, who did know how to open the register, finished his call to the police and came up front. He handed the thieves about $800 in cash. Casey tore the gold chain from a worker's neck, and the robbers fled.

The machinery of policing worked efficiently. Officers speeding to the area immediately spotted the men sprinting with their bags of cash in hand. After he and his buddies split up, Casey headed for the backyard brambles. An officer chased him, just a few steps behind. Squad cars ringed the block, sealing it off. A police helicopter, already aloft and conveniently nearby, joined the search. Darkness lent the fleeing thieves no cover. Using an infrared scanner, which detects body heat, officers in the helicopter directed their counterparts on the ground. One tackled Casey, and they struggled. Another cop ran up and drew his gun. The fight was over.

The search for evidence began. One officer noticed Casey's pocket was hanging inside out, and checked the bushes. He found wads of cash, the gold necklace, and Casey's small, toyish-looking chrome revolver, loaded with two bullets. (Casey had meant to remove all six bullets, in case he got arrested, but had been too high to accomplish the task.) On the ride to jail, Casey asked how much time he would do for the robbery. He also asked that they tell his wife where he was.

The officers did go to the Casey home, and talked to Nazim Sr.'s wife, LaTanya. She invited them inside, where they found Baggies, straws, balloons, and razor blades—all signs of heroin use, and perhaps dealing—in a room strewn with toys and children's clothes.

Around ten P.M. that night, in an interrogation room downtown, Casey waived his right to a lawyer and confessed to the robbery. The answer to his earlier question, about how much time he would serve, came two months later in a hearing at Oakland Municipal Court. Casey pleaded no contest—essentially the same as guilty—to second-degree robbery, with a sentencing "enhancement" for using a gun. His conviction was as efficient as his arrest. In the hearing, Casey uttered twenty words. He said, "I would like to get sentenced today." He said, "No contest." He said the word *no* once, and the word *yes* ten times. The judge gave him six years in state prison. With credit for good behavior, he would be eligible for release when Nazim Jr. was twelve. Already though, the boy was old enough to understand the situation, and what price he would pay for his father's drug addiction and violence. In a visit to the prison, he asked his father, "Was what you were doing worth leaving me?"

It was hard to see much good in the locking up of a twenty-five-year-old father. But it did lend some consistent structure to Nazim Jr.'s life. His grandfather would now assume full responsibility for him. The grandfather, Askia, didn't welcome this new task. He preferred a life of quiet semiretirement, watching French cooking programs and C-SPAN in his tiny apartment. A tired man, annoyed by interruptions as tiny as the ringing of his phone, he had no wish for a second round of parenting. And if he were any good as a father, he bitterly observed, his son wouldn't have been in prison. But he didn't see much choice. He chafed at the boy's frenetic energy, his seeming inability to obey. But at least Askia Casey was a stable presence in Nazim's life. And now that he had full control of his grandson's situation, he started thinking about making some changes—among them, leaving Parker Elementary. Askia Casey had never liked the school, which he saw as a dank, depressing place filled with lurking drug-dealer types. Back in the summer, when Auntie Monique mentioned that a new charter school was getting started down the street, the idea of a change had made sense to Askia Casey. He signed up his grandson without hesitation.

Now, though, young Nazim had become a symbol of the trials for a new teacher and the disciplinary challenges of an entire newborn school. The little academy would have to fix those problems if it was to realize the hopes of its parents and founders. And for the moment, solutions seemed far off. Valentín Del Rio was removing Nazim from class with increasing frequency, usually sending him to Laura Armstrong's office. While the boy was gone, the class ran with an unfamiliar smoothness. The room would get quieter, the kids would settle in more quickly, and Del Rio would relax. Had Nazim left for good, another miscreant might well have risen to take his place. But for the moment, Nazim's visits to the office brought much-needed peace to Del Rio's room.

Behavior, however, was not the only matter threatening the dreams that Del Rio held for his class, and which so many parents held for the school. When Del Rio mulled over the academic struggles ahead, they loomed dauntingly large. In English, the kids were defeated by their attempts to use a dictionary; they had taken an entire hour to look up a dozen spelling words. And for much of the curriculum, Del Rio largely had to fend for himself. In social studies, he had to devise his own materials and tests, which meant a book of readings and fill-in-the-blank exercises on California history that he had bought at the local teacher supply store. As for art—a subject he was supposed to address—he had nothing at all to offer. School Futures had adopted a curriculum called Core Knowledge, but Del Rio knew little about it. And parents were starting to complain. Robin, his top student, sat bored while he ministered to his less-accomplished kids. Eric's mother, who had never visited the class, had called to grouse about the behavior problems.

What was more troubling was Del Rio's sense that he wasn't getting any real help. Armstrong seemed aloof from the predicament of her new teachers. It wasn't that she didn't know what was going on; as a former teacher, she had an accurate sense of how the discipline problems were playing out in the various classrooms, and how the teachers were reacting. Del Rio in particular had been honest with her about the behavior problems in his class. She had responded, enigmatically, that he should expect to use all of September to address the behavior problems, but that by October, "I better not walk in and see kids messing around."

Yet with September nearing its end, it was hard to imagine how Del Rio would accomplish such dramatic changes. Each time he banished Nazim from the classroom, the boy's appreciation of the power of mischief just seemed to grow. Late one Wednesday morning, after a penalty period in the office, Nazim strutted back to class with the attitude of a spoiler, a miniature John Wayne. The rest of the class noisily heralded his arrival, and soon they had been docked a minute of recess.

Then, as the class moved on to social studies, Nazim managed to stay at the center of attention, proving he could be as relentlessly entertaining as he was troublesome. As one of the students struggled to pronounce the Native American name Snohomish, Nazim leapt into action.

"I know that word," he interjected, and then butchered it. "It's Sonhomish. I know that from Indian."

LaShay was impressed. "You been to India?"

Nazim wasn't one to brag. "I've been to Indian Town."

The door opened, and Laura Armstrong strolled in to announce there would be pizza for the teachers at lunch. Some of the children wanted pizza, too, but Armstrong explained that she was rewarding the teachers for their helpful presence at back-to-school night.

Nazim felt left out. "I wasn't here!" he complained.

Smiling, Armstrong said, "We know."

Chapter 6

Weak Links

On the last day of September, Valentín Del Rio was not happy.

Paychecks, due that day, failed to arrive. Knowing that he would face a late fee on his overdue Visa bill, Del Rio flew into a rage. Health insurance hadn't kicked in, either. He wanted to visit the doctor, but had no confidence in School Futures' promises to reimburse him for out-of-pocket expenses. And those worries paled next to his rising panic over the state of his classroom. A day earlier, he had assigned a set of three-digit subtraction problems. Most of the kids got nearly all the problems wrong. When he went to the board to explain the answers, the class would not pay attention. And according to Armstrong's offhand command, today was the last day she would accept disorder in his room.

At a loss for other ideas, he rearranged the furniture, hoping that "cooperative learning" groups would improve the situation. Scrapping the standard rows, he created four little desk-islands, each made up of four desks. Nazim's stood alone. But if the idea was to instill peace by separating and isolating problems, it wasn't working. The various desk-continents kept sending out delegations of disturbance, and the potential for conflict in the heavily traveled shipping lanes was high.

By raising his voice, Del Rio could establish momentary calm. But as a new teacher, he had not yet mastered the art of efficient acts, be they transitions between activities or distribution of stickers. The ensuing dead time invited chaos. That took the form of boys turning somersaults on the floor and kicking each other's rear ends. By day's end, as the kids wasted twenty chatty minutes copying down sixteen math problems, Del Rio's classroom felt like the inside of a popcorn popper. The furniture experiment, he concluded, had just made matters worse.

From Principal Armstrong, Del Rio needed more useful help than ultimatums and deadlines. But Armstrong was overwhelmed with the daily crises that accompany the opening of a new school: sewer leaks, bathrooms that still didn't lock. When pressed on the issue of how she would rescue her flailing beginner teachers, she admitted that her thinking hadn't progressed that far yet. So while she had discussed discipline with Del Rio, she had offered him no techniques, no strategies, to improve the situation. Instead, she was counting on Carol Fields, the official master teacher, to mentor the fledgling staff. But Armstrong had given Fields—who had a full teaching load of her own—no extra time to play mentor. More to the point, Fields lacked the perspective on her own craft to explain what she did so well. She had a remarkable knack for keeping her kids engaged and well behaved. But she was like one of those gifted Olympic champions who could not explain how she did what she did. And though she lent Del Rio curriculum materials, he had little time to read them.

Perhaps the most distressing aspect of the behavior problems was that they were creating a racial wedge between Armstrong and one of her teachers. Armstrong directed her indictment at Emily Deringer, a white woman raised amid the arboreal elegance of upstate New York, who had just months earlier graduated from Princeton University. Deringer, who hoped eventually to work as a lawyer protecting children from violence, was presiding over a spectacular classroom disaster. Her students either ignored her or shouted in her face. They vandalized the room, and—most horrifying to Deringer—hurt each other, tipping each other from chairs onto the floor and fighting in the aisles. Deringer sat in her classroom and sobbed every day after the children went home.

Armstrong, however, had little sympathy for the twenty-two-year-old white teacher. Deringer had said that many of her students couldn't read, and concluded that they needed special-education classes. To Armstrong, Deringer's views embodied the sort of low expectations she deplored. Armstrong had known too many white teachers in San Francisco who slapped labels on black boys who did not sit still—labels that shunted them into special-education classes, which to Armstrong meant a certain dead end.* Armstrong believed Deringer's students could read, albeit poorly. Deringer's students were merely living up to expectations, Armstrong figured; Deringer didn't think they could perform, and so didn't ask them to.

Likewise, Armstrong believed that Deringer's failure to control her students suggested that the young teacher did not believe her black and brown children were capable of behaving. Both Armstrong and Fields had offered Deringer advice, and saw no evidence she had followed any of it. They harbored suspicions about why Deringer seemed to ignore advice from her two black leaders.

The conflict had surfaced publicly at a faculty meeting a day earlier. September 29 had been a grim day marked by a convincing, gory prank involving fake blood, and unanswered questions about the teachers' health benefits. School Futures had delayed setting up payroll and benefits systems until it had signed a business agreement with the district, in hopes that the district would agree to handle those tasks for a fee. For the moment, the company was paying the school's bills from its own savings, because the district hadn't turned over a dime of the public funds earmarked for the school. (Walton's money was meant to finance development of schools and leasing of buildings, but public funds were supposed to cover the cost of actual operations.) Put off by the company's stance of blaming the district for their pay problems, the teachers spent much of the faculty meeting talking about their frustration with School Futures.

---

* Special education is often used in common parlance as a synonym for education for those with severe learning disabilities, but in fact very mild learning disabilities and other minor handicaps are far more common.

With tension already high, Armstrong chose that occasion to vent her feelings about white teachers who didn't display confidence in children of color. "Just because they're African American, just because they're Latino, that does not mean that they cannot sit still," she told her teachers. "And when I see that happening in your classroom, then I think that you believe that just because they're black children, they don't have to sit still." Vehemently, she added, "They have the same abilities as any other child, and I expect high performance from them."

Soon after Armstrong's diatribe, Troy Brookins, a public school veteran, wondered aloud whether, as in his old district, teachers could unilaterally suspend children from their classrooms for three days. Armstrong told him no, sharply.

But, as the concerns over behavior mounted, Armstrong knew she was going to need a plan.

If Valentín Del Rio wanted a bit of reassurance over the behavior problems in his classroom, he needed only to open his door and glance across the hall. There, the bedlam of Deringer's class made his own room seem like a regimented British academy. On the first day of October, Deringer was attempting to line up her class for lunch. The scene, had it been less excruciating to watch, would have been comical. Deringer pulled those who were talking out of line, but there were so many that the process threatened to go on forever. Deringer's fury, concealed under a gossamer shroud of self-control, contrasted with the boisterous, uncaring cheer of her students. Her collective punishments and rewards—five minutes of recess added or subtracted—were meaningless next to the all-day recess the kids created for themselves through their mutiny. Entire class periods disappeared. "It did take us too long to get lined up, so that we missed P.E.," Deringer was saying. "However, I like the way that you are lined up."

The order didn't last. Someone had appropriated the stickers she intended to award for good behavior; someone else had stolen a red marker and given himself high marks on the class behavior chart. This whole new crisis only underscored the distance from that idealistic vision that had brought her to teaching, in which the children would see that she cared for them, and be motivated to learn because of her caring. And Deringer, amid her desperate and painful efforts to achieve some semblance of discipline, resented the suggestion that her failures stemmed from racism. She was certain her students could learn. But she admitted, openly, that she didn't know how to teach them.

Carol Fields's classroom, after the school day, served as E. C. Reems's analogue to the Situation Room at the White House. Here, teachers could discuss the weightiest of matters, air their unvarnished opinions, and map strategies to avert or contain disaster. With its big windows and cool breezes, the classroom offered a refuge on the first days of autumn, which ranked among the hottest of the year. Today, the most pressing question was how to help the flailing first-year teachers.

Armstrong had saddled Fields with an enormous responsibility, making her, essentially, an instructional leader and trainer for the entire staff, on top of her full-time teaching schedule. Fields, however, had remarked privately that she felt ill-placed as a sort of chief of pedagogy. Despite her eight years in the classroom, and her clear mastery of her craft, she didn't savor "modeling" how to teach a lesson, and because her control of the classroom came so naturally, she framed her advice in ways that didn't translate easily for struggling neophytes. She advised "equal respect" between teacher and student, but that had been a starting point for Deringer and others. She suggested plans that assumed a certain suppleness of classroom organization, such as having stronger students coach weaker ones. She advised putting students in groups, so that each group could take responsibility for its behavior, but as Del Rio had found, that just seemed to make things worse in his room. Deringer, for her part, saw groups as suicide—she wanted to keep her kids as far apart as possible. In any case, Fields knew the school would require more than the spare time she could offer, her tidbits of qualified advice, the occasional periods when someone sat in her class so she could visit someone else's. The school needed professional staff development.

Armstrong wandered into Fields's room and settled into a student desk. She was thinking about the predicament of the new teachers. It was past five in the evening—meaning Armstrong already had spent more than ten hours in the building—but no one was going home soon. Armstrong addressed the particularly rowdy situation in Cherlon Simms's classroom with her usual irony. "They're flying off the ceiling," she said with a cavalier chuckle. "It don't bother her." Then, mulling over another sore point: "I'm going to free up Landry to go into Kalka's room tomorrow." In a sign of the chaos there, a mother had alleged that Kalka had spit in her child's face. Armstrong, suspecting a bit of interpretation at work—perhaps the teacher had leaned in close while shouting and there had been a bit of spray— suggested the mother enroll elsewhere. The mother said she had no- where else to go; the child stayed.

But battles over discipline—and Armstrong's muscular handling of them—weren't the only issues of concern. Fields artfully switched the subject to the need to work with the new teachers, and to the shortcomings in curriculum. Armstrong sounded glad that Fields had raised those subjects.

"Now," Armstrong said with emphasis, "it's time."

"People don't have curriculum," Fields said.

"There hasn't been time," Armstrong said, a bit defensively.

Christine Landry walked in. She wanted to talk curriculum, too. She proposed meetings for the lower-grade and upper-grade teach- ers. That idea, too, struck the right note with Armstrong—a solu- tion to some of the problems that had been troubling her. "That's very much needed, very soon," Armstrong agreed.

Matter-of-factly, Landry mentioned that her students were strug- gling with the reading books she had been assigned. She wanted to start using books meant for younger children.

Almost casually, Fields sided with Landry's proposal. "Is that OK, if we all shift down?"

With "high expectations" an inescapable education buzzword, one might have thought Landry and Fields's momentous proposal—

to allow all the teachers to assign books meant for younger students than they were teaching—would have required great and rueful consideration. But Armstrong entertained few hopes of rapidly catching students up to grade level when they started well behind. She felt that she could guarantee a year's progress for a year's schooling—but nothing more.

It wasn't that Armstrong was simply giving in to her students' poor preparation. In fact, she wanted to establish a tutoring program for kids badly behind in their reading. She figured, however, that the children needed to start with books at their own level. So in answer to the question of whether the teachers could lower their academic requirements, she said nothing. She just nodded yes.

•   •   •

By the beginning of October, the problems of the E. C. Reems Academy fell into three categories: the behavior problems, the academic dilemmas, and the growing hostility between the school staff and School Futures. It was the last of these that would create the greatest woes for Laura Armstrong.

She helped to fuel the conflict when she told her staff, frankly, that the blame for many of their frustrations lay in School Futures' home office. Her bosses, who wanted her to stand up for the company that employed her, saw betrayal by a franchise manager. So when Don Gill dropped by the weekly faculty meeting on October 4, the scene quickly escalated into a confrontation.

On this gray day, the mood in the building was somber and tense. Gill, a curriculum expert accustomed to upbeat staff meetings, had no idea what was in store for him. The teachers were upset, and they wanted answers. Armstrong had directed their frustrations toward Gill, perhaps justifiably—many of the problems were truly outside her control—but also perhaps unwisely. In many good schools, principals either find ways to solve outside problems themselves or serve as a buffer between teachers and the system. Here, Armstrong acted as a conduit.

The first complaints surrounded the missing health benefits, and paychecks that—when they did arrive—fell below district levels, despite School Futures' promises to match Oakland's pay scale. Gill, in what was to become a pattern, gave a lengthy explanation that cast the Oakland district as villain and obstructer. "This is another example of the kinds of trials that you have to go through to work in a charter school," he said. "For any inconveniences, I apologize." But he promised that Armstrong would fix the paycheck problems.

Emily Deringer brought up the lack of special education. For a handful of her children, the aspiring children's advocate said, it was "basically immoral to have them in school without getting services." That, she argued, was because they were "so profoundly learning-disabled"—here, Armstrong peered at her intently—that they must get services. Gill deflected the question into the dark corner of uncertain future arrangements with the county.

Troy Brookins, who had accepted the role of informal shop steward and labor organizer, attacked the "lack of professionalism" School Futures had demonstrated in paying the teachers too little, too late. "If you expect us to be nonunion," he warned, "you guys have to step up to the plate and take care of these things."

Gill, who thus far had maintained his affable manner under continued fire, began to look around uncomfortably, avoiding eye contact with Brookins. After a pause, he replied, "That was a statement, right?"

Alan Foss suggested that a liaison with the district might solve some of these problems. Gill replied, "We rely on our principals to be the link."

Armstrong, who had been tugging at the collar of her white turtleneck, glanced up. But Gill continued.

"When we put this sort of thing behind us, we move on to the business of educating children," he preached. "We don't want you to be too concerned about issues like salary."

Valentín Del Rio hadn't been able to pay his Visa bill on time. He was concerned about issues like salary, and he wasn't alone. But no one spoke.

After a moment of awkward silence, Gill looked around. "I'm seeing sullen faces," he intoned, accurately.

He checked his watch; he was late to catch a plane back to San Diego. He talked for a moment about the strain of their hurried opening, and said, "I'm going to chalk it up to the extra stress."

Then he hefted his black nylon briefcase and strode from the room, murmuring, "This is a hard group to read."

•   •   •

At the same time as the chasm between the Reems Academy and School Futures was deepening, Armstrong turned her attention to the battle over Nazim's behavior. She had sent him home once already, after he had mouthed off repeatedly in class. Del Rio, after investing considerable energy and focus on Nazim, was beginning to despair. So was Nazim's grandfather, who had come to E. C. Reems hoping for a change. Reluctantly, the grandfather had arranged for Nazim to be tested at the well-regarded Children's Hospital, and he needed Armstrong's signature on the request. Long opposed to the drugging of African-American children, Armstrong agreed to have Nazim evaluated, but refused to sign any form that permitted medicating him.

On Tuesday, October 5, Armstrong and Del Rio met with the grandfather, Askia Casey, in Armstrong's office, and Armstrong explained that she was going to draft a behavior contract for the boy. It would stipulate that if Nazim was suspended three times, he would be expelled. Armstrong also advised that Casey drop by the school unannounced to observe Nazim in class.

Nazim's good behavior lasted exactly six hours.

At 2:05 that afternoon, feeling that he was being ignored, Nazim jumped up from his seat and stood at the door of the classroom. "You don't listen to me!" he bellowed. "You listen to every other motherfucker!" He then said he was heading to the office so he could be sent home.

Del Rio ordered Nazim back to his seat several times; finally, the boy sat, and sobbed. Del Rio ignored him.

At 2:12, Armstrong arrived in the classroom with the behavior contract in hand. The mood was grave. "Did somebody die?" asked the eternally morbid Chante. Armstrong ordered her back to her seat, tapped Nazim's desk with the sheaf of papers, and told him to see her after school.

The contract required Nazim to listen to his teacher, raise his hand, obey all school rules, complete his class work, and stay in his seat. It warned, "If he breaks a rule and is sent to the office again for the second time on the same day, he will be sent home. The third time he is sent home, he will be suspended for three days. After three suspensions, expulsion will be considered." In an earlier draft, Armstrong had written "Expulsion will be automatic," but she wavered. "He needs as many breaks as he can get," she admitted privately.

But he wasn't getting a break that day. His scene before the class had earned him his first suspension. Plus, Armstrong had to travel to San Diego the next day for a meeting of the School Futures principals. If she couldn't be at school, she figured, he might as well stay out, too.

•   •   •

Eugene Ruffin's vision did not include late pay, disgruntled employees, and boys who wouldn't behave. On the contrary, the CEO's notion of well-ordered, high-performance schools revolved around principles of efficient business management. His was an encompassing, ambitious plan—one that, if successful, would deliver major changes in inner-city education. On October 7, a few days after Gill's tense go-round at E. C. Reems, Ruffin laid out his vision for all his principals during their monthly meeting at headquarters in San Diego.

"I think we will build one of the finest delivery systems that I've ever had the chance to be a part of," Ruffin asserted, displaying a gift for oratory that might have come from the pulpit. Indeed, he had been heard to remark, "I'm not a minister, but I am black." Today, he was asking the principals to "accomplish a miracle," namely the creation of schools that would serve as a catalyst for change in their respective cities through exemplary performance.

Sixty-one years old, with nine grown kids, a glamorous new wife, and a taste for golf on exotic islands, Ruffin had plans to foment a revolution in schooling based on his experience in sales and marketing—plans that, if successful, would make him rich. At IBM and Xerox, Ruffin had worked on the systems that marketed the first PCs to the American public. It was no new technology, really—just a new package and a new way of getting lots of copies of that package to lots of people, cheaply. Yet it was a breakthrough that moved digital technology from the basement computer room to the desktop, fundamentally altering the way the world lives and works.

Ruffin wanted to do for schools what he already had done for the computer business. The expertise on good schooling already existed, he figured; it was just a question of delivery. Ultimately, Ruffin envisioned a network of inner-city schools, freed from the bonds and politics of bureaucracy and union domination, rationally operated by business principles and dedicated to satisfying their customers. These schools would bring excellent education to the urban masses the way the PC revolution had put computing might into so many offices and homes. Such schools, he believed, also would make entrepreneurs rich, just as the PC had. Ruffin planned to be one of those entrepreneurs. The nonprofit structure of School Futures was a politically useful starting place. Schooling, to Eugene Ruffin, was a business worth $384 billion annually in the United States. Handled right, this venture promised explosive profit potential. Education, he sometimes said in presenting his business plan, would be the next Internet.

Clad in his usual combination of plaid shirt and patterned necktie, Ruffin tilted his chair back as he explained that thanks to "equity research," charter schools finally had found a place "on the investment horizon." The key connections for the movement, he explained, would be "the black ministers—God-blessers."

Indeed, Ruffin needed those pastors badly. Their churches frequently owned unused land and even classroom buildings—a scarce commodity in many inner-city areas. The pastors also lent instant neighborhood legitimacy and automatic enrollment. Ruffin, for his part, was a fine messenger. He used his black identification to advantage, dropping references to the recent Baptist convention he had attended, winning easy entrée to the pastoral inner sanctum.

That strategy had worked well with Ernestine C. Reems at the Center of Hope. But now, that school was floundering, along with its Oakland sister, Dolores Huerta. He sounded a warning that everyone at the table immediately grasped.

"None of this is going to be any good if we have one school that is unsuccessful," he intoned. "We can't stand any weak links. We won't have any weak links." And, in a reference Armstrong could not miss, he added, "The buck stops with you. Don't pin it on someone else." He mentioned, almost casually, that he enjoyed talking with teachers at his schools. He didn't like to interview them about the performance of their principals, he said—"but I do."

Armstrong, chin on hand, was sitting directly across the square conference table from Ruffin. At the direct assault, she smiled slightly, but she pursed her lips to hide it, and looked away. Coates remained grimly tight-lipped.

Ruffin's salvo wasn't the only one putting the Oakland principals on notice. In the afternoon session, School Futures' lawyer, Brian Bennett, gave a presentation on special-education law. Although he did not know about Armstrong's ban on special-education students, his lecture left no doubt that she had placed her school in serious jeopardy. Bennett explained that hostile districts would use this "Achilles' heel" to close charter schools if they could find violations of law. In order to avoid shutdown or a disastrous lawsuit, Bennett explained, schools had to follow a three-step process. They had to search for and identify students who needed special help; they had to review each identified case, which in a new school meant reviewing every child; and they had to document that review within thirty days of the school's opening. He sternly reminded them: "You cannot screen out, you cannot cajole out, you cannot press out" any special-education student. If anyone did attempt to do that, he said, "you're in violation of federal law, and your charter will be yanked."

After the meeting, with some time to kill at the Hotel Circle Hilton, Coates and Armstrong joined another principal for a drink. All had been affected by Bennett's warnings. Coates confessed that she had turned away three children in wheelchairs because the school building lacked elevators. "We're going to get sued," she said.

For her part, Armstrong didn't worry much. Special education would happen, she figured, when School Futures finally struck a deal with the district. It was a tricky business; federal funds didn't cover the entire cost of educating special-education students. States handled the matter in various ways, but in California charter schools, districts typically paid only part of the cost. As a result, a single very expensive case—say, a medically fragile child who required a full-time attendant—could bankrupt a small charter school. For the moment, though, Armstrong assumed—perhaps wrongly— that no services would be available from the district until a deal was sealed. So she figured she was excused. (It was that same breakdown over a business agreement, of course, that had prevented any money from flowing from the district, leading School Futures to fund the school entirely from its own bank account for the moment. Had it not been for advances from John Walton's well-lined pockets, it was hard to imagine how the school would have survived.)

The outright ban on special education at E. C. Reems was unusual. Nationally, educators debate the question of whether most charter schools enroll their fair share of special-needs students.[9] The largest national study reports that charters schools serve a lower proportion of students with disabilities than do other public schools, but not by much—8 percent versus 11 percent. Some claim, however, that the numbers are underestimated, and that many charters go out of their way to recruit special-needs students. Whatever the truth, the situation at E. C. Reems hinted at the thorny role special education can play in the life of a charter school. In the Oakland school district, about 10 percent of students were identified with special-education needs. If the same pattern held at E. C. Reems, nearly thirty children should have gotten services. In fact, by year's end, only two requests came into the central district. No one there thought to wonder why.

• • •

The day of Nazim's suspension had tested the limits of Valentín Del Rio's tolerance. After all his efforts to improve Nazim's behavior, through rewards and punishments and endless chances, Del Rio said, with rueful finality, "I don't want to stop caring about him, but I guess I have to."

Yet in truth, despite Del Rio's frustrations, neither he nor Armstrong was really ready to give up on Nazim Casey Jr. Armstrong in particular saw both the promise and the tragedy of the boy's young life. In her complex personal moral code, she viewed parent involvement as a foundation in her school, but she was willing to stretch the rules to save children whose parents met only the biological definition of the word.

Askia Casey had not given up on Nazim, either. The grandfather resented the forced responsibility of a second round of child-rearing, but he honored his agreement and showed up in Nazim's classroom, uncomfortably folding his lanky six-foot-three-inch frame into a child's chair and desk. It was a jarring sight—the bearded Casey scowling behind rectangular mirror sunglasses, next to his tight-wired, irrepressible grandson. But as Del Rio tried to guide a lesson on nutrition on a warm October afternoon, the grandfather's presence seemed to rein in the boy's behavior.

Del Rio was laboring to explain the difference between butter and margarine. He asked if anyone had churned butter, an improbable proposition in one of America's most urbanized areas.

Nazim's hand shot up, just for a second. A moment later, he withdrew it.

The boy turned to his grandfather. "I never churned butter before, did I?" he asked. The older man glared at him.

On the board, Del Rio was making a list of milk products, beginning with ice cream and butter. He asked for other suggestions. "Buttermilk," Nazim offered. For once, his answer avoided the rocky shoals of the weird or the irritating or the offensive, and Del Rio put buttermilk on the board, nodding his approval. Charged by his success, Nazim turned to his grandfather with another suggestion. "Peach milk!"

Casey stared at him. Even in hushed tones, his voice hit a high pitch of incredulity. "What the heck is *peach milk?*"

"It's like strawberry milk."

Across the room from Casey vs. Casey, Del Rio switched subjects. As he introduced a unit on geography, he attempted to elicit a definition of geography from the class. He asked, "If I say we're going to study geography, what are we going to study?" he asked. It was a new teacher's clumsy phrasing, and the children served up the answer without hesitation.

"Geography!" they chorused.

Except for one lone voice—Nazim's. With relentless enthusiasm, he declared, "Corn!"

•   •   •

The School Futures Research Foundation knew about the frustrations over behavior and teaching at the E. C. Reems Academy, and it had no intention of allowing the school to fail.

In truth, there was no way the school's struggles could have stayed secret. There were too many visitors, too many parents complaining, too easy a conduit from parent to pastor to Ruffin and Gill. While many parents were more satisfied with the Reems Academy than with their previous district schools, they remained dismayed about discipline, especially in the chaotic classes of some of the new teachers. And as Ruffin often remarked, a lousy school would damage the entire effort. Each year, each school's standardized test scores were published in School Futures' annual report; low numbers would narrow its horizons. So the company took action. Soon, the bosses were treating the Reems Academy and its runty twin, the Huerta Academy, like infants born fragile and sick after a difficult pregnancy, and the Oakland charters ended up in a neonatal intensive care ward of sorts. Recruited to oversee the operation was the estimable Bernadine Hawthorne.

Hawthorne, like Don Gill, had held an administrator's post in a large school system, but she carried credentials he lacked. A longtime San Diego principal with a reputation for success through tough management, she knew the all-important standardized tests like the cupboards of her dining room. She was godmother and main adviser to Donald Evans, School Futures' most successful principal. And Hawthorne was black, which probably made it easier to gain Armstrong's trust. She understood her mission: to save the school from mediocrity. That mission did not include evaluating Armstrong, but it would prove impossible for her to visit without forming some strong opinions on Armstrong's ability to handle the job.

On October 12, Hawthorne caught the early flight to Oakland, and Armstrong made the short drive to the airport to pick her up. By the time they returned to the school, Hawthorne was in full lecture mode. She started with Armstrong's attitude, telling her, "You're going to be the cheerleader, even with all this stuff falling down. You're going to have to be the cheerleader for the kids, for the school, and for School Futures." Armstrong swallowed hard on that advice, but she kept her peace, and they moved on.

By the end of two hours, Armstrong and Hawthorne sat amid half a dozen pastel-colored stacks of pretest booklets that rested in the corners of Armstrong's office like rectangular house pets. Although the October test didn't count in any official sense, it was key to School Futures' vision of "data-driven" teaching. That notion involved using tests to determine each child's strengths and weaknesses, and then designing a program matched to each child's needs. In addition, since this was a new school with no previous test scores, the October numbers would serve as a "baseline" to demonstrate the children's growth over the year, for audiences ranging from parents to the media to, perhaps, investors in a Ruffin for-profit venture. And with loose talk of bonuses circulating, it was reasonable to assume that such growth would have direct advantages for the teachers. The test may have been practice for the kids, but for the grown-ups, it was as serious as a tax audit.

With the test books in order, Armstrong and Hawthorne moved

on to other key issues: discipline and the new teachers. Hawthorne recited some old-time wisdom that would have chilled Del Rio to his core.

"If they don't have good classroom control by the end of the first day, or at least the first week, it's not going to get better," she said plainly. "In fact, it's probably going to get worse." She advised Armstrong to persuade teachers to take responsibility for the behavior of all the children in the school—not just the ones they taught. She told Armstrong to deal with the mischievous student "door monitors," who were creating more trouble than they were solving, and to buy longer jump ropes, because the kids couldn't double-Dutch properly. Armstrong jotted notes on a thick yellow legal pad.

Then Hawthorne broached the core matter: classroom teaching. She advised Armstrong to make classroom visits a high priority, through not just casual visits but formal teacher observations and evaluations.

"When should they start?" Armstrong asked.

"Since you haven't been doing them, I would say as soon as possible," Hawthorne said gently. "If you don't get into the classrooms, you're sending a very strong message that that's not what's important."

Hawthorne questioned Armstrong on her vision for the school. Armstrong did have a vision of a sort, though it was not likely to impress Hawthorne or any other experienced educator. Armstrong wanted to hire caring, committed teachers and then foster an environment where teachers would feel supported. If she could keep them happy, they would do good work, she reasoned. But she didn't say that. She knew Hawthorne had won distinction for leading high-performing schools. So Armstrong talked about her target. "I want all of my kids to perform academically at the eightieth percentile on the Stanford Nine," she said, referring to the standardized test. Ultimately, she wanted the E. C. Reems Academy singled out as a California Distinguished School. It was a fine thing to aim for, but a vision entailed more than just hoping for high scores. Hawthorne suggested they create a calendar of return visits so she could keep working with Armstrong.

• • •

With the ides of October came the advent of the pretest, which offered a foretaste of the Big Test coming in late spring. The Big Test
carried unimaginably great import. Newspapers would run stories
judging not just the school but the charter school movement by the
scores. It would not matter that the Reems Academy was one year
old—an infant. School board members, policy makers, pundits, prospective parents would examine the scores. Realtors would use them
to set local housing prices. The school would win or lose grants and
state aid, and ultimately would earn a secure or tremulous future.
The numbers also would weigh heavily with the executives of School
Futures, which was part of a fast-growing movement to use test
scores as a basis for merit pay. Under School Futures' plan, teachers
whose students' test scores rose would receive pay bonuses that
could run into four figures—a substantial sum for college graduates
earning less than $40,000. The pretest was key to any calculation of
improvement.

The company's passion for test scores placed it within a new
cadre of school managers deeply enamored of such numbers. For
School Futures, testing represented a tool for teachers and principals to address each child's deficits and strengths. Indeed, the notion
of "data-driven" instruction was rightly finding a respected place in
education. Yet the intense focus on standardized tests worried critics, who pointed out the many crucial areas measured poorly or not
at all by fill-in-the-bubble tests. These critics argued for using a
palette of different measures, including writing, verbal performance,
artistic expression, and so forth. These critics also were pained by
the number of class hours devoted to preparing for the all-important
standardized tests.

The desire for testing emerged from a reasonable impulse: parents
and the public, as well as school people, should know how well the
kids were learning. Yet it also seemed reasonable to wonder whether
the current era accorded an exaggerated power to standardized test
results. The most fervent edu-technicians sometimes talked as if

each child's intellectual development might be checked hourly, and then carefully adjusted, as if the delivery of algebra and literature could be controlled like the air-fuel mixture in a jet engine.

All those calculations, all that seriousness, all those bonuses and curriculum adjustments, and newspaper stories, depended on the test accurately measuring students' abilities. So it was, perhaps, a curious decision to administer the test starting in kindergarten. The state of California did not require testing until second grade, but School Futures had purchased tests even for the five-year-olds. Kindergartners, after all, are not expected in October to know their letters and numbers, nor much of anything resembling formal learning—indeed, their school career is only a month old, and kindergarten is not even a required grade in California. So the question arises: Just how does one give a multiple-choice test to kids who don't know their letters or numbers? Harcourt Educational Measurement, the manufacturer of the statewide test, had an answer. It had devised a kindergarten version of the test, with familiar objects like ducks and puppies instead of question numbers, and unusually large bubbles for the children to fill in. Theresa Bade had to figure out how to get her kindergarteners to sit through it. Although skilled at maintaining order, she felt that some things were developmentally inappropriate for five-year-olds. But she mustered her energy to carry out the plan.

"OK, you see the picture of the pirate?" asked a strained Bade shortly after lunch on the first day of testing.

"You see the pony?" one of her girls asked. A boy stood and danced, while another girl drummed on the table.

Bade read from the test book. "You will see a picture of something that starts with the same letter as *pirate*." She told them to fill in the bubble, raising her voice above their chatter. She moved to the next question. "Point to the row with the house." She instructed the children to find a picture of something that rhymed with *house*.

"Yo, mama!" said a boy named Michael. "I got the dress for the mama and I got the dress for me!" He draped himself over one of the adult proctors.

Jasmine couldn't contain herself. "Miss Bade!" She held up her test book for Miss Bade and everyone else to see. "House! Mouse!"

The next question called for finding a rhyme for *cub*. Michael had another announcement.

"I got *tub*," he called out. He penciled a thin line—which the scoring computer might or might not see—through the circle he was supposed to blacken completely.

Bade, at top volume, could barely be heard. "Next to the ship, you see a whip . . ."

One boy scribbled out the entire whip. Another bubbled in the circle perfectly. One marked a light X through the circle. Sedrick crossed out the entire page. LaKeisha turned surreptitiously to the neighboring table and exchanged test books wholesale with the nearest girl.

Bade murmured to herself under the din, "Oh my God. This is going to be the worst week ever."

•   •   •

On Sunday, the last day of October, after careful and agonizing reflection, Emily Deringer phoned Dr. Armstrong. She had taught for the better part of two months, and could count two hours when she had been happy. Concluding, remorsefully, that she was doing little good for her children and needed to take care of herself, she told Armstrong she was resigning, effective in two weeks.

Armstrong accepted the resignation without pity or rancor, and set about looking for a replacement. She found one, conveniently enough, in Wilma Cornish, one of the two teachers benched at Dolores Huerta until the still-uncertain opening of the San Antonio–Volunteers of America School. Cornish had two decades' teaching experience, including a few years in the immediate neighborhood, and Armstrong trusted her immediately. Cornish visited Deringer's class, remarked that "somebody should have helped her a long time ago," and promised, "That class is going to be totally turned around." Armstrong liked Cornish's assurances that she would eliminate behavior problems in the class, and sought her advice on other discipline problems. She looked like a natural match.

But the problems in Deringer's class were not over. Around the time Deringer turned in her resignation, Armstrong suspended the most difficult child in the class, Carlton. The boy, who had wild eyes, a chapped face, and a disturbing, otherworldly smile, was universally seen as troubled, and as one of the school's toughest cases. Armstrong figured no progress would occur until she had gone face-to-face with Carlton's grandmother. So, testing the limits of legality, she had suspended him indefinitely, until his grandmother showed up along with him in the school office. Suspension—rarely more than a vacation for any student—proved an especially ill-chosen step with Carlton. He lived less than a block from school, and reveled in the opportunity to stroll by during recess and lunch and antagonize his classmates from the other side of the steel gate. On November 2, after a week out of school, he raised the ante. He hinted to his classmates that he had a weapon.

The teachers on the yard, unaware of his threats, shooed him away. Walking around the corner to the street behind the church where the teachers parked, Carlton climbed to the roof of Roland Anderson's bright purple Jeep. Seating himself there, Carlton kicked his heel against the windshield with remarkable force until the window imploded with a muffled crunch. Then, eerily, he kept swinging his heel into the empty cavity.

Sam Harrell, the school handyman, stepped out of the church and spotted him.

Still kicking, Carlton looked him in the eye. "I didn't do it," he said.

Harrell and Lawrence Tottress, the school secretary, dragged the struggling Carlton bodily into the school office. He screamed as they carried him across the yard.

By this time, word had made it to the school office that Carlton was armed. Armstrong sat Carlton down, and called the police on the eight-year-old. Then she asked if it was true that he had a weapon.

Yes, he said. He had a knife.

She asked him whether she could feel in his pockets and take it. He said yes. Armstrong retrieved a small box-cutter with a retractable razor for a blade.

What do you use this for? she asked evenly. He hunched his shoulders and began to cry.

Armstrong offered him tissues and water, but he would take nothing. He buried his face in his jacket and sobbed.

Two police officers—a man and a woman—arrived. Tottress walked across the street and escorted Carlton's grandmother to the school. The cops talked to everyone and filled out a report. As they were preparing to leave, Armstrong intimated that she was ready to expel Carlton. She felt for the boy, but she didn't know how to help him.

The woman cop advised her to keep Carlton. The grandmother was in no position to help him, she said, but maybe Armstrong could. "Give it another try," the officer said. Then, grasping the flip-top aluminum case that held her report-writing notebook, she strode back to her patrol car.

The other cop, the man, stayed behind. He had different advice.

Get Carlton out if you can, the officer said. By the time he's sixteen, he'll be a murderer.

Later that afternoon, Deringer sent another student to the office, this time for raising his middle finger to her. On his way out of the classroom, the boy hit another student. Armstrong hinted that she was going to kick him out of E. C. Reems and asked him where he was planning to go to school next. Was he going to find another school in the yellow pages?

Yes, he said sullenly.

"No you're not," she shot back cruelly. "You can't read."

She didn't mean it to come out as nasty as it sounded, she realized later. She had meant to teach him a lesson about why it was important to pay attention to his teachers. At the time, though, Armstrong just laughed, hard, for quite a while.

Less than a year later, in the summer, Carlton was arrested for the first time. Wielding a rock, he had tried to take another child's bicycle. The police, who branded him "a little terrorist," hauled him in for robbery, attempted robbery, and assault with a deadly weapon, but he was never formally charged with a crime. One wondered how long that would remain true.

Emily Deringer taught her last class three days later, on November 5. Her rout was complete. She had already made arrangements to move out of town early the next week, and back to her parents' home in upstate New York. Now she needed to tell the children that she wasn't coming back.

Minutes before the end of the school day, Deringer made her announcement. "Principal Armstrong has found someone who's going to be coming in here," she said.

Even for her swan song, Deringer couldn't get a polite audience.

"Is it your boyfriend?"

"Is it your girlfriend?"

"You got a boyfriend?"

Deringer tried to restore some dignity to her final speech. She told them that they would not see her again after Monday.

"Nooooo!"

The children stormed her as if she were the uprights after a football game, nearly knocking her over. The gesture may have appeared affectionate, but it violated that final zone of Deringer's dignity, her own body. Deringer, however, had not given up on her grail, an orderly line.

"We are going to walk out of this building much nicer than we walked to P.E. today," she declared. She reached for a pile of papers that would explain her departure to the parents.

Steven then darted across the aisle and lifted another boy out of his seat, and dumped him onto the floor. One boy grabbed another and held him in a headlock with his knees. The children were screaming, and now, in the final minutes of her brief career at E. C. Reems, so was Deringer.

"Let him go!"

•   •   •

By early October the challenges before Laura Armstrong loomed painfully clear. She needed to energize and accelerate the learning of 268 children who, mostly, had arrived at her school woefully behind, and she knew she must achieve her goals before her San Diego bosses ran out of patience. Yet for all its wrenching birth pains, the E. C. Reems Academy was not the most urgent worry for School Futures executives. That dubious honor went to the company's other outpost in Northern California—the Dolores Huerta Learning Academy.

Dolores Huerta had opened its doors on Monday, September 20, a week after E. C. Reems and two weeks after every other public school in town. The first day found Felicitas Coates excruciatingly tense, seemingly certain that disorder would break out at any moment, and determined to frighten away the forces of chaos through sheer will. She had run the children through a rehearsal of their lining-up routine the week before, but on opening day she wasn't satisfied with their performance, and let them know in stern tones. She sent home a child who had showed up out of uniform. One parent compared her manner to that of a prison guard.

After a series of recess periods that had not conformed to her expectations for order, the principal produced a police whistle and blew it liberally. The teachers grew visibly more frazzled at each blast. At day's end, in a "debriefing meeting," the teachers relieved Coates of her whistle, and by the next day she did seem to be yelling less.

Yet even with the yelling, the tension, and a psychotic fire alarm, this tiny pink-painted school, with its 140 students, felt like a sweet, friendly place. The kids seemed eager to please; they were strikingly obedient before the experienced teachers, smiling sunnily up at them each morning. Most dressed quite neatly, and a few boys even donned neckties for the first days. True, they tested the new teachers in all the traditional ways, but there was no venom behind their antics. Since the secretaries and custodians were all either parents or well known in the neighborhood, there was little separation between the staff and the families, contributing to the sense of community—a sense that had been sorely lacking at Jefferson.

Despite those good feelings, great hurdles lay ahead. Like Del Rio at E. C. Reems, the Huerta teachers found few students working at the level expected for their age. But as tension grew between the staff, the parents, and the increasingly erratic principal, it became evident that academic concerns would not occupy the center stage. Instead, the key issue was the question of Coates's control—of the school, of the children, of the staff, and of herself.

Most worrisome was Coates's singular focus on appearances. The weeks before school opened found Coates picking out tablecloths for the school dining room and arranging fruit baskets while most of her teachers had not been hired. What really set her up for conflict with her bosses, though, was her discovery of the color of floor tile that was being laid at Dolores Huerta.

The afternoon she walked into the skeletal school building and spotted the tile, she sped back to the Volunteers of America building and steamed around her office, spewing profanities. She heaped scorn on the checkerboard pattern of "titty pink" and "cheapy beige," and vowed to "rip it out myself if I have to." Then she lit out for the unfinished building again, camera in hand to record the atrocity. On the way out, she explained to her office staff that she had nothing else to do anyway—a remarkable and distressing statement from someone trying to cobble a school together within a few months.

Don Gill arrived in town and dropped by Coates's office. By then, her anger had reached high boil. "How's everything look?" Gill asked. "Like shit," the principal snapped. Gill had visited the school, and by contrast praised its looks. Coates was outraged. "The school looks great? You're insane," she stormed. "It's gotta be changed."

In the midst of the fight over floor tile, Coates demanded—and won—a week's delay in the opening date to hold training sessions for her teachers. Yet she ended up scheduling less than two days of seminars, much of it noticeably unsophisticated. Indeed, the simplistic presentation of a truly complex challenge seemed boldly displayed in a diagram that Coates posted: a circle of words linked by arrows that read "Happy teachers–>Happy students–>Happy parents–>Happy administrator."

The administrator, however, was anything but happy. She couldn't let go of her fury over the paint and tile colors at the school. Certainly, she had good reason to want an attractive school. Parents were fleeing a district that had put their children on campuses scarred by graffiti, and play yards trashed with broken glass and syringes. But there was also a matter of balance and priorities. In talking with her bosses, Coates made no secret of her disgust, nor of the fact that the color of the school was dominating her thoughts. Indeed, she threatened to resign unless the problem was fixed.

Throughout September, Don Gill received ceaseless complaints about Dolores Huerta and its principal. Mostly, the objections cited her brusque impatience—if not outright nastiness—with a startling number of children, parents, teachers, contractors, and others. Meanwhile, teachers lacked materials; the school lacked a handbook that parents could take home. School Futures had no intention of putting up with such antics. Three weeks into the school year, Gill returned to Oakland on a mission of warning. He delivered a four-page single-spaced letter containing a lengthy chronology of Coates's alleged misdeeds, most of them acts of disrespect, defensiveness, and insubordination. As she listened stoically, Gill recited the charges out loud. But a single sentence in the document revealed all she really needed to know: "Your inappropriate behaviors and actions towards your supervisor, parents, teachers, students as well as direct and indirect employees of School Futures Research Foundation, if continued, will result in your termination as principal of Dolores Huerta Charter School."

The other school that Coates was supposed to run—the San Antonio–Volunteers of America School—showed no signs of opening in October, as originally scheduled. Unfortunately, the frequent delays to the supposed starting date created havoc for the families who had enrolled, and for nearby district schools, which had to absorb the children when they found out the charter wasn't opening on time. Primarily, it was Garfield Year-Round Elementary—the district school that Coates had left—that bore the brunt of the burden.

The opening date for the San Antonio–Volunteers of America School had been delayed several times, and plans grew hazy amid phone calls and faxes and voice mails between Gill, Hammer, Coates, Harris, and Ruffin. School Futures and OCO fumbled the job of communicating the news to those most affected: the families who had enrolled during the summer, and the school district, which stood to gain or lose hundreds of students. Admitting that the school would not open in the fall would carry a high price; once the children went back to the district, they might not leave midyear, and the charter would lose the thousands of dollars that accompanied each child. Yet the school couldn't possibly open on schedule; renovations hadn't even begun. Finally, in mid-September, parents began to get word the charter would not open on time, but an official letter to that effect didn't go out right away. Neither School Futures nor OCO seemed overly worried about the headaches the late notice would cause for the district. But, as usual, the children would pay the price of the adults' disorganization and selfishness.

Most of the students who had signed up for the VOA school came from Garfield. Garfield, like Jefferson and other schools in that crowded swath of Oakland, ran year-round on four staggered "tracks" in order to accommodate as many children as possible. Ena Harris, the principal at Garfield, heard rumors in mid-September that VOA wouldn't be opening on time, and assigned the forty-three children in limbo to the D track, which started school October 4. But with only two weeks' notice, Garfield had neither enough room nor enough teachers to handle the additional kids. Worse, Cycle D was reserved, for scheduling reasons, for students who required Cantonese bilingual teachers. Nearly all the VOA students were Spanish speakers.

Noontime on the day of reckoning—October 4—found a substitute teacher who spoke no Spanish trying to communicate with twenty dispossessed VOA children, many of whom spoke no English. It was an improvement from earlier that morning, when the hapless substitute had simply sobbed. The principal, Ena Harris, had managed to find classroom space for everyone, but finding teachers proved harder. All the Spanish-speaking instructional aides were on vacation. There were no Spanish-speaking teachers to spare throughout the district. And to make matters worse, the district's mainframe computer had taken to randomly deleting children from Garfield's enrollment list, which was tottering at 998 children.

It was unclear when the VOA refugees would get a permanent teacher. The downtown district office was sending one, but that teacher wanted a full-time position, not a substitute post. The principal could afford to do that if these children, and their public school funds, stayed at Garfield. But she had a right to wonder: what if the charter school opened and the kids disappeared again?

•   •   •

By late fall, the scorecard for OCO's charter schools looked like this: one school—despite having established itself as a parent-friendly place with deeply committed teachers—had a principal fighting for her professional life. A second school—though it enjoyed some of the same strengths—was struggling with issues of order and academic solidity. A third school had repeatedly missed its announced opening dates, and a fourth and fifth hadn't even made it to the planning stages. So it might have seemed strange that OCO was using that experience as a launching pad for its most dramatic political event of the year—one aimed at creating better schools for many more children than the charters would serve. The charters had represented one notion for expanded school choice, but OCO understood all along that the charter idea had limits. It would serve, comparatively speaking, only a handful of students, and it didn't do much to answer the powerful call for reform within the existing district schools. So OCO was working on a second track as well, keeping alive its original plan for small schools within schools. Of late, OCO had devoted more attention to that plan, given the obvious signs that the charter schools would not be instant, resounding successes. Now OCO set to work on the sort of grand event for which it was famous: a giant "action," with thousands of its members present to watch as promises were extracted from the city's most powerful politicians. This required delicate negotiation: blending the agenda of OCO with that of its education partner, the Bay Area Coalition of Essential Schools, and then forging goals to which the politicians would agree.

In early October, Hammer, Lopez, and other OCO leaders had gathered around a burnished oak table at the Wells Fargo human resources department, where Lopez worked. They targeted politicians in City Hall, the school board, and the statehouse, whose backing OCO wanted. But looming over all was the outsized influence of the governor-turned-mayor, the scion of the state's greatest political dynasty, Jerry Brown. The meeting dwelled on how to convince him to focus not just on charters, his pet concept of the moment, but also on new small autonomous schools. "He thinks that charter schools are going to fix everything, and that's just not the case," said Lopez, who sat on Brown's education advisory board. "How do we get that through to him?"

All agreed that Brown would not walk away from charters. Indeed, at one point Brown had talked of bringing two hundred charters into Oakland—a virtual impossibility, everyone figured. Moreover, OCO felt charters were unpopular with teachers, and the coalition needed the support of teachers to anchor its agenda inside the district. But could OCO leaders persuade Brown to think in terms of sixty new schools?

The answer emerged from Brown's own office. The mayor had managed to install his lieutenant, George Musgrove, as the school superintendent—Carole Quan's replacement. Yet, after ten months in office, Brown had nothing to show for his campaign promise of education reform through charter schools. With its newly opened charter schools, OCO was poised to steal his campaign issue. Brown's education aide pushed him to lend OCO his support, and Brown agreed.

Brown met with several OCO members in early October. After some preliminaries, the OCO leaders presented a map showing crowded schools in the flats and small schools in the hills. They asked him to attend their action on November 8. Then they rolled into testimony about their New York trip and how they needed help with facilities.

Brown cut them short. "What can I really do?" he asked. "I don't run the schools."

The OCO people talked of a small-schools plan that would affect more children than charter schools could, of igniting a movement that could affect the country. They even suggested the small schools might figure in Brown's "legacy."

Brown's attention seemed to flicker, but he agreed to show up on November 8 and throw his support to the plan. Before the OCO group left, though, he asked, "There aren't going to be any surprises, are there?"

●　　●　　●

Autumn is the one time of year when coastal Northern California regularly stays warm after nightfall, and November 8 turned out to be a pleasant evening. OCO's campaign would reach a climax that night, and the feeling inside the vast St. Elizabeth's gymnasium was ebullient, celebratory, like an election-night rally for a candidate who was certain to win. In truth, the comparison was not far off. The political work that had begun two years earlier, when Matt Hammer read Deborah Meier's book, would come to a head that night. Before an audience of two thousand voters, several powerful local politicians would be asked to commit their support to OCO's plan for small schools. To say *no* on that stage would risk high political costs.

As the bleachers at St. Elizabeth's filled and the festive din increased,

Jerry Brown described his appreciation of the movement for the benefit of a radio reporter. Brown, who called his nonprofit-political headquarters-warehouse-commune-home "We the People," was saying that "the power of the people" came through in small schools.

"They're more effective," he intoned into the reporter's microphone. "There's a more face-to-face encounter." His voice, as always, was earnest and hoarse, as if he had made a loud speech minutes earlier. "The entire framework is within the control of the teachers, the parents—it's a more human scale." He added, "The schools with a thousand, it's outrageous; it's obscene."

Ron Snyder, OCO's senior organizer, had laid plans for the evening as if it were an invasion. "How the press hears this is crucial," Snyder had told the leaders. "We don't want them talking to someone in the seventy-fifth row or out in the parking lot about what the purpose of this action is. We want them talking to you, because you can articulate it most clearly." They would roll out a map showing schools of three hundred children in the wealthy hills, and of a thousand or more in the flats. "The basic message is: things are not fair; things need to change," Snyder said. And the key to victory was backing that message with emotion. "Testimony is about people's emotions and guts," he said. "Testimony is not about information and stories. This is about raw emotion, getting out the feelings. People can dispute facts. They cannot dispute emotions and feelings."

At seven P.M. exactly, the announcement came for all to take seats. Earlier, music and song had added to the warm and festive feeling in the room, but now it was time for business. Ken Chambers, the athletic-looking pastor of a small West Oakland congregation, spoke before the opening blessing. "We are here, two thousand strong, for a very special purpose tonight: our children," Chambers said. "We have three things we want. Number one, end overcrowding. Number two, start new small schools. Number three, build new school facilities. Do you agree with that tonight?"

The two thousand agreed—loudly and at length. They were black and brown, mostly; some were Asian and white; many were of humble means. The two thousand were largely of the sort that America believes are difficult to bring into community organizations and collective action; the kind who, supposedly, don't stand up well for their own rights, let alone those of others. OCO, by bringing out these two thousand, had put the lie to notions that such people will not devote sustained energy to community change, and that they will not build bridges across racial lines. These were the people without money for lawyers, without the education that translates constitutions and codes and statutes into freedom and power. These two thousand supposedly did not support their public schools, back their teachers, attend report card conferences, read with their children. Yet here they were, in the flats of Oakland, black and brown, packing the seats and thronging the aisles, tossing their arms above their heads in applause, cheering for the ideas of a Jewish educator and her school in Harlem. They had power, and it came not just from their numbers, but from the righteousness of what they wanted.

In a grand version of the strategy that had worked so well at Jefferson two years earlier, OCO's leaders sought to harness anger over injustice to create an emotional momentum for change. To this end, Sandra Frost, an OCO officer, presented a "research report" based on visiting with "thousands of parents and hundreds of teachers." She recited the charges, potent if familiar: "Our schools are too big, overcrowded and unsafe, our test scores are low and the dropout rate is too high, our teachers are demoralized and want to leave Oakland. Our children are falling through the cracks." Lecturing with the tone of a stern and dissatisfied matron, she made reference to a national survey that showed Oakland's parents more unhappy with their schools than those in any other major city besides Cleveland. Smaller schools, she said, offered a solution.

Slides projected on the wall told the rest of the story: A color version of the famous hills-versus-flats, small-versus-big school comparison, flanked by photographs of verdant, lovely schools amid the woods and of others, dilapidated, on unrelieved stretches of concrete. "We want an end to overcrowded schools!" Frost said. The crowd rose to its feet in a spontaneous wave of cheering. The demand was translated into Spanish. The crowd exploded. *"Sí se puede!"* they chanted—"Yes we can."

The room grew hot as the "testimony" continued. To the podium came parents, community activists, teachers. "I refuse to return to these conditions," a teacher named Deborah Israel said, "unless some changes are made." Then came the most powerful speakers: the children. Among them was Leslie Santiago, a fifth grader at Dolores Huerta and the daughter of Xochitl Garcia, the school secretary. "I like to thank you, Mayor Jerry Brown, for supporting our school," Leslie said hesitantly into the microphone, reading from her neatly hand-printed speech. Losing his faraway look, Brown leaned forward to listen. "I wish that my friends from Jefferson had a better and smaller school like the one I have."

A mother closed the testimony. "Two of my sons got hurt in school," she said. "Even though I live in this country, I don't feel safe."

The evening reached its climax with the grilling of the politicians. Would they promise to establish new small schools? To help find the necessary funds? To end the crowding, the hated year-round schedules? Would they tear down the crumbling shell of a long-abandoned Montgomery Ward and transform it into a school? Would they move the district administration out of its offices and convert that building into a school?

No one dared say no. Brown even won a standing ovation for his promises—which he translated into Spanish himself. Then, red in the face and smiling bashfully at his own hokiness, he led the crowd in a chant of *"Sí se puede."* His lieutenant, Musgrove, exhorted the crowd like an activist. "Are you angry about the condition of the schools you go to right now?" he asked the crowd. "Well, stay angry, and hold us accountable."

The evening closed with a prayer, offered by Reverend James Abner.

"Lord, we thank you for this victory," he prayed. "We pray, Lord, that you'll lead us from grass roots to green pastures, from overcrowding to overachieving. We ask for a better future, and not better excuses."

Despite their rough beginnings, the charter schools had lent force to the night's events. Hammer believed that the threat they posed to the district had forced top officials to the bargaining table. It had given OCO and its partner, the Oakland-based Bay Area Coalition of Essential Schools, a voice. Once, the OCO parents had felt impotent before the immovable monolith that was the district. Now, Hammer figured, the potential threat from such independent schools had shocked the district into paying attention. The movement, too, had demonstrated the appetite for better schools among supposedly apathetic parents. And despite the difficulty of securing buildings, Hammer was investigating new partnerships with other companies that could start more charter schools and thus magnify the danger for the district. Of course, that threat was meaningful only if the charter schools were attractive. In an article previewing the action, the *Oakland Tribune* quoted Lillian Lopez, the OCO leader and Dolores Huerta parent: "I've had my kids in very small schools—it's so different. It's more like a community. Smaller is better."

It was ironic, then, that even as the big political evening was getting underway in Oakland, Don Gill was meeting with lawyers in San Diego to draw up documents for the firing of Felicitas Coates.

Chapter 7

Comparisons

On a hot, hazy November 12, three days after OCO's climactic education "action," Don Gill arrived at the Dolores Huerta Learning Academy to fire Felicitas Coates. He had not scheduled the visit ahead, because he didn't want her to ask why he was coming. When he strolled onto the campus shortly after noon, accompanied by Bernadine Hawthorne, Coates had vanished.

"Daggone it!" he growled. "She smelled it!"

She hadn't needed an especially acute sense of smell. Conditions at Huerta had worsened dramatically after Gill delivered his October warning. He had attended back-to-school night, which turned into a venomous shouting fight, mostly over matters under Coates's control. Gill had found it necessary to schedule a separate meeting with the angry parents. On other visits, teachers complained of lingering problems reminiscent of the district schools: sweltering classrooms with windows bolted shut; books and materials still missing. Coates's surliness with children and staff persisted. The teachers, bereft of the security and calm that emanates from strong leadership, became so divided that in mid-October they sat down for a round of peace talks. Even after that, tension between the teachers—some of it racially tinged—lingered. Dolores Mena, the grandmotherly school secretary whose moral gravity and dignity had earned wide respect, described herself as "shaking like a child" before each workday. And Gill heard it all; he had invited staffers to call him with their complaints, and they did, daily, going over Coates's head and making her irrelevant even before her dismissal.

Her firing would mark the end of a quick, steep journey to disappointment. Just five months earlier, Gill, Matt Hammer, Lillian Lopez, and the rest of the OCO leaders had seen Coates as a great prize. Now, the same parties found themselves aligned on the need to dump her. Even Lopez, who worked in the human resources division at Wells Fargo, was puzzled and frustrated at the scale of the mistake.

The experience highlighted the difficulty of finding a strong leader for a new urban school. Coates's qualifications had made her a tempting prospect; her résumé listed a considerable range of skills and experience, and she enjoyed community support. Moreover, the landscape is not teeming with terrific candidates to lead urban schools. Yet, Lopez and others now realized that in their haste and hunger to hire a known, homegrown and ethnically appropriate chief, they had ignored warning signs. Some parents at Garfield had murmured that Coates yelled a lot. School Futures had never talked to her current and former supervisors; at least two would have given strong warnings if asked the right questions. Perhaps School Futures should have interviewed Coates more times. Perhaps there was some better way to introduce her to the depth and complexity of her job. School Futures, however, never really learned lessons from the experience—a fact that would haunt them in the coming months.

The whirlwind romance between School Futures and Felicitas Coates raised questions about the company's claim of bringing solid business practices to education. Yet, her firing also underscored one of the areas of claimed superiority for charter schools. A November dismissal of a principal was nearly unheard of in the district, and even at the end of the year, a problem principal might well have been reassigned to a small, quiet school where fewer parents would complain. But at the charter school, the managers could remove Coates swiftly—a painful but quick surgery that put the needs of children above those of adults. Gill needed only to wait until she returned to campus.

Around 1:30, an hour after Gill had arrived, Coates appeared. She had been at the chiropractor's, she said. She acted surprised to find Gill there on a Monday, which was not his usual visiting day. "It's not Thursday," she said, looking blank.

The appointed hour had come and the noose was strung, but there was a delay. The heavy ceramic sink in the boys' bathroom had fallen from the wall and shattered. No one was hurt, but the shards presented a safety hazard. Hawthorne and Gill climbed the stairs to view the disaster. As they pitched in to clean up, Gill sliced his finger on a sliver of the ruined basin.

When he finally took a seat in Coates's cramped little office, blood still oozed from his finger. He winced as a drop landed on his suit. "Doggone it, I didn't want to get it on my pants," he said, dabbing at the dripping blood.

Coates, who by now had a pretty good idea why Gill was there, couldn't hide her amusement at his condition. "You need some help?" she asked wickedly.

Gill, trying to be pleasant, looked like he would have amputated a limb before he accepted a Band-Aid from her. He turned to the business that had brought him there.

"We've had several conversations about your performance here as principal," he said in a tone that was strangely, disconnectedly friendly. He had observed, he added, that she had not completed the tasks required of her. "What I've done," he said in an offhand way, as if he were explaining a correction to some obscure financial record, "is prepared a severance package between you and School Futures." The words *fire, terminate, let go,* had not been uttered. One had to listen carefully to realize that Coates had just lost her job. She registered no reaction, her lips pursed in a mild frown. She perused the agreement: "Employee shall be relieved of all responsibilities as Principal of Dolores Huerta School on November 12, 1999, and shall not return to the School thereafter, except as specifically agreed with Dr. Gill to return on a onetime basis to collect her personal belongings."

Gill tried to sound affable. "As of today, I would like you to collect your keys and give you time to get your personal things out," he said. If she wanted to pick up her belongings at night, he said, "I'll support you." He added, "If there's anything I can do for you, I'll be open."

"No," she said in a weak voice. "I'll talk to my attorney."

She swallowed her anger and tried to maintain her composure. But when Gill left, she started, ever so quietly, to cry.

The phone rang. On the other end was Bob Spencer, the former school board president, returning her call. She had planned to invite him to sit on the board of trustees for her school.

"Actually," she told him, an ironic smile on her lips, "I just got fired." And despite herself, she began laughing.

Coates set about emptying cabinets, and soon found herself holding a passel of paintbrushes. She wouldn't get to paint the school during Thanksgiving after all.

It wasn't long before she began to wonder how long her compatriot and competitor, Laura Armstrong, would last in her job.

•   •   •

Because it aimed to make a political point, School Futures faced singular pressure to turn out high test scores, even at its first-year schools. As in the case of Felicitas Coates, that urgency translated into pressure on principals to perform or get out. The same ax could fall on Armstrong if she failed to set her school on course for test success.

December marked the passing of a third of the school year. At Dolores Huerta, the situation actually had improved after Felicitas Coates's departure, and the teachers were doing a credible job of running the place themselves, though they squabbled at times. Armstrong's school, however, felt like a battleship that had weathered some nasty broadsides. Although still seaworthy, still in the fight, it was listing a bit, its gleaming newness replaced by scars and leaks. Indeed, the gloss had quite literally worn off, the hallways now scuffed and unshiny. The parents had started to grouse about the dirt. Certainly, the teachers' hopeful honeymoons had ended long ago. They had not, even once, been paid on time. They had set up an after-school tutoring program for children with serious reading problems, but they earned no pay for the extra teaching. The kids, with their noise and disrespectful antics, exhausted them.

Wilma Cornish, who had replaced the routed Emily Deringer in third grade, offered a rare note of progress in the discipline campaign. Almost miraculously, she had established model behavior in that troubled and volatile class, without ever raising her voice. But for the school as a whole, the battle ground on. Armstrong frequently found herself delivering stern reprimands, often coupled with threats of return to the regular public schools. She lectured kids one-on-one, in handfuls, and even, on occasion, a dozen at a time—for mouthing off to teachers, for throwing around racial epithets, once for tearing a teacher's blouse, and once for removing their pants and mounting each other during kindergarten nap hour.

Armstrong wasn't the sort to consider all her troubles at once; her mind had a way of performing triage, delivering no more than one issue at a time. The others got held in a hopper, outside her conscious thoughts. Underlying everything, however, was her race to make her school perform. She had to move swiftly before the big standardized tests in the spring. Her first priority at the moment was spending time in the classrooms, to observe and coach her floundering virgin teachers. But even now, with the advent of December, she had yet to conduct even one formal observation of a teacher—a process that was standard in most public schools. She had let other matters slip as well—crucial matters, like establishing a board of directors. The school still offered no special-education services of any kind.

Much of Armstrong's energy, improbably, had been diverted into managing a weeks-long candy sale campaign. Pastor Reems had ordered the fund-raiser from the heights of her pulpit, to pay for a trip to see *The Nutcracker*, and maybe even to Disneyland. By now, though, with candy lost and money uncollected, the project had stalled; the school might not even make back its original investment.

At the end of November, signs had appeared that Armstrong's job was in jeopardy. After a couple of spats with Don Gill, she knew she had a formal, written warning on the way; yet she allowed the feud to escalate on December 1, when she traveled to San Diego to visit some of School Futures' campuses. She was grouchy enough to her host—School Futures' senior principal—to cause him to talk to Gill. At the end of the day, she found herself, by unlucky coincidence, sharing a plane with Gill back to Oakland. She snubbed him in the waiting area, and then chose a seat a dozen rows away from him on the flight. In her mind, she was simply avoiding an inevitably ugly conversation. But the growing tension between her and her boss ratcheted up the pressure on her to demonstrate some success at her school.

Armstrong tried to stay focused. Everyone—the pastor, OCO, the parents who had fought for the charter—was relying on her to create an educational result far different from the other schools in the neighborhood. The scope of the task would become fully evident when the scores from the October standardized pretest arrived in another couple of weeks. Armstrong, however, didn't have to be a prophet to guess what they would say.

The best predictors, sadly, were those maddeningly reliable "family characteristics"—race, income, parents' education level, single and teenage parenthood. If such "risk factors" behaved like radiation, the students at the E. C. Reems Academy had grown up in neighborhoods that represented the core of a nuclear reactor. Most of them, moreover, had enrolled after years spent at some of the city's worst-performing schools. Citywide, 27 percent of fifth graders read at the national average, and at schools in the hills, that number soared as high as 87 percent. But E. C. Reems drew largely from its neighborhood schools, whose scores lay at the bottom of the list: Webster (13 percent), Whittier (16 percent), and Parker (15 percent). Reports from the classrooms confirmed what the numbers predicted. Without some great course correction, the kids might face the same academic fate as those who stayed in the neighborhood schools.

As the principal of a charter school, Laura Armstrong had taken on the task of changing the kids' trajectories. Even in the first year—often a ragged year for charters—she would be tagged as a failure if the Reems Academy didn't outperform the regular schools nearby, such as the Webster Academy, Reems's neighbor a handful of blocks to the west.

The comparison hinted at many of the fundamental differences between regular schools and charter schools. To be sure, such a comparison presented problems. It made little sense to talk about "typical" charter schools, since each school was defined by its uniqueness. Many charter schools were very different from E. C. Reems, whether because they were run by more efficient companies, or no company at all, or served very different communities, or had taken more time in their planning. Yet, placing the two schools side-by-side offered a window on the daunting problems of a school like Webster, and on the presumed advantages of a school like Reems.

By virtually any measure, the Webster Academy was one of the most disappointing schools in Oakland. Its standardized test scores ranked it as one of the lowest-performing in California. Even compared to other schools for the very poor, it scored a one on a scale of ten. The state had officially targeted Webster as an "underperforming school"; even in tough neighborhoods, many district schools worked much better than Webster.

America as a whole had suddenly taken an interest in schools like Webster—and the inner-city education "crisis," with all its economic and moral urgency. The parents at Webster themselves, however, had never seen much mystery in the dimensions of the problem, or its consequences. They knew that their kids didn't read well and didn't study advanced subjects. And they knew what failure in school might mean. Their son might become the teenage boy who sold dope on the corner and died in a drive-by shooting. Their daughter might become the woman shuffling and muttering to herself at the rescue mission soup kitchen. But the question nagged: Why didn't Webster, and schools like it, work better?

Newspapers and television often linked the problems of schools like Webster to the woes of the big, troubled district bureaucracies. The Oakland district, like many throughout the country, struggled with its failings—sluggish service, absurd policies, misspent money, corruption, and patronage. The system often tolerated nasty treatment of poor parents, and it had trouble accomplishing basic tasks like maintaining safe buildings, delivering textbooks to classrooms, and keeping the heat on in the winter. Its test scores ran too low and its dropout rates ran too high.

Like many big-city systems, Oakland's school board often had responded to the problem in the system by replacing the man or woman in charge. Such moves depended on the assumption that, with a better CEO, the company would turn out a better product. The Oakland district had gone through five superintendents in the previous ten years. Yet, if the strategy had produced real and lasting improvement, the Webster parents had missed it. Indeed, the problems at Webster seemed separate from those of the district—the ones so frequently cited in public discussion. For all its woes, the Oakland district ran some schools—in affluent neighborhoods—where kids performed admirably. At Webster, barely one student in eight read at the national average.

Those numbers took a toll on the spirit of Webster's staff. It was hard to escape the sense that—for all the individual and small victories—the overall venture was failing. Confronted each workday with that poisonous knowledge, some teachers blamed the very people they were trying to serve: the children and their parents. The argument that the students would have done better with more support at home made perfect sense. Yet in the mouths of some teachers, the complaints occasionally assumed an angry, racist tinge.

Such teachers directed their ire at a breakdown in society, morals, and traditions of parenthood. They knew that their teaching techniques would work fine in suburban classrooms. They got fed up with aggressive, loud kids with absent fathers and with mothers who undermined their discipline efforts. They chafed at the hundred tiny assaults they endured each day, from rude, angry, foulmouthed students who anonymously roamed the campus. They fumed over the "crack babies," the emotionally disturbed special-ed kids "mainstreamed" into their classes, who did not understand the lessons and would not sit quietly. They tired of children who turned studying and behaving well into a kind of cultural treason. They saw the trashed bathrooms, the graffiti, as the handiwork of a marauding force of youngsters who had never learned respect. And the staff itself was fractured by a racial cold war. There were white teachers at Webster who said, privately, that black kids with "mental problems" were making the classroom pointless and the playground dangerous for better-behaved Latino kids. "The schools aren't failing the kids," one Webster teacher said. "Society is failing the schools. We are put in the position of being social workers and care providers for kids who aren't ours."

Many teachers, however, soldiered on without rancor toward the students and their families. One was Barbara Purdom, Webster's counterpart to Valentín Del Rio. Purdom, too, was young, idealistic, and relatively new to teaching. Webster was her first public-school assignment, after two years at a private elementary school in Japan and another stint at an afterschool college preparation course in San Diego. Like Del Rio, she enjoyed a natural rapport with her children. And she, too, battled over discipline and order—before a class that was far tougher than Del Rio's, as a visit demonstrated with painful clarity.

The boy with tufts of lint in his short nappy hair, and tears coursing down his face, was named Choyce. Over and over he wrote, "I will control my temper in class and do my work." Lines by the dozen were a standard punishment at Webster, as they were at E. C. Reems and many other schools. It was recess time for Barbara Purdom's third-grade class, in portable P-26 on the distant reaches of the Webster blacktop. But no matter how many times Choyce wrote his sentence, it didn't look likely that it would hold true. Purdom, who was too young to be as motherly as she seemed, examined Choyce's incomplete page. "You need to finish your work," she said evenly.

Choyce started mouthing off. One of the girls in the class stopped him, seeing that Ms. Purdom had an adult visitor.

"You're embarrassing Ms. Purdom," she warned.

"No I'm not," Choyce shot back, miserably. "I'm embarrassing myself."

A colossus of more than a thousand children set amid the residential expanses of East Oakland, Webster backed up against a good-sized park with a baseball diamond. The school itself followed the standard formula: a traditional two-story building of white masonry, its large asphalt play area now larded with portable classrooms. Across the blacktop, the buzzer signaled the start of class, but it took several minutes for Purdom to get all her students seated. She relied on a system of check marks on the board to track misbehavior for the day, but it didn't look promising. Choyce already had eight checks, and a boy named Chris had twelve. There were fifteen children in class that day, but enrollment had swung wildly, from a high of nineteen on the first day of school to a low of twelve, mostly as the children's families had moved, gotten evicted, or suffered other tragedies. The kids who entered later, to restore the enrollment, were inevitably a difficult lot. One had enrolled in the school seven days ago, and had served four of those days on suspension. Now he had returned.

Tropez, the best-behaved boy, asked the class, "You all remember our promise?"

Chris called out, "I pledge allegiance to the flag, and I promise not to be bad." On the strength of that dubious vow, he marched to the front of the room for no apparent reason. After four others recited a more traditional pledge to the flag, silence reigned, and Purdom seized the moment to teach. "Plus and minus are both different, but—"

Tropez called out, "They're both operations!"

Purdom ignored him. A girl raised her hand, and Purdom called on her. "They're both operations!" she repeated.

"Right," Purdom said, calmly. "Thank you for raising your hand."

The lesson on subtraction went on. Perhaps half the children looked like they were paying attention. Choyce played with a pro wrestler doll with its head ripped off, drilling a pencil's point into its hollow skull. Choyce, who in the past had threatened suicide in class, was one of a handful of students who, in Purdom's opinion, needed psychological help. But she had learned that the official channels at her school didn't work. The last time she had tried, with another child, the administration acted as if it had never heard of a special-education referral. Never, in her time at Webster, did Purdom locate a referral form for special education. Maybe the holdup stemmed from the district's effort to reduce the number of children of color in special education, or maybe simple bureaucratic inertia. Whatever the reason, teachers such as Purdom faced daily struggles with those few children whose academic needs were eclipsed by bizarre, troubled behavior.

A boy named Kenzo, as if to drive the point home, got Purdom's attention. He asked whether he could "go holler outside."

Ms. Purdom acted as unsurprised as if he were asking to sharpen his pencil. "You may not holler outside," she said. "You may go outside and think a holler." Kenzo headed for the door, murmuring, "Gotta let it out. Gotta let it out." He opened the door. A restrained "Whoo!" could be heard.

Purdom got back to teaching. She reviewed a recent test on choosing the right operation for a problem—subtraction, multiplication, and so forth. Many students, she said, had chosen addition simply because they liked it best, not because it was the correct operation. The public-address system broke in. A voice announced that all the students working as "conflict managers" should go to the office. Four students strode out the door, Choyce among them. Chris ran after them. "Choyce," he called, "you forgot your pencil!"

In the ensuing pause, Purdom was able to teach uninterrupted for two minutes, until the conflict managers returned. It turned out the meeting was canceled that day. On their return, the chaos boiled over. Kenzo picked up the easel and held it over his head. Purdom tried to get him to sit, but he stormed around the room, and began harassing another boy. Finally, Purdom lost her temper. "No!" she shouted, grabbing him by the arms. She led him toward his seat. Another boy rose. "My pencil broke!" Purdom divided her attention. "Honey," she said, still struggling with Kenzo, "how do you take care of that?" Another student stood outside the door, waiting to enter. Kenzo, now free of Purdom's control, leapt up to hold the door closed, and Choyce dashed over to pull Kenzo away. The boy outside forced the door open, and Kenzo pushed Choyce into the outdoors. Purdom, flushed and upset, dispatched Tropez to find a security guard. Then she took a breath and recovered herself.

"OK," she asked the class, "do you all want my help with this?"

Kenzo didn't. He walked to the overhead projector and stole the diagram that formed the core of the lesson.

Purdom refused to surrender. "It's all in my mind," she told him matter-of-factly. "I do not need that paper. You cannot stop me from teaching my class."

Of course, that wasn't entirely true. Kenzo had indeed derailed the class, a fact that highlighted the differences between Purdom's class and Del Rio's. Critics assert that charter schools "skim the cream," recruiting academically accomplished, well-behaved students, while leaving the rest behind. The principal at Webster, Sandy Shapiro, had little doubt about that. She knew that schools like E. C. Reems asked parents to sign a contract promising to commit time and support. By law, Webster couldn't do that. "We take a broader range," she said. "We have to take kids whose parents may have no commitment beyond, 'Take my kid off the street.'" And indeed, during the course of the year, E. C. Reems dumped a couple of its worst-behaving kids back into Webster. Moreover, Webster's distinction as one of the lowest-scoring elementary schools in town had made it a last resort. Parents enrolled their children there, in many cases, because they could not afford private school, and didn't know how, or lacked the motivation, to find their way into a better public school.

Unquestionably, Purdom faced a tougher task than Del Rio. Her class was a dumping ground of sorts regardless of the nearby charter, and even within Webster itself. The bilingual teachers there, by and large, faced a more manageable task, because their classes typically included at least a few students from countries where children unflinchingly obeyed the *maestra*. In addition, Purdom's newness at the school gave her little pull in the student-assignment sweepstakes. Two of her students were homeless; three were pinballing through the foster care system. Despite Purdom's pleas, Choyce's foster parents refused to have him tested for special education. Del Rio, so far as he knew, had no homeless students, and only one child with foster parents.

Attendance in his class ran noticeably higher than in Purdom's. That was not, however, to say that his kids lived easy lives. Had anyone believed that, an assignment Del Rio gave to write letters to the mayor put that to rest: "Dear Mr. Mayor, In my neighborhood there are a lot of people selling drugs . . . The cop's said they wer coming, but they didn't come . . . We do not get sleep at night becaues of all the shooting . . . I am scared to walk outside at night . . . Police chase the young men on the corners, beat them up and take their money and the boy never goes to jail . . . I'm ashamed of our area where I live . . . Can you help? It will not cost much."

By the usual statistical measure of poverty, the two schools stood roughly equal. At Webster, 84 percent of students qualified for a free lunch, as compared to 78 percent at E. C. Reems. Del Rio, though, had only one truly constant troublemaker: Nazim. Barbara Purdom had three or four. That fact raised a key question: Was the charter school recruiting, on the whole, easier-to-teach kids?

It is a measure of America's tolerance for inequity that private schools brag about their exclusive enrollment, while charter schools speak of selection in shamed whispers. But charter school student bodies often are not a cross section of their neighborhoods. By law, charters are open to all, like the vast majority of public schools. Many charter schools, however, are built around a particular mission, community, or theme, and families enroll accordingly. There are charters for kids in the juvenile justice system, and Afrocentric charters. Technically, they might be open to all, but only certain children enroll. The E. C. Reems charter was identified with a black church, and its enrollment was overwhelmingly Christian, and 85 percent African American. Nationally, however, most charters roughly reflect the makeup of their surrounding districts. Studies also suggest that charters do not cream off the easiest kids, and perhaps even draw lower-performing students than the regular schools.[10]

But "creaming" takes many forms. Did E. C. Reems recruit the families that were already most involved in their children's education? Yes and no. Some E. C. Reems parents were counted among the most involved in their previous schools. Bob Latson, one of the first to sign up at E. C. Reems, had played a remarkable role at Webster, distributing free food to the needy and encouraging black parents to seek common ground with Latinos there. He had come to Reems at the encouragement of Margarita Soto, another Webster parent and active OCO member who had been his partner in distributing food. But other E. C. Reems stories were achingly similar to Nazim's—the child academically behind; the family largely absent.

Whatever the makeup of the class, the key differences between the schools involved what each carried in its educational arsenal. The armaments came in a variety of forms: the expertise of the principal; the experience and energy of the teachers; the amount and quality of on-the-job training and support they received; the quality of the curriculum and materials. In all those areas, the two schools ranked surprisingly even—with an edge, in some, for Webster.

Webster's principal, Sandy Shapiro, had a good bit in common with Laura Armstrong. A more experienced administrator, Shapiro probably knew her curriculum better. But both were prickly people, given to making enemies when they didn't have to. Both were new to their current posts, and both had seen their jobs threatened. Armstrong knew hers was on the line for her behavior toward her boss and for her school's performance; the Felicitas Coates experience taught her that here employers weren't skittish about pulling the trigger. Shapiro, on the other hand, had won her job at Webster following a capricious demotion and a successful grievance that required the district to return her to a principal's position. The superintendent, looking for a place to put her, found a space at Webster, where the previous principal had departed with no explanation or warning the previous May. Shapiro would last one year there before a new superintendent transferred her again.

Probably the most important question, though, revolved around the quality of teachers at each school. Purdom's colleagues had more formal training in their careers by far, but that didn't automatically make them more effective. Webster's staff held the edge in teaching credentials; 58 percent of the teachers there had one, as against 28 percent at E. C. Reems. (Credentials tracked closely with student performance; at the city's top-scoring schools, between 90 and 100 percent of teachers had them.) Webster's teachers also had more experience; only 13 percent of them had just started teaching that year, compared to 64 percent at Reems. Nationally, charter school teachers are younger than those in districts, with fewer hours in the classroom. They have experience in a wider range of occupations than district teachers do, and have attended more competitive colleges.[11] Many of those comparisons appeared to hold true between Reems and Webster.

Yet the numbers didn't tell the full story. There was also the matter of morale, and therein lay crucial advantages for the charter school. Despite their relative youth and lack of training, Del Rio and his fellow teachers acted as a team, with considerable unity. The teachers' sense of working in a special place, toward a special mission, mattered. Webster's staff was divided, particularly along racial lines, with the deepest distrust between Spanish-speaking teachers of bilingual, mostly Latino classes, and black teachers of mostly black classes. Teachers had drawn battle lines over a reading program, which some of them saw as beneficial for English speakers and harmful to Spanish speakers. Webster's staff meetings were not usually pleasant, and the building was mostly empty by four in the afternoon. At E. C. Reems teachers hung out, working and talking, until dusk and beyond.

Moreover, the teacher quality question raised another key issue: the union. Like the large majority of teachers in public school districts, Purdom belonged to a union; like the large majority of charter teachers, Del Rio did not. When School Futures paid Del Rio too little, too late, he might have wished for collective bargaining. Yet the absence of a massive, long-negotiated contract made possible inno-vations like the longer school day and year that School Futures had promised (though not, as yet, delivered). Likewise, the charter's po-sition outside the system made it easy to do things that would have been crushingly difficult under large-scale collective bargaining. The charter could explore merit pay and bonuses, and in theory could hire the best teachers rather than the most senior ones, and fire those who had ceased to teach well.

As for the crucial issue of support and continuing training, Bar-bara Purdom and Valentín Del Rio shared some unfulfilled wishes. Both wanted more help with their teaching, and more expert train-ing. Both attended frequent faculty meetings, which dwelled mostly on matters of business, not curriculum or teaching. So-called in-service training for teachers was a proven element of effective urban schooling, but neither school received a lot of it. Purdom's staff at-tended such sessions a bit less than once a month; Del Rio's had them slightly more rarely.

As a charter, E. C. Reems enjoyed considerably more freedom than did Webster in choices of curriculum and methods. Such free-dom allowed schools to experiment with the ways teaching and learning took place. If charter principals and teachers wanted to train the kids in Urdu, teach percentages by showing students how to fill scuba tanks, or open a school inside an art museum, nothing stopped them. While some charter schools capitalized on that free-dom, Reems, amid its first-year disorganization, did not. Armstrong, largely free to pick curriculum, had not gone far afield from the mass-produced materials that the neighboring schools used. And while her seasoned teachers were doing strong, often creative work, Del Rio and other new teachers were merely trudging through that curriculum. Fill-in-the-blank handouts were no one's idea of engag-ing teaching, but they did help the kids stay quiet. In social studies, where the school had no textbook, Del Rio simply chose a book off the shelf at the teacher supply store in his assigned area—California history—and started making copies. At Webster, Purdom enjoyed somewhat more support. The third-grade teachers met as a group to work on their teaching. At least this year a science program existed there. At E. C. Reems, as at Webster the year before, there was no science beyond what the regular teachers happened to do in their own classrooms.

In a nutshell, the interesting classes at both schools usually reflected the industry and innovations of individual teachers. Moreover, there was never any mechanism to accomplish what some charter advocates envisioned: the transfer of creative methods from the charter laboratories to the big system. Even if the conduit had existed, it would have been hard to imagine Webster's teachers taking lessons from their upstart competitors at Reems. Moreover, the experience of school choice in other countries has raised doubts about how successful charters will be in supporting classroom innovation, especially when parents demand traditional visions of teaching.[12]

E. C. Reems, however, carried one other potent advantage over Webster: its sense of community. Because of the power that Reems had given to its founding parents, and because of its ties to an established community institution—the Center of Hope Church—the charter promised to close the distance between parent and school. At Webster, parents sometimes felt unwelcome, and had few meaningful roles to play. It was no wonder, some argued, that these parents failed to support discipline, check homework, or volunteer in the classrooms, as was the norm in places where education worked better. In charters, the advocates said, parents would *be* the school, sitting on boards of directors, rendering decisions on policy, choosing the principal and teachers. A larger number of adults in the school also could mean more tutoring and better supervision. Moreover, the generally small size of charter schools would enable that community to flourish. (The typical charter school had 137 students, while the median regular public school had 475. Webster was about four times the size of Reems.) And for a grim reason, school size was perhaps the most significant advantage of all. Smaller schools, by and large, are safer schools. Purdom was sick of walking onto the blacktop as kids clustered around a fistfight. Del Rio never had to deal with that level of ugliness. Certainly, kids traded insults, got up in each other's faces, and sometimes shoved and hit, but fistfights with audiences did not occur at E. C. Reems. The small school may not have had recess monitors, security guards, or much more than a postage-stamp play area, but it did avoid real violence.

E. C. Reems was not typical of every inner-city charter school, any more than Webster typified urban district schools. Indeed, even within Oakland, one could see the vast range that the freedom of a charter permitted. One school, in a neighborhood even tougher than Reems's, benefited from years of planning, and admitted only two classes' worth of students—fifty children in all. It had no corporation behind it, just dedicated parents and teachers and community activists and it was performing fairly well, despite an extraordinarily difficult student population. Another, also years in the planning by dedicated parents, was facing eviction and revocation of its charter over its unlicensed teachers and financial problems. A third charter, based on a nineteenth-century German education philosophy called Waldorf, had practically mutinied against its principal. And a fourth, which enrolled mostly adult students, was quietly churning out honorable high school equivalency degrees for onetime dropouts. As for the question of academic results, the situation largely mirrored the national picture: most agreed it was too early to draw any firm conclusions. There were reasons for cautious optimism, in spots, especially in charter schools focusing on the students who were furthest behind. No charter in Oakland, however, had yet drawn notice by outdoing the district's average test scores. Indeed, it seemed that the lessons of Oakland might hold quite broadly: some terrific charter schools exist, but if parents expected a charter to be an automatic ticket to excellence, they stood to be disappointed.

• • •

As December rolled on, Valentín Del Rio noticed some encouraging signs in his classroom. His kids seemed to be reading better, and they had found a comfort zone that allowed them to write more creatively and at greater length and with more skill. They seemed, finally, to grasp what he was saying, and he was more sensitive to their moods and abilities. Yet, he held sadly modest hopes for their learning. He saw promise in developing their character, but figured they would advance their academic skills only slightly. "How," he wondered, "do you work with somebody who spells *and* wrong all the time?"

Despite his improving relationship with his class, he joined the rest of the staff in a sort of battle-worn frustration. Some of Del Rio's troubles were his own. He still felt he belonged at Dolores Huerta, with its high Latino population. Also, his secret hope that his new career would multiply his dating possibilities had been utterly dashed. There were few romantic options available to him at E. C. Reems. Yet most of Del Rio's irritations stemmed from the disappointing state of the school. He had expected a contrast to the public school system; he expected a school where he could get an overhead projector when he needed one. There were no substitutes available; when a teacher called in sick, Armstrong dispersed that teacher's students among all the other classrooms. There was no reading teacher to help the less-skilled students. The teachers still didn't have health benefits, and some had drained their bank accounts to the last $5 when rent bills arrived and paychecks didn't.

Even so, for Del Rio, a taste of success in the classroom could compensate for a lot. Unfortunately, that success did not extend to the headache named Nazim Casey Jr. In his best moments, Nazim was funny and chatty and loud, trying to answer every question in class, sometimes with brilliance, usually with nonsense. ("Why do the earth go so slow?" he asked one day.) In his worst moments he spewed fury and tears. Del Rio flip-flopped in his attitude toward the boy. He knew Nazim had a behavior contract that allowed the principal to expel him after three suspensions, and he knew Nazim had exhausted that limit. Del Rio didn't understand why he wasn't gone. But he genuinely cared for the boy. And he sensed that no nine-year-old's troubles could be of his own making, no matter how hateful his actions might appear. Nonetheless, he could not continue to halt class at each outburst and to soak up the boy's abuse.

Armstrong, however, resisted putting him out. It was disturbing to ponder what might happen to him if she did. In Nazim's neighborhood, a solid education was the exception, not the rule. With his charisma and determination, the boy was destined to make a deep mark on his world. Without an education, it was hard to imagine the mark would be a good one.

Two or three generations earlier, it would not have mattered as much whether a child like Nazim completed school. Nazim's great-grandparents had come to Oakland during World War II as part of the massive migration that, in one decade, swelled Oakland's black population to forty-eight thousand from eight thousand. So plentiful were wartime jobs that Oakland's shipbuilding companies were handing out train tickets in Louisiana, Texas, Oklahoma, and Arkansas. Without a high school diploma, let alone a college education, a worker still might establish a comfortable life. Nazim's grandfather—who did attend college—had worked on the railroad, that vast machine that, rather literally, had put Oakland on the map in 1869 when the city became the terminus of the transcontinental routes. But in modern times, low-skilled and semiskilled jobs had withered, ushering in an era of poverty and joblessness. Nazim's grandfather now lived in a hovel attached to the back of someone else's house. Nazim's bed was a narrow mattress on the floor, pushed up next to the identical one where his grandfather slept. They lived behind a steel-plate door and a tall, padlocked gate, the walls of his junk-strewn concrete walkway topped with loops of barbed wire. Nazim's father, who never finished high school, was pissing away his most vibrant years in a steel-barred cell.

On the afternoon of December 10, Del Rio sat down with Nazim's grandfather, Askia Casey, to review the boy's report card. The chat became a mutual sympathy session for Nazim's two chief caretakers. Both were deeply alarmed over the latest development in Nazim's behavior: an elaborate, frightening fantasy life which he reported as vivid fact. At home, Nazim had reported burglars, robbers, more men with guns. Three times, Askia Casey took him seriously enough to call the cops. All the scares turned out to be products of Nazim's imagination.

Nazim had been inventing tragedies in class, too, Del Rio lamented. "Last week," Del Rio said, "his sister died, and he was in Chicago." Casey bowed his head and shook it sadly. "He's even been seeing things," Casey said, and talked about one of the gun incidents. "It's horrible."

Del Rio began, "His lying is so consistent—"

"—that there's no truth," Casey finished. "I can't believe anything he says anymore. Anything he says, I have to take it as a lie first."

Del Rio listed some of the other problems. Nazim had frequently yelled at him, and he walked out of class at will. "I don't know who he thinks he is," Del Rio said. Nazim threw tantrums all the time, and fake sobbing fits. Under no circumstances, he said, could he get Nazim to study on his own, and it was affecting his grades. "This is the work I get from him," he said, holding up a report card that ranged from C-plus to F.

"He's going out of his way to do bad," Casey groused.

Del Rio offered a commonsense observation: Nazim might be acting out to get attention. Surely, he received precious little of that from his exhausted grandfather. But Del Rio did not take the thought further, to talk about why Nazim might so desperately crave attention. In any event, Casey had explained that Nazim was already receiving counseling, though the grandfather saw little benefit from it.

Finally, Casey reluctantly brought up a solution of sorts. "You say Dr. Armstrong has the form about A.D.D.?" he asked. He was referring to attention deficit disorder, the hyperactivity label so frequently attached to black boys in the inner city. If doctors tagged Nazim with that diagnosis, they might well recommend behavior-modifying drugs, an idea Casey and Armstrong had long resisted. "I know she doesn't believe in it, and I don't, either," Casey said. But, he said, he had reached the point where his grandson might need to "take something."

Casey speculated about the roots of Nazim's behavior. He mentioned that Nazim's father was in jail—the first in his extended family to land behind bars, he said. The woman Nazim once treated as his mother had died a few years earlier, but that was actually his grandmother. Nazim's mother, he explained, was still alive. "She lives so close by that she often walks by here," Casey said. She had borne four other children, but had as little contact with them as she did with Nazim, he said. "You see those nature programs where gorillas sometimes reject the babies?" he asked bitterly. "I think that's how she is."

"I think that has affected him a lot," Del Rio offered. "But we need to find a way where he can learn."

Neither of them, unfortunately, had many useful ideas. Del Rio wanted the boy involved in some activities, but Casey was hesitant to sign him up for the weekend baseball league, feeling it would come as a reward for misbehavior. Grandfather and teacher looked over the four days of absence listed on Nazim's report card. "Those may have been suspensions," Del Rio said. "I don't know what else to do."

"Neither do I," said Casey.

Casey seemed serious about pursuing the attention deficit diagnosis. After bidding Del Rio good-bye, he walked downstairs and waited twenty minutes for an audience with Laura Armstrong. She received the talk of a medical diagnosis for Nazim with skepticism. "So you think some drugs is going to change his behavior and stop him from lying?" she challenged.

"I don't know," Casey said.

"But you're willing to try."

"Absolutely," he said. Armstrong agreed to sign the forms, though she continued to oppose actually drugging the boy. "He needs psychological help," she said.

"He's getting that, and I don't see any improvement," Casey said.

Casey left, letting the heavy door to the principal's office swing shut. Armstrong picked up the phone on her desk and dialed Del Rio's extension. "You remember that form I gave you about Nazim?" she said. "I want it in my box by Monday."

•   •   •

Nazim Casey, and his potential drugging, presented one reason for Laura Armstrong's anxiety. But she had plenty of other reasons. The E. C. Reems parents may have enjoyed the safety of their new school, but that didn't mean they were putting in their required forty "volunteer" hours, signed promises notwithstanding. Even with the involvement of the founding parents' group, and even with the church as a bridge, a lack of parent involvement had become one of the chief concerns at E. C. Reems. If parents couldn't put in the volunteer time, the school allowed them to pay instead, at a rate of $12 for each hour they missed. By November, however, it seemed obvious that most parents were unlikely to fulfill the promise. Indeed, the situation at Reems was little different than in most schools, where a handful of parents are heavily involved, while most barely are at all. Some parents complained that they worked on weekdays, and could not help during school hours, so Armstrong arranged a Saturday workday in late November. Easily a hundred families were behind in their hours, but fewer than a dozen showed up. Armstrong and the active parents grew increasingly resentful.

The tension came to a head in early December. The first signs were a rift between the founding parents' group and Armstrong, along with her right hand, a mother and sometime business college student named Fanessia Williams. A spirited and cagey fighter, Williams had rung the opening bell by accusing the committee of doing nothing for the candy sale and the *Nutcracker* fund-raising. "The founding group of parents is a sorry group of people," she said. "Honest confession is good for the soul." Armstrong backed her up, saying the parents were failing in their responsibilities. "I have a very serious problem with any type of excuse," she said. Although angry, the committee members agreed the full parent body wasn't doing its part. One of the group members, Telicia Hooker, argued for a mass letter warning that if parents didn't deliver on their obligations, their child would not be welcome the following year.

As the school's frustrations mushroomed, it increasingly used threats to force involvement. In some ways, that coldness had dwelled within the Reems Academy all along, despite the community feeling. Even in its architecture, the school kept parents at a distance. A wall with windows separated the office from the school's main hallway. The office staff often kept the door locked, and shut the service window at lunchtime. In the teachers' bathroom, a sign read, STOP. IF YOU ARE NOT A PART OF THE STAFF, PLEASE LEAVE THIS BATHROOM IMMEDIATELY. IF YOU ARE CAUGHT USING THIS BATHROOM, THERE ARE CONSEQUENCES. And perhaps most dramatically, the founding parents had voted in penalties of $1 per minute or more for parents who arrived late to pick up their children from the school's afternoon day care. In cases of extended or repeated lateness, the parents had suggested calling the child welfare people to take the children away.

Yet now, the threats to kick out the laggards were gaining force and frequency. They surfaced repeatedly at the next general parent meeting, on December 8, ultimately provoking a backlash from the targeted parents. Hooker invited the small group of heavily involved parents to introduce themselves, and then assailed the others for doing too little. "That's not what our school is about," she said, her voice somewhat lost in the boomy, loud basement cafeteria. "Our school is about parent participation. If you're not going to help our kids, we're not going to help your kids."

Another mom reinforced the point. There was to be a "reenrollment process" the next year, and those who did not participate would not be allowed in.

A father named Solomon Isom was outraged. He had taken his children out of the Berkeley public schools to come to E. C. Reems, and he felt that in a white community, parents would not be fed a diet of threats. But Bob Latson, one of the most involved parents, stepped to the school's defense. Latson—who often patrolled the school hallways, endearingly reminding children to tie their shoes and act right—was a fierce advocate of a "fast-track" school. An Air Force brat educated in England, Latson offered no apologies for demanding private school exclusiveness. He wanted bad actors thrown out, pronto. "I got a simple plan," he explained one day. "If my son has a problem, I'll take care of it. If every parent adopts that plan, we'll be fine."

But even with the threats, many parents weren't attending meetings, and most weren't volunteering in the school. Among that group was William Stewart. He had been suffering sleeplessness and panic attacks. His late wife's family had dragged him to court repeatedly in a bid for custody of Malory, who was doing lackluster classwork. They had traded accusations of "stealing" the ten-year-old. On top of that, he was plain worn out from his struggles at Whittier with OCO. He knew about the threats, but he didn't believe them. He did believe that parents should be present at school, so their children will realize that education is a high priority. He felt guilty about his failure to spend time at school. He just wasn't up to it right then.

Armstrong wasn't really planning to expel the families who had failed to fulfill their "volunteer" hours. She didn't have the heart for it, and anyway, such clear-cutting of the enrollment lists would have left the school empty and broke. In theory, she already had less money to work with than the regular schools did, because her school had to pay for its lease and renovations out of its per-student funds, while district schools received extra funds to cover those costs. Plus, the charter wasn't entitled to all the special-category money that a regular school was. The loans and grants from Walton helped to cushion the school, but even so, its classrooms were half the size of Webster's, its lunchroom almost nonexistent, its tiny library stocked with a 1965 encyclopedia. And on top of that, Armstrong had far less support than a district principal did. Sandy Shapiro, Armstrong's opposite number at Webster, didn't have to worry about arranging food service, custodians, security, maintenance, payroll, and all the other things that came with a central bureaucracy.

None of that deterred Laura Armstrong in her mission. It was her job to outdo the "competition" down the street. But she had a million little jobs to figure out, for the first time, before she could attend to the core matters of teaching and learning. And she had a hard time delegating tasks and responsibilities. As she reflected on this difficulty, she wasn't sure whether to trace it to the departure of her father in early childhood, or some other trauma, but she had a very hard time trusting other people. She preferred to rely on herself. She drove a big Lincoln Navigator, a high-up, muscular sport-utility that symbolized her independence. The license plate, which read LDA-TYJ, named the two people she counted on the most: Laura Denise Armstrong; Thank you, Jesus.

•   •   •

In mid-December, the results of the pretest arrived, causing a small flurry of curiosity. Of course, the tests had been administered, back in October, under what statisticians might politely call nonideal conditions. After two months, though, Armstrong didn't think about the chaos that had prevailed in some classes on test day. She largely took the scores as gospel. But gospel means good news, and these tests didn't carry much of that. Across the board, class averages lay below—and generally well below—the thirtieth percentile, which meant that more than 70 percent of American kids had performed better than the kids at Reems. In fourth grade, 2 percent of the students read at the national average. In third grade, 18 percent did. The numbers in math were even worse. And in the other grades, the numbers were similarly devastating. Among Del Rio's fourth graders, precisely one child had reached the national average in reading and in math. Nazim Casey was reading like a mid–second grader, and doing math somewhere near the end of first grade. Asia McGehee had similar scores. Several students did even worse.

Laura Armstrong knew she needed to devise a plan. She had started, a week earlier, with her first formal observations of teachers in their classrooms. Fanessia Williams was helping her with her people skills, and had posted reminder signs in her office that read simply, HUMBLE. Armstrong knew she needed to examine the test results closely. Already, she was making the after-school tutoring a reality. The building was looking better, and Armstrong had left the nonsense of the candy sale behind her. She was going to need better teaching and better discipline if she hoped for strong results on the real test in May. Now, she was in a position to focus on that plan, just so long as no major disasters came along.

Unfortunately, in a first-year charter school, that was too much to hope for.

The biggest disaster yet to strike the E. C. Reems Academy of Technology and Art began innocently enough, with a reading light. It was one of those portable lights with a spring-loaded clamp, mounted above an overstuffed couch. On Friday, December 11, at the end of school, someone left the light on. Apparently, the custodian didn't notice. In fact, no one paid it any attention until 9:25 P.M. the next night, when an alarm sounded at Oakland's downtown fire dispatch center.

Firefighters quickly arrived at the school and peered through the glass front doors. Thick smoke coiled along the hallway and stairwell, billowing under the night security lights. The firefighters smashed one of the doors and made their way to the second-floor hallway, where water gushed from a ceiling sprinkler. That stream of water, pouring in under a door, had confined the blaze to one classroom. With the windows and door closed, the intense fire that started in the couch had smothered. It could have been much worse, certainly, but the damage was serious. The classroom was gutted and unusable. Much of the rest of the building had suffered smoke and water damage, and contractors had to remove a good portion of the materials inside—including textbooks and student work—so repairs and painting could take place. The recovery would require planning and arranging, energy and time.

It was precisely what Laura Armstrong couldn't afford.

•   •   •

Dr. Armstrong firmly believed in the saying that the Lord will never present you with a challenge larger than you can handle. The fire squared nicely with a Biblical tradition of trials and tests. If there was a flavor of divine providence in the events, it was enhanced by the fact that the fireproof doors and sprinklers that restrained the blaze had been installed just weeks earlier. Armstrong made a keepsake of the melted electric cord from the rogue light, had workers stretch yellow caution tape across the doorway of the ruined room, and went on. The fire would cost her valuable days during the Christmas break, dealing with insurance adjusters and identifying materials boxed for storage, but it did not shut her down.

It was no secret, however, that School Futures was losing whatever faith they once had in Armstrong. Pastor Reems's confidence in her was dwindling, too. Reems—who of course had selected Armstrong—talked regularly with Ruffin. Although a woman of the cloth, Reems was a businessperson. She was troubled by reports from her congregants who had children at the school—complaints that detailed not only the discipline problems but also Armstrong's surliness and her difficulty managing what amounted to a good-sized start-up business. Reems believed not in fancy degrees but in what she called "mother wit"—what some call common sense. She was beginning to suspect that Armstrong didn't have enough of it. She feared that Armstrong, for all her deep-down goodness and passion and hard work, was not the person to bring the pastor's dream to reality.

Bernadine Hawthorne's coaching work culminated in a grand presentation that Armstrong delivered to her staff after the Christmas break, on January 12, exactly a month after the fire. Armstrong had prepared for the meeting with a fervor unmatched since the opening day of school. Well into a winter night, she reviewed the tests student by student, a feat unimaginable in a large district school. In strategy sessions with Fanessia Williams, Armstrong had focused on her purpose. "The whole issue is how I'm going to motivate the teachers to motivate the kids," she told Williams. "Bottom line is, we've gotta raise our scores." But she was confident that it could be done. Repeatedly, Williams reminded her that style mattered, too.

Armstrong was going to have to abandon her distant, sardonic front and act enthusiastic.

When the day came, Armstrong left nothing to chance. She attended carefully to the arrangement of seats in the room where the faculty met. (The space was rather hopefully known as the computer room, in expectation that one day the school would buy computers.) Armstrong set up an overhead projector. She pulled in students to arrange the furniture, but she was so distracted that she kept stopping in mid-direction, thinking aloud. Finally, when the tables were clean, she was ready.

Valentín Del Rio arrived, without his test scores. He spotted someone else's folder, and groaned. As usual, he had forgotten something. "You better have your test scores," Armstrong admonished, in her fondly grumpy way.

Bernadine Hawthorne walked in and immediately rearranged the tables. Armstrong looked perturbed. "Isn't this a U?" she asked.

With Hawthorne in the room, Armstrong switched to a version of herself that few had seen before. "Thanks, everyone, for another day of hard work," she said, smiling broadly. "I want you to know, your hard work doesn't go unnoticed." In confident tones, she reminded her staff of the importance of the May test. Newspapers would publish the results, she warned, and the whole point of the charter was to improve student performance. Everyone needed to understand the results, and to explain them to parents and kids.

But her confidence faltered as she tried to explain the statistical terms on the score reports—stanines, NCEs. She soldiered on, handing out sheets with a bell curve drawn on them, and asking teachers to note where their students' scores lay. The teachers murmured with concern. "That's terrible," Cherlon Simms said. The most hopeful remark came from Carol Fields: "They're at the top of 'below-average.' "

Wilma Cornish chalked up the low scores to illiterate, drug-abusing parents. "The environment does play a really big part in the child's learning." Armstrong tried to redirect the conversation; if the scores were the parents' fault, it would kill her push for improvement. "That merits further discussion at a later time," she said breezily.

She handed out index cards. On them, she asked the teachers to write down the level they expected their children to reach when the test was given. "Think about setting a goal," she said. "Where will you take them?"

Quietly, the teachers studied their cards. They wrote digits on them, privately, indicating great hopes—climbs of twenty, thirty, forty percentage points. Armstrong told her teachers to tuck the cards away in envelopes. These were confidential dreams.

Then she invited the teachers to offer proposals for changing the grim state of performance at their school. The ideas poured forth: tutoring for poor readers, repeated practice tests for everyone, a literacy and math night for parents, classroom tests that looked like standardized tests with little bubbles to fill in, vocabulary from the tests posted on the walls and used in class discussions. It was all productive, but even so, Bernadine Hawthorne harbored deep concerns about Armstrong's capacity as an instructional leader. Despite the impressive show that day, Hawthorne doubted that Armstrong had the expertise to guide her teachers toward the goals they had inscribed on their index cards.

By that time, though, School Futures already was plotting the school's next chapter. One day earlier, Don Gill and Gene Ruffin had held a quiet meeting at a restaurant near the Dolores Huerta school with a candidate for a principal's job. If he won the position, he would oversee two schools: Dolores Huerta and E. C. Reems.

The candidate—a bald, charming African-American man near retirement age—had not visited the E. C. Reems school. But he knew it well enough. After all, he had run it when it was a private school. His name was John Cleveland, and he was Ernestine Reems's brother.

PART III
Promise

Chapter 8

Power

Who was in charge of the E. C. Reems Academy?

As signs loomed that the School Futures Research Association might remove Laura Armstrong from her post, once-theoretical questions became more and more relevant. In a so-called community school, could School Futures swing the ax without consulting parents and teachers?

In a regular school, no one would have thought to raise such questions. The lines of authority there are as clear as in an army or a police department, a legacy of the turn-of-the-century rationalist reformers. The principal serves at the pleasure of the district superintendent, who in turn reports to the school board or the mayor. Teachers and parents may offer advice, but usually have little formal power.

In a charter like E. C. Reems, however, the lines on the organizational chart can twist and blur. The idea is to extricate the school from the daily control of the big bureaucracy, but what results is a complex web of power based on law, money, and politics. Legally, the local school board has little involvement, except to enforce basic promises through the sledgehammer threat of closure. Day to day, the school's own governing board holds the aces. But it is the principal who is expected to run the school, and with responsibility goes authority. Morally, the parents and community people who put their sweat into building the school—often literally—deserve some say. The charter, or a contract, may award power to yet some other party, such as a management company. And often, especially in the inner city, a community organization or church may quietly exercise profound control, especially if that group owns the building. In times of discord, these blurred lines can cause endless, exhausting confusion over who gets to make the vital decisions.

The E. C. Reems Academy now stood at the center of just such a vortex. Legally, final say belonged to a governing board that still had not been created. School Futures, however, held both the management contract and the cash, placing it squarely in the driver's seat. Supposedly, the company had "empowered" Laura Armstrong to make major decisions, together with parents, teachers, and "the community." Morally, the founding parents and OCO, who had fought to get the charters passed and laid the groundwork for the school, felt entitled to some say. And Pastor Reems, who held the title to the building and power in the neighborhood, wielded enormous influence. She had already selected one principal. Now, it seemed, she might get to do it again.

Principal Armstrong did not fully understand the jeopardy her job was in, because she didn't see the school as having big problems. Some start-up woes were inevitable, she figured, and to her mind, the school was in fair shape. Still, she saw the urgency of dealing with big-time miscreants like Nazim and bringing up the performance of her school. Moreover, Armstrong was scheduled for major surgery in early February, which would keep her home for six weeks—most of the time when the children were supposed to be preparing. All those pressures fused to produce an extraordinary spasm of activity, largely aimed at driving up test scores, and much of it carrying real benefits for children. Armstrong roped her young, still-energetic staff into creating an after-school literacy tutoring program for the poor readers, and an enrichment program—with offerings like cooking and hiking—open to everyone. And she brought life to yet another surprise from the Reems pulpit: an announcement, without warning, that there would be school on Saturdays. Armstrong didn't know how she would pay for it, but she set about establishing a new program for low achievers that would mix academic help with fun.

At the same time, Armstrong began consolidating her base of control, hoping to brush away a source of frustration and bring some convenience and efficiency to the school's operations. She had long squabbled with the school's most powerful body, its founding parents' group. In January, she sidelined that group and created a new committee in its place. In her struggle for survival, that decision was to prove one of her worst mistakes.

The rift between Armstrong and her founding parents had opened in November, over the pettiest of disputes. The disagreement revolved around a $40-a-month water cooler she had wanted to buy for her teachers. Armstrong still had no discretionary budget, however, and the San Diego headquarters handled all the finances. So she asked the half dozen women who constituted the founders' group to allot some money for a water cooler. That group controlled a bank account funded by fees from the after-school day care program, which was technically separate from the school. But the parents rejected Armstrong's request, arguing that diverting the money might shortchange the day care program. Armstrong, always reluctant to trust or to ask for help, took the founders' refusal of her request as a betrayal. She ordered the founders out of her office, and kept most of them at a chilly distance afterward.

In the weeks that followed, Fanessia Williams—Armstrong's self-appointed volunteer assistant, and her most frequent confidante—made a project of rebuilding diplomatic relations between Armstrong and the founders. Williams wanted to buff away Armstrong's curt, sour exterior and replace it with warmth and friendliness before School Futures deemed it too late. She persuaded Armstrong to take the founding parents out to dinner, and her HUMBLE sign still hung on Armstrong's office wall. Yet Williams herself had helped to create the schism with her memorable December broadside, telling the founders, to their faces, that they were "a sorry group of parents." And when rumors spread that they—and some less involved parents—were griping about Armstrong and her school to the church higher-ups, it was more than either woman could stand.

On January 20, three weeks before Armstrong was to leave for her surgery, she executed her power play. She created a new top group, the School Site Council. SSCs—groups of parents and teachers—are common in regular public schools, and Armstrong had always planned on instituting such a group. The move was not directly engineered to do away with the founding parents, but it was hard to miss the fact that the SSC—all of whose members were appointed by Armstrong—would assume much of the decision-making power that had once belonged to the founders. At the group's first meeting, Armstrong made clear what she thought of the dissenters who had brought their complaints to the church. She knew there were "all kinds of rumors out there" about the school, and she had one thing to say about them: "I personally feel a parent should not have a voice if they have not been active in the education of their child."

Laura Armstrong's wishes notwithstanding, the parents, of course, did have a voice. And whether she meant to or not, she had shut their complaints out of the school. It was natural, perhaps inevitable, that some parents would then carry their complaints to the church. They knew where the real power lay.

Yet for all the growing discord, everyone—principal, pastor, and parents—shared a single goal: a high score on the spring test. This desire now dominated the life of the E. C. Reems Academy. On walls and doors, lists of test vocabulary words had sprouted. Teachers converted their daily quizzes to multiple-choice, fill-in-the-bubble form. There was talk of a raffle to lure parents to the test-prep session. No meeting was complete without a discussion of plans for the test. And the teachers showed the kids their score reports from the October pretest, illustrating how far they had to go.

Valentín Del Rio handed out scores before the end of the day on a Friday. The score reports were a mishmash of percentiles and charts, most of it mysterious to the kids. But one part—a little graph, with a dot for each subject—revealed how the student had done on a scale of one to one hundred. The higher her performance, the closer her dots were to the right side of the scale. For most of Del Rio's students, the dots were clustered well to the left, in the thirties and below. For Nazim, they practically touched the left edge. Almost all his scores were under ten.

Nazim glanced at the sheet for a moment. With no surprise in his voice, he announced, "I got a bad grade." Then he looked away.

•   •   •

Laura Armstrong's view—that her school was basically in good shape—was not widely shared at School Futures' sterile, office-park headquarters in San Diego. There, CEO Eugene Ruffin listened to reports from the field with increasing alarm. A pair of his most trusted deputies—Donald Evans, the star principal, and Bernadine Hawthorne, the consultant and godmother—had logged dozens of hours with Armstrong, trying to keep E. C. Reems from becoming the "weak link" in the company's chain. Their evaluations were distressing. They could have forgiven some growing pains; even Evans's school had weathered a rough first year, complete with racial strife and a roof collapse. Both of them, however, believed that Armstrong lacked the gifts to guide her students and teachers to excellence. Hawthorne expressed puzzlement over how Armstrong had landed the job in the first place. "It's so important to have a vision," she said, "and I'm not quite getting that she's acting on a vision."

Of course, Armstrong's perceived lack of skill was only half the problem. The other half concerned her notoriously surly manner, most particularly with her immediate boss, operations chief Don Gill. The animosity between them was so palpable that it was uncomfortable to be in the same room with them. Indeed, their nasty feud had taken on a life of its own. In phone conversations, Gill tried to get Armstrong to swear obedience to him and loyalty to School Futures, and Armstrong delighted in frustrating him. Plus, she was openly grousing with her staff about the company. Gill demanded, over and over, that Armstrong stand up for School Futures before her staff, but she refused. CEO Ruffin, accustomed to the rigid ladders of deference in giant corporations, found the whole situation bizarre.

Pastor Reems's opinion, too, had shifted. The key point had come on January 8, when Ruffin, Gill, and Jeff Harris met with Reems in her office. Also present, though mostly silent, was Reems's older brother, John Cleveland, an elementary school principal in San Francisco. Harris did much of the talking, letting Reems know how displeased School Futures was with Armstrong. Ruffin and Gill were surprised to discover that the pastor was nearly as frustrated with her protégée as he was. Reems had wanted to see excellence, tight discipline, and high parent involvement in the school. She saw none of those. And she felt that Armstrong didn't have the people skills to unite a team. Reems genuinely cared for her passionate disciple, but Armstrong had separated herself more and more from the church leadership, giving Reems less and less to say in her defense. It wasn't so much that Reems approved a change in the principalship, but that she no longer could put up much of a fight for Armstrong.

Later, though, when School Futures said it was searching for a new principal to replace Armstrong, Reems offered a candidate. Her brother, John Cleveland—the one who had sat in on their meeting in early January—was looking for a new job, she said.

Ruffin's list of complicated issues, however, went well beyond a single problem school in Oakland. Ruffin wanted to build more schools, but his sole funder, John Walton, and the rest of the School Futures board had stepped firmly on the brake. Walton had visited the schools and called School Futures' two Oakland charters "an embarrassment" that should "be improved drastically." Moreover, he had poured millions more than he had expected into the operation, at Ruffin's behest, and was still subsidizing the operations of schools that were supposed to support themselves with per-student funds, to the tune of a projected $4.7 million overrun. In Southern California, one school needed money because it was operating under unclear legal auspices even though its charter had never been approved. In Oakland, School Futures still had not negotiated the details of its business relationship with the district, and therefore had not gotten a penny of the money intended to fund the school. School Futures had advanced $328,000 to cover costs there. At the Volunteers of

America building in Oakland and at another site in Fresno, School Futures was paying for leases with no school operating.

Yet as these existing charters wallowed, Ruffin's grand expansion plans were devouring still more cash. Half a year earlier, he had budgeted $500 per month to sign up new churches and write new charters. Now, with Brian Bennett conducting negotiations in fourteen states, that figure had soared to $133,000 for December alone.

Walton imposed a spending freeze and demanded an immediate end to expansion. He wanted Ruffin to focus on improving the existing schools, not on building new ones. Ruffin, on the other hand, wanted to answer the call he was hearing from pastors in so many urban centers. So he set off in a new direction. With more than a half million dollars from Walton plus some of his own money, Ruffin started a new company. Good Schools for All would create inner-city charter schools, too, but without a fussy no-growth edict. Ruffin would not leave School Futures, for the moment. But under the banner of his new company, he finally would realize his long-cherished dream: an education management organization without limits.

In pursuing that dream, Ruffin would be fortunate to avoid frustrations like the ones that persisted in Oakland. School Futures had five approved charters, but had opened only two schools. The most promising third possibility had been delayed again and again, as the San Antonio–Volunteers of America facility proved too expensive to renovate. Parent interest in that school had dwindled; attendance at some meetings about that school totaled two. Matt Hammer, the OCO community organizer, was leaving to head a community organization in his hometown, San Jose. And the fourth and fifth schools were dead issues entirely. Dolores Huerta still had no principal. And, to judge by test scores, the largely Spanish-speaking kids at Dolores Huerta needed help badly as well. At Huerta, only 13 percent of the fourth graders and 4 percent of the fifth graders were reading at the national average. The principal's position remained unfilled at that school, two months after Felicitas Coates's firing.

And now, a new development: a surprise announcement from Laura Armstrong that she would take a six-week medical leave in February. Once she returned, only a couple of months would remain in the school year. Ruffin and his associates decided to use the opportunity to put one new principal over both schools—a more competent principal, with stronger people skills and closer relations with the home office. The move would end the principal void at Huerta, and avoid one at Reems. And it would provide Armstrong a smooth exit, by calling her departure a medical leave and offering her some training in the future, plus the hope of applying for a future principalship. It was an elegant solution to the nagging Oakland problem.

So Ruffin had a couple of tasks before him. First, he had to hire the replacement principal. John Cleveland had impressed him; Cleveland said his former students from the Hope Academy were now practicing medicine and law. The company had received tips that Cleveland came with baggage—there were rumors of a sexual harassment case in his current job—but Ruffin had no evidence, and few other candidates. If Cleveland was hired on a month-to-month contract for the few remaining months in the school year, Ruffin reasoned, he could boot him at the first sign of trouble. Ruffin was optimistic about moving forward with the charming, grandfatherly Cleveland.

The other task before Ruffin was entirely familiar from the world of big business. He would have to tell Laura Armstrong, face-to-face, that she was no longer needed at E. C. Reems.

•   •   •

As she drove to her lunch meeting with Ruffin and Gill on January 26, Laura Armstrong had no idea what was coming. Her bosses would often stop in or call her away with little warning, but they rarely required her to drive as far as Palo Alto—a full hour away—as they did on January 26. Also, the timing was terrible; she had put herself on a furious schedule of planning and arranging as her surgery approached, and Wednesdays like this one were crucial, because the faculty met on Wednesday afternoons. Today, she would be presenting the final Saturday school plan, the keystone of her scheme to raise scores: an intensive program, targeted at the sixty lowest-scoring children. Now it looked like she would be late to her own staff meeting.

She pulled her Navigator into a parking space at the Sundance, a well-heeled steak house with candles and burnished mahogany walls. Gill and Ruffin sat at the table, along with Pastor Herma Ross, a deputy of Pastor Reems who handled many of the school details. They devoted much of the meal to the kind of chitchat that Armstrong generally tuned out, including the details of their travel that day. Only as the lunch drew toward a close did Ruffin change the tenor of the conversation. He offered sympathy to Armstrong for her upcoming surgery. Then he said that he wanted to bring someone in to run both E. C. Reems and Dolores Huerta. Armstrong, who had uttered barely a word through the meal, was caught utterly by surprise. Quietly, she tried to explain that she had prepared a team of teachers to stand in for her. But Ruffin said he needed a more formal arrangement. She asked if he knew who would take her place. Ruffin hedged, saying he was considering a couple of candidates, but told her that one of them was John Cleveland.

The usually impassive Laura Armstrong could not hold back her tears.

At E. C. Reems, with Dr. Armstrong away for a lunch with her bosses, Carol Fields convened the staff meeting. Since Armstrong wasn't there to present her big plan, the session became a clearinghouse for problems and questions. Teachers had been sending kids to use the copier for them; supervision on the play yard was falling short. Theresa Bade felt that the school was giving the test too much emphasis, especially with her kindergartners. After waiting at length for Armstrong, many teachers gave up and went home. Finally, at 4:30, Armstrong entered the building. She issued a couple of crisp commands about removing some boxes from the foyer, and then proceeded to Fields's classroom, where the two set to work on a grant application, barely exchanging a word. They finally broke their grim silence after more than half an hour, when Armstrong tried to pull a staple with her fingernail, and cut her thumb. Fields offered a Band-Aid.

"No thanks," Armstrong replied. "I must complete my task."

An hour later, Armstrong, deep into a meeting of her newly formed SSC, was slowly regaining her biting, witty charisma. After some talk about discipline, new committees, and extra help for the low-scoring kids, she delivered some news.

"One more thing," she said. "February 8, I will be having surgery and I will be out for six weeks."

Bob Latson, the school's most active father, was worried. "Who's going to take over your position?" he asked.

"Nobody's going to be taking over my position," Armstrong answered evenly. Her team of three teachers would be in charge, she said, and she would be available by phone and fax. She moved on to her next meeting.

The next day, the question came up again as she outlined the Saturday school plan to the faculty. In the same meeting, she told the teachers about her upcoming surgery. "Are you going to be back for the testing?" asked teacher Michelle Kalka.

"Right before," Armstrong said. "I'll be back to administer the test."

The same day, kindergarten teacher Roland Anderson read a story to his students called "Satchmo's Blues," about the legendary jazz-man Louis Armstrong. After he finished, he probed the students' comprehension. "Do you know who this is about?"

A boy named Jonathan raised his hand. He thought he knew the subject of the story.

"Dr. Armstrong?"

In the days that followed, Laura Armstrong continued to promise her staff and parents that she would be back. She believed it was true. She had puzzled it out on the drive back from Palo Alto, trying to figure out what had gone wrong in her divinely chosen destiny. She knew for certain that she had been betrayed. She did not think that her leader and protector, the pastor, had supported her firing. She believed that School Futures had chosen John Cleveland in order to pacify the pastor, who—Armstrong imagined—must have been angry over her removal. But God's will, she reasoned, would overcome the foolish actions of men. Their decision could not stand. She even allowed herself to hear in Don Gill's words an assurance that her "interim team" could run the school after all. She ratcheted her pace of work even higher, looking for ways to serve her staff and her parents better than she had in the past.

School Futures' executives left it to Armstrong to announce the change. While she remained there, they never came to E. C. Reems to talk to the staff. They had intended to do so, but events intervened. Armstrong and the church got caught up in preparing for the hugely attended funeral for Pastor Reems's husband, Deacon Paul Reems, five days after the firing luncheon. So it happened that on February 8, Laura Armstrong left to have surgery without telling a soul at her school that she had been instructed not to come back. In San Diego, everyone simply assumed that she had communicated her news to the Reems community. No one bothered to check.

Both sides had the capacity to head off a catastrophe. Neither one did.

Word that there was a new principal in town hit E. C. Reems on February 9, as Laura Armstrong lay in a hospital near her suburban home, recovering from her surgery a day earlier. School Futures had officially hired John Cleveland the same day as Armstrong's operation. Although Ruffin and Gill had made the decision earlier, they extended their formal offer to Cleveland at the Oakland airport, where they were waiting for a plane to San Diego. Evidently anxious to close the deal, Cleveland had rushed to the airport to meet with them in person. In the moments before they had to board the plane, they told him he had the job. At no point, however, had anyone asked him some basic questions, such as: Why, if he was employed as a principal in San Francisco, was he answering his phone at home during the day? What school was he the principal of, and why wasn't he there? Why was he even interested in a month-to-month job if he already had a full-time gig? Had he ever been fired from a principal's job before? Evidently, the wish to please the pastor, and the hurry to put a principal in place, had once again trumped caution.

So, the next day, it fell to the consultant Bernadine Hawthorne to call over to E. C. Reems and ask Carol Fields for some space on that evening's parent meeting agenda to introduce Cleveland. Fields, taken completely by surprise, treated the move as a coup while the leader was laid low. She spun into a rage. Hawthorne, meanwhile, quickly realized that the new principal was news at E. C. Reems. Sitting inside the Dolores Huerta office, where Cleveland already had taken up residence, she asked him not to come that evening. He obliged happily. "I wouldn't want to walk into that anyway," the dapper, shaved-bald Cleveland said easily, as rain began to pelt the windows.

Hawthorne hurried through the cold drizzle to E. C. Reems to see if she could get a few minutes to talk at the parent meeting, but Fields shut her out. After a long discussion of test-preparation ideas, Fields told the assembled parents, "Dr. Armstrong had surgery yesterday, and she'll be out for a few weeks. We've got a very strong interim team in place."

With that salvo, Fields called the meeting to a close and agreed, finally, to meet privately with Hawthorne. She brought along the rest of Armstrong's "interim team": Christine Landry, the friendly, young second-grade teacher; Alan Foss, the tall, slender first-grade teacher; and Fanessia Williams, Armstrong's volunteer assistant. Hawthorne uttered some apologies for the confusion, and then dropped the bomb for those who hadn't heard: a "consultant" would be coming to take charge of the school. From there, the discussion quickly devolved into nastiness, as the group—particularly Foss—fired anger and vulgarity at Hawthorne. She absorbed the group's fury, repeatedly apologizing for the awkward way the news had been delivered. "I understand how you're feeling," she assured Foss. "No, you don't," he snapped.

The group was livid that Armstrong would be cut loose even as she was being cut open, and they painted dark pictures of the future if the change was allowed to stand. "You might as well start looking at ways to rebuild," Williams said, "because everything is going to crumble to the ground." Foss asserted that the pastoral staff at the church had known of the change before the teachers did. Fields—Armstrong's closest friend on the faculty—promised an even deeper split between the teachers and School Futures. "This is divisive," she said, raising her voice. "This is fucked up. I don't have another word for it. I hear your apologies, but I'm not feeling it."

After more than an hour, Hawthorne retreated to the home of her godson, Donald Evans, to spend the night. There, she washed the pile of dishes in his bachelor's sink, just to feel that she had accomplished something that night. Although she couldn't tell the teachers so, she was sympathetic to their side. She thought they had some good points, and she had registered their anger as well. With Evans's support, she told Don Gill that the interim team should be allowed to run E. C. Reems after all. Cleveland, she said, should handle only Dolores Huerta. But Gill was having none of it. Just because Armstrong hadn't fulfilled her responsibility to announce her departure was no reason for him to change his plans, he reasoned. But, he said, he and Ruffin would visit the following week to chat with the staff.

Within a day, as word spread through the school, the staff switched into full battle mode to prepare for the arrival of the corporate enemy. Teachers already had compared their relationship with School Futures to a colony's relationship to a king. Now, revolution was brewing. In meetings that consumed their afternoons and evenings, the teachers came together to share their outrage and to make plans. Indeed, this was the one event that had completely unified them. Until her ouster, Armstrong had been a complicated figure, loved by a few, respected by some, tolerated by some, hated by a few. But no one could stomach the way they believed she had been junked, sneakily, while in the hospital. She had become a martyr.

Valentín Del Rio liked Armstrong personally, though her leadership had never impressed him. Now, though, he was furious, and wanted to stand up to the bosses. "If they're kicking her out just 'cause they don't like what she's doing, then they're hurting kids," he said, and threatened to use up his remaining sick days. With no substitutes available, it was a potent threat. It mattered to Del Rio that Armstrong was the one who had started the school, and he wasn't ready for more chaos. "I accept the bumps here and there, but this is like an earthquake," he said. "This is like a tornado coming through." It wasn't enough that School Futures had paid the staff late again and again, messed up their taxes, and fumbled their health benefits. Now the company wanted to change principals midyear. "It's horrible," Del Rio said. "It makes me not want to be a teacher." Many others felt the same.

The E. C. Reems teachers ended the week with a Friday afternoon meeting where they discussed School Futures' misdeeds at length; then, the teachers developed their own list of "demands." Sounding like college students at a campus protest, they decided to threaten a "walkout"—a strike, really—if their demands were not met. Over the weekend, they agreed, they would call parents and tell them to keep their children home on Wednesday, the day after Ruffin and Gill were to visit. If the company met the demands, the teachers would spend their student-free day planning curriculum. If School Futures failed to agree, the teachers would go on strike for the day.

On the Tuesday when Ruffin and Gill were to visit after school, Fields and Landry drafted the petition of demands. As others passed out fliers announcing the day off, the two teachers toiled over an ancient Apple laptop at the back of a classroom, while their students watched the movie *Toy Story* on video. The letter, which was circulated for teachers to sign just before the end of the school day, set the battle lines for that evening. It catalogued a variety of demands, from corrected W-2 tax forms to overtime pay. But its key point was "Item 1": the return of Laura Armstrong to the principalship of the

E. C. Reems Academy. "In her absence," the petition demanded, "the team of Carol Fields, Alan Foss, Christine Landry, and Fanessia Williams will act on her behalf as previously decided and planned." And it issued an ultimatum:

> The staff and SSC unanimously agree that each of these conditions must be met by the specified dates. We expect that an agreement will be signed by School Futures today, February 15, 2000, outlining and accepting these conditions. If Item 1 is not agreed upon, the staff, with the full support of the SSC, will walk out, effective Wednesday, February 16, 2000.

The growing tension at E. C. Reems spoke not just to the management skills of School Futures, but also to the heightened expectations that can surround a charter school. Teachers and parents expected a voice in big decisions; they expected to own and run the place as few parents would inside the district. When a school raises those expectations and then fails to live up to them, the results can be dramatic. Indeed, an air of final reckoning hung about the school as the meeting-time approached, as if before a prizefight or court verdict. As with all big contests, the important players had assembled—the entire staff, minus of course Laura Armstrong, plus a handful of parents and a few of the church pastoral staff. On the stroke of four, Ruffin and Gill strolled through the door to the "computer room" and took seats at one end of the narrow, crowded room. John Cleveland quietly took a seat on one side of the room. Carol Fields opened the discussion by calmly recounting her shock at the announcement of a new principal. The spotlight turned to the men from San Diego.

Gill delivered the news. About ten days ago, he explained, he and Ruffin had met with Dr. Armstrong and Pastor Herma Ross. "At that meeting," he said, "we discussed a couple of things. The first thing we talked about was Laura's desire to take a medical leave for the remainder of the year." The teachers exchanged befuddled glances; it was the first they had heard that Armstrong even knew she was out for good, let alone that it was her idea. Gill went on. "We accepted that request, and discussed a transition plan," he said. "Laura," he added, "was to come back to the staff and explain to the group that she was taking medical leave for the remainder of the year, and a new interim director would be placed in the position."

Fields, incredulous, challenged Gill, emphasizing her words to make sure she had heard right: "Dr. Armstrong said she desired to go on medical leave for the *rest* of the *year*."

"Mm-hmm," Gill confirmed.

Fields wanted to set this one to rest. "Does anybody have a cell phone?" she asked. Nobody offered one, so Lawrence Tottress headed for the office to call Armstrong in the hospital.

In the pregnant moment of waiting, Gill remarked on his confusion over the confusion. "I don't believe this should come as any surprise to Dr. Armstrong, because we sat in meetings several times and talked about the transition plan," he said. "I'm not sure really why that communication was not made."

Alan Foss wanted to know why School Futures hadn't spoken about the changes earlier. "You could have asked to come to a staff meeting," he said.

Ruffin, who had expected to meet only with the interim team, was angry over having the tense conversation in front of twenty people, including parents. The insubordination from Foss—who was irreverent, gay, angry, and unimpressed by the chain of command—was starting to scuff at Ruffin's corporate and Marine roots. "You don't really have to ask to come to a staff meeting," he said. But he admitted, "I don't think this was handled very well, or we wouldn't be having this meeting." There were murmurs of agreement, but they were not friendly. Trying to be conciliatory, Ruffin said he wanted everyone to play a role, somehow, in the school. But even so, he said, School Futures needed a principal for its two schools.

Bob Latson, a father and able negotiator, gently pushed the staff's agenda. "We liked working with Dr. Armstrong," he said. "Is this just until she returns?"

Gill interjected. "Dr. Armstrong asked to have medical leave for the remainder of the year," he insisted.

As if on cue, Tottress strode in.

"I just called Dr. Armstrong," he said. "She stated when I called her just now she never said she wanted to take medical leave until the end of the year." The memos he had typed for her, he said, were clear: she wanted to return in mid-March.

Cornered, Ruffin abandoned his game of make-believe. "That was a public statement that she was supposed to make that we both agreed was in her best interest," he said. A murmur of discomfort spread through the room. Ruffin explained that the choice to keep her out for the year had been his own, made in the interest of "the children in Oakland." The CEO added, with easy confidence, "We do that all the time."

From that moment on, the stunned staff was left to find compass points in an unmoored world. They now knew that Ruffin and Gill had lied. But had Armstrong lied, too? Could she have hidden her firing from them? The uncertainty magnified the teachers' consternation. They had walked in believing they would set the agenda; now, School Futures had upended their plans with the unambiguous statement that Armstrong was gone for good.

Bob Latson, as usual, drove to the heart of things. "Is she aware that she's not coming back?"

"Yes, she is," Gill said.

Theresa Bade, the kindergarten teacher, was on the verge of tears. "Obviously not," she muttered. She scribbled a private note to Christine Landry: "Can they legally make Laura leave?"

Foss tried a different tack, hoping to retake control of events. His bungled paychecks were not Armstrong's fault, they were School Futures', he asserted. Likewise with his W-2 form, which still hadn't arrived. "If I don't have one by the end of the week, I am calling the IRS," he snapped, the haughty tone in his voice a thrown gauntlet.

Ruffin, who had maintained his otherworldly calm through each previous skirmish, finally lost his temper. "You can make a decision of where you want to be employed, but you are employed by School

Futures," he warned. "We probably should have closed this school thirty days into existence because we haven't gotten paid one dime for operating the charter by the Oakland school district. The fact that you got a check at all is a blessing."

The room reeled from the statement, but Foss wasn't cowed. It was his understanding that the county was supposed to be handling the finances, he said.

Ruffin cut him off. "You have a lot of understandings that are inaccurate—sir," he said, spitting out the last word. "The issue is, we're mixing two mediums. We've got customers here and we've got employees. We're having an employee discussion in front of customers, and I really feel sad about that, but none of you do, so please feel free." He was sardonic and bitter, a mode few had seen before from him.

Donald Evans, who had sat silently with the School Futures crew, now delivered some hard news. "Not everybody's cut out for this particular job," he said, quietly and coldly. "And I'm talking about teaching as well as principal." He had told Armstrong about the many things that she needed to do, but she hadn't complied, he said. The payroll problems, among many others, had been hers to solve, not a buck to be passed. And the interim team, he said, "is not nearly enough to move this school to where it needs to be." The school needed a better principal. "There is an awful lot of stuff that needs to be done, that I've already talked to the principal about. And I haven't seen those things—"

Bob Latson interrupted, striving to play peacemaker. Evans's statements begged for an even hotter fight. But Latson could see this was not a war the teachers could win, so he steered the conversation toward a peace agreement that would allow his son, along with 267 other children, to keep getting an education. He explained why the teachers had felt ambushed. And he apologized, gently, for Foss's aggressiveness. "I don't want this meeting to end on a bad note," he said. "Our hearts are in the right place."

Ruffin relaxed visibly. "Our only purpose here is to get from where we are to where we need to be for the kids," he said.

Don Gill spoke at great length, trying to convince the teachers that the short, late paychecks were the sort of "minor irritants" that come with "freedom" from the foul bureaucracy. But the real action was at the end of the room, where Ruffin and Latson were making jovial, whispered conversation. The two businessmen had recognized their own kind, and as a deeply trusted parent, Latson could safely act as ambassador. Meanwhile, someone wanted to know when the new principal would start. Abruptly, Gill turned formal. "The person I'd like to introduce to you right now," Gill said, "and to the staff, the faculty of E. C. Reems school, the parents, community members, and clergy of the Center of Hope Church, is Dr. John Cleveland."

"Good Afternoon!" Cleveland boomed with mock cheer. "What a Welcoming Meeting!" Some answered his mock schoolmaster-before-the-class greeting, but few teachers would make eye contact with him.

Cleveland spoke at length, describing how he opened a private school in this building in 1978 and oversaw it for a dozen years. "I'm excited about charter schools," he said. "I see this as a chance for poor people to have private schools." And he vowed to support the teachers. "I'm here to work with you, if you will allow me to." Slowly, as he spoke, a few parents and even a few teachers began coming around. When he promised to "set the tone so you as a teacher can teach," one teacher nodded, and a mother from the SSC murmured, "Yes." By the time he was done, he even won some applause.

Befuddled, the teachers asked the School Futures crew to leave them alone for a while, and Ruffin agreed. Foss wanted to call Armstrong again. Fields was confused. "I have a hard time believing that she knew all this and told us something else," she said. "Maybe I shouldn't be stuck there, but I'm stuck there."

"We're all stuck there," said Susan Adams, a mom.

Some wondered whether Armstrong just couldn't bring herself to relate what had happened. "In my eyes God gave her a way of escape, through her sickness," one mother said. "I just believe in my heart she couldn't come and tell you guys she was leaving."

Latson was watching the clock. He asked what the group wanted to do. No one knew whether the petition, with its strike ultimatum, had made its way into the executives' hands.

Pastor Herma Ross pressed the real question. "Are you going to stick with the school until June?" she asked. "School Futures has lost sight of the main interest, and that's the students. They can't get teachers." Elysa Christy, a first-grade teacher, confessed her fears that if they went on strike, she wouldn't receive the money she was owed. "I don't know what my rights are," she said. "Either way I'm scared."

Ruffin craned his head into the room. He was due for a meeting at OCO. "Do you know how much longer you'll be?"

Three minutes.

"This is a nightmare," Fields sighed.

At 6:13, when the meeting was better than two hours old, Ruffin and his posse walked back in. Fields spoke for the group. They didn't want Cleveland to start immediately. They didn't understand how a principal divided between two schools could be better than one who supervised just one school. And they needed to keep talking the next day. Ruffin accepted that. "I would urge you to try to come together as a group, because the kids need you," he said. He handed his business card to Bob Latson and headed to his next meeting, leaving behind a group of shell-shocked teachers and parents.

Now in private, they talked a bit longer. There was talk of a hurried call to a union or a labor lawyer. But the real issue—whether the teachers would remain, or would "walk out," or even quit—would wait for the next day.

Ruffin and Gill had received the teachers' ultimatum letter during the meeting. But in the rush of events, they didn't read it until after midnight, on the plane back to San Diego. Amazed and amused, they chortled about what would have happened if they had read the letter during the meeting. Had the teachers gone on strike, Ruffin and Gill vowed, they would have locked them out with relish and found substitutes to fill the classrooms. Gill said he would have enjoyed doing some teaching himself.

The horrid task of deciding whether to leave the school midyear dominated the staff's all-day meeting the next day. Official business opened with a stunner out of a soap opera: a letter Armstrong had dictated from her sickbed. Fields, fearful she would cry, handed it to Fanessia Williams to read aloud:

> I know you have a lot of questions, and so do I. Let me tell you first that I do not have clarity on a lot of these issues, even though I have asked many times verbally and in writing. School Futures does own the charters, and therefore can make these types of decisions at their discretion. Unfortunately, I have fallen victim to such an occurrence. I have not agreed to anything, but I don't think this matter is the end. I will let you know that things have been said about the school which are not true, and I have not had the opportunity to hear the concerns, address the issues or face the accusers. I have defended the efforts of the staff, and your rights, and this is the end result.
>
> Shortly after I informed School Futures of my medical needs, a meeting was called. Don Gill, Gene Ruffin, Pastor Ross and myself were present. At the end of lunch, I was informed that School Futures wanted to extend my leave. When I inquired as to why, they said that School Futures needed stronger leadership in Oakland. They wanted someone to oversee the three schools, and they felt that it was not fair to give me that responsibility. I said that E. C. Reems Academy was doing fine, and that I had everything in place for test prep, et cetera. I also said that I would not want the responsibility of three schools with 500 to 800 students. They also said that they had some concerns and felt that I could use that time for professional development. I asked who would be that person, and when they told me, I expressed my concerns from previously working with that person. Needless to say, I was overwhelmed.
>
> They had to rush to another meeting, but said the discussion would continue, and no one would be placed in that position until further discussion. I got a memo regarding this meeting that I felt did not

disclose everything discussed and requested a corrected response. I did not get a response. Instead, on Friday, February the fourth, I received a message to call Don Gill. He asked if I thought if Carol Fields, the head teacher, could handle running the school. I told him that was my proposal, along with the team leaders and staff support. He confirmed the arrangements with me while I was on my surgery, told me not to worry about a thing, and that his word was good. The rest is history.

Take this experience and learn from it. We have a vision and we have had many successes. I hope that you will continue as a team and complete the school year. I will be in touch, and more than likely, visit you sooner than I should. But I want to see you keep the faith and keep the commitment to education and, *I still have a vision.* I cannot let anyone or anything stop me. I have learned a lot in the past three months that will help me on my journey. I wish that I could truly express my gratitude for all of your hard work and sacrifices. Just remember that your labor has not been in vain. You, we, have already made a difference in the lives of our children.

The letter altered the debate completely. No longer was it a question of whether Armstrong had been ambushed, or whether she had known a change was coming. No longer was there any real hope of getting Armstrong back in the principal's chair. The only question that remained was whether the teachers could live within this harsh new world.

Shocking though it seemed at the time, their dilemma was almost predictable. A year earlier School Futures had sold Oakland, OCO, and the churches on the notion of a school controlled by community members, parents, and teachers. That idea was enshrined legally in the charter, in the form of a five-member board where School Futures had only one vote. To be sure, the company had always argued that it weighed the community's wishes by paying close heed to the church. Yet, in times of conflict, the notion of control by parents and teachers held little interest for the executives. To Ruffin, the CEO, the parents were customers. For the E. C. Reems faculty, on the other hand, the parents were an indispensable part of a living organism. It was a clash of two utterly different visions—the top-down management of a franchise, and the grassroots collective control of a community school. The two could not work together. To play bait-and-switch—to sell the community vision and then handle a crisis top-down—was a recipe for revolution. Now, on a day when they should have been teaching children, E. C. Reems's faculty had to figure out what to do.

It was a conversation among friends—just the school staff and a couple of parents—and it was to last all day. Positions soon became clear. The true Armstrong loyalists, who happened to make up the interim leadership team—Alan Foss, Christine Landry, Carol Fields—were furious about what the company had done to Armstrong. They could not bear the idea of continuing to serve the people who had savaged her, and they wanted publicity and revenge. They wanted to quit, or to stage rolling strikes, or to go to the news media to expose the story. They wanted to cut off the extras they had given for free— the after-school tutoring, the enrichment, the long days they had voluntarily worked. They wanted support from lawyers and unions in their struggle with the company. Some even wanted to file a new charter, start a new school, and take the kids there, even if it meant teaching in some basement or garage. On the other side were teachers and parents who saw the children as the victims in any upheaval. Few teachers wanted to return for a second year, but several saw great damage for the kids if they shut the school down now. They counseled compromise.

To the great good fortune of everyone, the room was blessed with a few articulate peacemakers. With his political wisdom, the senior organizer from OCO, Ron Snyder, reminded the teachers that the battle would be won by those who staked out the moral high ground. To hold that ground, he said, the teachers must put the children's interests first. Bob Latson, master of deals legal and otherwise, pondered the situation like a chess game. If the teachers planned to strike, he said, they had better be prepared to stay out until they got what they wanted, which could be a while. Few were prepared for that, particularly without a union and a strike fund. Troy Brookins, the teacher who frequently had talked about joining a union, put the focus on children. He had been ready to leave in October, he said, but had remained because of his commitment to the students. "The students come to me and talk to me about teachers that they've had that really never gave them opportunities," he said. Those teachers, he added, "treated them like dirt." Pointedly, he asked, "Are we really thinking about the kids, or are we thinking about ourselves and our own egos?"

But if there was one moment that gave the long day its flavor, it was a remark from Theresa Bade, the kindergarten teacher. Bade, true to her Midwestern roots, was a plainspoken person; she never put on airs, and claimed no sophistication. She seemed to feel the pain of the school, and its children, more deeply than anyone else. She had appeared close to tears for much of the previous twenty-four hours. She had said little during the discussions, withdrawing to a windowsill with her doodling pad. Now, after everyone else had their say, she spoke.

"No matter how confused we are," she said, "the point is our vision. I came here to work at a community-based school. I came here to work with parents as my co-teachers. Whatever we decide here, I want the parents to know everything; I want them to make the decision on what is best for their children. . . . What is best for their children, that is what I will do."

Bade's position carried the day. There was little enthusiasm for continuing the tutoring and the other extra efforts. But there would be no strike, no quitting, no calls to the media. School would go on.

•   •   •

For all the chaos associated with the change in principals, the decision exposed not just the potential trouble zones in a charter school, but also the freedom and strength that come in the bargain. Laura Armstrong's vision arguably fell short. Her notion of simply establishing a pleasant, supportive place for teachers, and encouraging them to help each other, was inadequate to the task of building a successful school in a neighborhood where failure is the norm. Indeed, even Armstrong's own private hopes had not included lifting her students up to grade level. She may have been on a holy mission, but she was no miracle worker. It was good that School Futures felt intense, urgent pressure to see the children make progress, and good that they were willing to make whatever staffing changes that might require. In the neighboring public schools, as in schools across the country, that sort of decisive action was hamstrung by contractual protections and simple weakness and loyalties that placed the needs of adults above those of children. School Futures' business approach had its positive side.

But in exercising its power, School Futures also was doing what charter schools often must: satisfying the people who write the checks. The most direct control belonged to John Walton, for he held the strings to the largest purse. His demand for better schools before expansion meant pressure for rapid changes, but swift action was not necessarily the same as smart action. Likewise, in Gene Ruffin's company, there seemed no limit to the influence wielded by the pastors. In addition, School Futures at that moment was riven by a debate over whether to go for-profit, as Ruffin always had wanted. Bad test scores at E. C. Reems or at the other School Futures charters would not impress on a prospectus.

Indeed, the fortunes of many rode on the results of the Reems Academy and the other charters. School Futures was using its schools, explicitly, to advance an agenda of urban school choice. OCO hoped the schools would raise its profile, lending leverage to the small-schools plan, which the new superintendent supported. And of course, Jerry Brown still wanted into the charter game. He was proposing a pair of charters, one an arts school, and one a military academy. The charters, whether they had sought the role or not, had become political chess pieces.

It was not that the regular public schools were immune to the power of money and the power of power. For years in Oakland, before the Jerry Brown revolution, astute viewers had noted that the top echelons from City Hall and the school district attended the same church. It was whispered that few would stray far from the line of the pastor there. Even so, the district schools served an elected board, which made its decisions, for the most part, in public. The charter's masters were much less visible, veiling the forces that pushed and pulled the school. John Walton rarely appeared in Oakland.

And while a sense of urgency about improving student performance was welcome, the ever-present hurry was costing the school. It had cost when Armstrong was selected in the first place, despite School Futures' doubts. And now, it was going to cost again. Thanks to the urgency to replace Armstrong, School Futures' executives had failed to learn quite a few relevant things about John Cleveland, some of which would have been pretty easy to find out.

Cleveland's employment history was deeply troubling. In 1993 he had made the newspaper in Oakland when he was demoted from a public school principal's post over allegations of misusing funds and ignoring district policies. "In additional documents and a series of interviews," the story said, "clerical staff, teachers and parents accused Cleveland of a wide range of misconduct including sexual harassment and racism." (Cleveland's response, quoted in the story, was thought-provoking: "If I am guilty of the charges, why have me in the district at all?") He soon moved on to the San Francisco district, where he won a new posting as a principal. But the reason he was at home to receive School Futures' calls—and the reason he needed a job—was that he had been placed on leave. The district, at the time, was investigating a claim that he had sexually harassed an employee at that school.

Two months after taking the School Futures job, on April 11, Cleveland signed an agreement to resign from the San Francisco district, effective June 30. But because the district had put him on paid leave through that date, the sexual harassment case perversely freed him to receive two paychecks at once—one from School Futures and one from San Francisco. Meanwhile, the San Francisco district shelled out another $40,000 to the victim to settle the harassment complaint. (Pastor Reems had heard a little about the case, but considered it "a farce," and never knew it had led to a payout.) For School Futures, unearthing that information might have required a bit of digging. But the company, which never bothered to ask even what school he was principal of, had not performed due diligence in hiring Cleveland. It was a position hard to square with a deep commitment to the needs of children.

•   •   •

Dr. John Cleveland spent his first day at E. C. Reems on February 24. He had already served two weeks as the head man at Dolores Huerta, where a staff anxious for leadership had received him warmly. (They had been without a principal for more than three months.) Cleveland had quickly won over the teachers and students there, leading children in song and taking action on discipline problems. At E. C. Reems, of course, he had a far trickier campaign to wage, but his strategy was sound, at first. He invited each teacher to talk with him alone, and asked all of them what they liked best about their school, what they were best at themselves, and what help he could give them. They told him that they adored the children and enjoyed strong bonds of friendship. Yet all the same, a picture emerged of a school laboring under heavy strain. Most urgently, there was a simple shortage of adult bodies, a consequence of an extremely tight budget. The teachers had little time to themselves; they had to watch students on the yard, even during their lunch hour. Books and supplies were lacking, discipline problems were pressing, and the new teachers still were woefully short of training. As Cherlon Simms memorably remarked in her one-on-one with Cleveland, "I don't have no clue how to teach reading." As a consequence of all those disappointments, morale was sagging. "It sounded Utopian," Troy Brookins told Cleveland, recalling when he first heard the charter school described. "It sounded like all the problems I had in public schools were going to be gone. To be honest, there are more. It's made me reconsider the profession, reconsider charter schools."

Cleveland promised to solve the teachers' problems. He would bring in the books, the supplies, the substitutes, the yard duty supervisors. He would correct the back-pay problem. And he set about making peace between the warring bodies that had brought about Armstrong's ouster. He brought together the SSC and the founding parents, heard their mutual complaints, and sought to calm them. He drew some odd looks when he blamed the squabbling on skin color—"we as black people," he said, "have trouble looking at the positive." But he gained some support when he promised high test scores and new elections for a parent committee. The parents liked him even better when he said he would suspend the worst-behaved kids. He instituted a monthly awards ceremony for students with good attendance, behavior, and academic achievement. He tried to make the office more welcoming to parents. The staff was still suspicious, but he was beginning to win people over.

Unfortunately, this auspicious beginning was not to last. By the early days of March, stories were circulating at both schools of strange and inappropriate actions by the new principal. At E. C. Reems the talk mostly involved his chats with students, which teachers alleged to be both sexist and sexual. Troy Brookins reported him talking before the sixth-grade class about his position as a sixty-three-year-old man with a young wife. "What do the women want?" Brookins quoted him as saying. "They want money."

On top of that, Cleveland wasn't fulfilling his main duties. He didn't have any magic answers, or really any answers at all, for the problems the teachers had complained about. He failed to come through with the solutions he had promised. He spent little time at Reems, where he faced wide hostility and suspicion from the teachers. And while a budget for yard supervision hadn't surfaced, Cleveland somehow found $1,300 in the school budget for a digital camera that he could plug into his computer.

In the absence of real leadership, matters at both schools went from bad to worse. At E. C. Reems Carol Fields and Wilma Cornish screamed at each other over supervising lunch on the yard. Cleveland's attempt to broker a peace just led to more shouting. That afternoon, Fields stood by a window and sobbed. Meanwhile, as teacher morale ebbed, student behavior deteriorated, and many kids stopped wearing their uniforms, which had great symbolic value for the parents. Support grew for more expulsions. "As one of the teachers who put a lot of energy into giving those kids another chance," Fields told Cleveland, "I want to say these kids do not deserve another chance." If they stayed, she warned, other parents would leave over fears that their own children might get hurt in fights. Lawrence Tottress blamed himself for not keeping the bad actors out in the first place. "Hopefully next year they'll be screened," he said.

At Huerta, a teacher quit in a dispute over whether she had given sufficient notice that she was going to be sick. Also at Huerta, Cleveland badly fumbled his handling of an apparent kidnapping attempt. Someone in a van tried to lure two children off school grounds. The school called the cops, but one boy's parents had to hear about it from their son, not from Cleveland. It just happened that the father was the pastor of the church that owned the school building. Cleveland had to leave Huerta that day while the police were still taking statements, because back at his other school, Wilma Cornish was threatening to quit after the fight with Carol Fields.

The angry divisions among the staff were not the only problems that required devoted, graceful leadership. Other problems were coming to light as well. Cleveland had asked that Armstrong turn in a complete financial statement for the school, but what he received was several line items on a few pieces of paper, which made little sense and didn't add up. Much to his consternation, he discovered that the after-school care dues had been used as a sort of slush fund under the control of the founding parents. What he didn't know was that those parents were themselves in an uproar over thousands of dollars that they could not account for. They were trying to keep the information from Cleveland, but they knew they couldn't hold out forever. School Futures' accountant had gotten wind of the situation and was pondering either a full audit or reporting the whole affair to a grand jury, raising the specter of criminal charges. At the same time, Cleveland discovered that teachers had suspended and even, in at least one case, expelled students on their own authority, which he rightly said was illegal and could not continue.

Only a gifted principal could have untangled the mess; Cleveland, who spent less and less time at Reems, wasn't the one to fix it. Around that time, John Walton dispatched a smart, knowledgeable evaluator to make what turned out to be a surprise visit. The consultant reported back that he was distressed by what he saw. Meanwhile, the staff loyal to Armstrong sent out a survey to parents asking how many intended to stay at the school the following year. About two-thirds said they would return, but the very fact of the survey indicated the division and hostility in the school.

In the midst of all this chaos and distress, Eugene Ruffin spoke at a conference on charter schools in Oakland, at the historic Beebe Memorial Church. The attendance list for the all-day event showed the success with which charter fever was sweeping the inner city. Some three hundred black pastors attended, along with Mayor Jerry Brown, and top representatives from OCO, the school district, and even the local teachers' union. (Brown, who had not deviated in his lines, opined in his speech that the "children don't belong to the state," and were being fed to a gigantic prison system by an education system that exploited rather than educated them.) Around the time that a fragrant roast-chicken lunch was being passed out to the crowd, Ruffin took the podium.

Ruffin's message included a tough warning. "There's no magic in the word *charter*," he told the crowd. The freedom of a charter provided an advantage over other public schools, he said. But that didn't mean everyone there could expect to start a strong school. "Maybe one percent of you—and that's not saying anything negative to the people in this room—will have the capacity and the will to have a successful charter school," he said. "But that one percent, if you step forward, you can change how we educate our black children in this country. That one percent can change for all of the children in the country, if you step forward, and do what you have the capacity and the will to do." He left no doubt whether his own company was up to the task, and he was happy to offer his services. "We have ten schools in this country. All of them are overachieving. They are distancing themselves from the schools that are in their community, academically, because of choice, because of freedom, because everybody there is there because of choice."

At E. C. Reems that same afternoon, eight children loitered in the waiting room outside the school office, all waiting to be scolded. A couple of other kids roamed the upstairs hallways. One claimed to be out of class in order to fetch the other one back to class. It was a Wednesday, the day that John Cleveland spent his entire day at Dolores Huerta. That left Lawrence Tottress yelling more or less full-time at the kids in the waiting room, none of whom had anything to do, or any work, and most of whom didn't have chairs. Meanwhile, Helen Seaport, the attendance clerk and after-school supervisor, was on the phone, reading over a draft of a letter she had written to Cleveland, detailing her own complaints about him. Cherlon Simms's kids were on the "playground," where many were roughhousing in a way that strayed close to fighting. A visitor who had been at Beebe Memorial earlier that day might have wondered whether all ten of Ruffin's schools were truly "overachieving."

A leadership vacuum allows bad things to happen, and E. C. Reems was beginning to feel like a roller coaster come free of its tracks. Rarely did it feel more so than on the night of March 22.

The founding parents had scheduled a meeting that night for two reasons: to examine some of the allegations against Cleveland, and to review the slush-fund crisis. As they waited for everyone to arrive, the parents gathered in the teachers' lunchroom, where Susan Adams—a talented cook who owned a small catering business—had provided dinner of pasta, salad, and peach cobbler. No teachers were in the building, but two staffers—Lawrence Tottress and Helen Seaport—were there. Well into the meal, an accusation arose that a third-grade boy had been "getting ready to" lick peach cobbler juice off the chin of a preschool-age girl. The boy swore he had done nothing, but his mother was furious. She borrowed a thick black belt from another mother and escorted the terrified boy to the computer room. Before long, sounds emerged: the smack of the belt, time and again, accompanied by the boy's screaming. A few moments later, she led him back down the hall, holding up his shirt to catch the blood that flowed profusely from his nose. She asked for ice. No one appeared disturbed; several of the parents seemed outright jovial over the whipping. Helen Seaport walked the boy to the office, where she larded his back and neck with ice packs, plus one for his nose. He looked like an accident victim.

The other parents were charged, excited, laughing loudly, and for a few moments it looked like the violence was going to be contagious: someone accused another boy of having sneaked down the hall to watch the beating, and his mother asked for the belt. She later relented. All the same, the parents evidently relished the spectacle of someone finally meting out old-style discipline. One mom recounted her daughter's threat to call 911 if she was beaten. She said she had told her daughter, in response, that if she ended up in court, she would tell the judge to keep the daughter. Bob Latson said his son had made the same threat. His answer: "What makes you think you'd make it to the phone?"

Corporal punishment was illegal in California schools. But it enjoyed a special, comfortable place in the hearts of many at E. C. Reems, as in similar neighborhoods all over. Faced with the chilling dangers of the street life, many parents saw it as the only sign of real seriousness in keeping children on the right path. It was the sort of situation that, amid all the fervent talk about letting parents choose the character of the school, showed that well-meant wish could cut two ways.

John Cleveland never knew what happened that night. As a man who had paddled children himself back in the days when that was permitted, he might not have been shocked. But he had a whole set of problems of his own: his professional survival was now on the line. With complaints about Cleveland mounting at both schools, a meeting was scheduled for the entire parent body, Cleveland, and the School Futures bosses on April 12. Even by the standards of this high-drama school, this would be a particularly emotional and difficult meeting. "Let's get ugly about it," Alan Foss said earlier that day. "He gotta have his posse with him."

For better or for worse, it seemed, everyone involved would find out on April 12 who was really in charge of the E. C. Reems Academy.

Chapter 9

Promises to Keep

A sense of sedate grandeur dwelled in the sanctuary of the Center of Hope Community Church. With its rich, powder-blue carpets, its blond-wood pews, and its airily high ceiling, it lent an atmosphere of luxury to a battered corner of Oakland. For those in the know, however, the evening of April 12 did not promise to be sedate. But many of the parents, as they settled into the pews, had no idea that this would be an angry meeting, with all the chips on the table. Some hadn't even heard that there was a new principal, let alone that he stood at the center of a storm. Only the initiated—the teachers and the inner circle of parents—knew that a showdown was looming.

Conflict is always a ready possibility at inner-city schools, built at the intersection where desperate hope meets generations of miseducation. At the heart of this particular impending fight lay the very thing that made a charter school different: promises. Promises—to teach children well, to fortify their character—are the pillars, the bricks, of the charter idea and the charter document. That notion sets charters apart from the district schools, which don't have to make promises, and often don't keep the ones they do make. A couple of years earlier, for example, an associate superintendent in Oakland had called a press conference to announce that within two years, 100 percent of third graders would read proficiently. Two years later, only 28 percent of third graders read at the national average. By then, few even remembered the promise, and no one was called to account. But if E. C. Reems broke the promises in its charter—to educate the children and serve their parents—the district could shut the school down. Despite all the anger, the mere fact of the meeting—and the fact that the parents felt that they deserved answers—suggested a level of accountability that might not have prevailed in the district schools.

Indeed, the parents at E. C. Reems held a good measure of power to enforce the school's guarantees. They couldn't close the school down directly, but as in any school of choice, they could walk away, draining the school's lifeblood—its per-student funding. It was a key argument for charters: that to stay alive, they had to please their customers, like any business in a free market. At the Center of Hope Church, School Futures had begun making promises almost a year earlier. Now, in the same sanctuary, parents would want to know whether the company had kept its word.

To some parents, the most important promises boiled down to an assurance of what Bob Latson, the ever-present dad, had labeled a "fast-track school"—a place that wouldn't trifle with kids who didn't act right, a school that would eject the bad kids so the others could thrive. Likewise, some wanted to give the boot to the many parents who had failed to put in their required "volunteer" hours. But more sweeping promises were up for discussion that evening as well: most notably, that parents and teachers would have real control over their school. That was the way School Futures had persuaded them to buy into the charter idea back in the spring and summer of '99. A year later, however, Laura Armstrong—herself the maker of some of those promises—was gone, with no consultation of teachers and parents. Now, John Cleveland, who had been chosen by the School Futures executives, was stirring controversy.

An unusually large crowd of perhaps a hundred parents had turned out this evening. Rumors were swirling, including one that School Futures might tire of the battle and simply pull up its tent stakes in Oakland. And the timing was crucial. It was now spring, the time when many parents think about whether to keep their children in the same school or enroll elsewhere. School Futures, which so often talked about pleasing its customers, had some delicate dancing to do.

A day before the meeting, Cleveland had tried to ease the situation with a letter to parents. "I would like to squash all rumors that there might not be a school here next year," he wrote. "School Futures spent almost $1,500,000 renovating this building . . . They are in this for the long haul." Yet the letter sparked more controversy than it quelled. After mentioning that many teachers might be leaving at the end of the year, Cleveland complained, "I have not been able to locate any of the school's financial records." He also claimed that "discipline and order have been restored at our school," when many felt events had gone in the opposite direction.

Telicia Hooker, the founder of the founding parents, opened the meeting in a tone of indictment that revealed the mounting tensions in the academy's daily life. Children were showing up out of uniform. From now on, children who failed to wear white tops and navy bottoms would be sent home. Likewise, there had been problems with parents arriving quite late to pick up their kids from the after-school day care. Two such offenses would prompt a call to the child-abuse authorities to pick up the youngster, she said. And with testing now beginning, the popular after-school tutoring would end, for good, the next day. Then Helen Seaport, who ran the day care, added to the list of ultimatums posing as announcements. Free breakfasts, she said, were available only to the before-school day care kids. Lawrence Tottress chimed in with an explanation: there wasn't enough staff to feed all the children.

The statement produced shock in the audience. Four out of five Reems students were poor enough to qualify for government-funded meals, yet the school couldn't get it together to feed them? And picking them up late would get the cops called? "To me, that isn't reasonable," one mother said.

The new principal hastened to step in. With his bosses watching, it had just been revealed that his school was denying children that most basic need—food—even when they were entitled to it under federal law. "Parents," he said affably, "I'm just for the first time understanding about the breakfast. I thought everybody who was wanting breakfast was getting breakfast."

His peacemaking salvo failed to end the conflict. The founding parents again lashed into the less active parents—the ones who had never done an hour of volunteer time, but didn't mind trooping into a meeting to complain about what the school wasn't doing for them. Next year, the founders warned, those who had failed to perform their hours might not be invited back.

But with Cleveland in the brawl, the focus of the evening was shifting. There were questions about why E. C. Reems had to share its principal with another school. Abruptly, the spotlight moved back to the principal.

Cleveland excelled at heartwarming speeches, and that evening, he did not disappoint. Dapper in a black suit and a black-and-white tie, he spoke of the crisis of education and of the black family, touching on themes sure to please many of the mothers in the room. He professed love and admiration for "these sisters" who escorted their kids to school, went to work, picked the kids up from school, and then fixed dinner, while "most black men are absent." He lauded the children at E. C. Reems as the brightest he had ever seen. He acknowledged the many grandparents who were raising their grandchildren. He thanked God for the founding parents, who "struggled with this before anybody showed up." He tried to persuade everyone to just get along. "You build a school on positive stuff," he intoned. "You don't build a school on criticizing each other." And he tried to turn attention to adding a seventh grade in the coming year, using the specter of the district middle schools to strike a note of fear. "It would be a shame to turn these little lambs into that craziness," he said. "We would have done better to teach them how to fight if you're going to send them somewhere where it's a battlefield."

Some parents seemed to soften at his well-turned words. But the regulars—including some OCO members—were unimpressed. They peppered him with accusations. Why was the school still dirty? Why didn't the classrooms have their full allotment of books? Why was Laura Armstrong gone? "When the school first opened, they said this was a charter school and the parents have say-so," a founding parent said. "You may not like me after I say this, but when Dr. Armstrong was here, stuff was together." The attacks on Cleveland began to heighten.

Don Gill whispered to Cleveland. Then Cleveland suggested the parents come talk with him in his office, later. Although there were murmurs of disagreement, Cleveland said he would address the parents' complaints the next day, privately, he said.

All the same, the challenges went on: It was now clear that most of the staff would be leaving at the end of the year. What would happen then?

"We have a waiting list of students and staff," Cleveland asserted. Whether true or not, the statement was a tactical mistake. If the parents were loyal to anyone, it was to their children's teachers. One teacher's sister, who herself had children at the school, sobbed as she spoke to the crowd. "I feel very sorry for my sister and what she has to go through," she said. Alan Foss, the first-grade teacher, was outraged by Cleveland's remark. "If we have a waiting list for teachers, how come we haven't had substitutes?" he asked. "We have the best teachers here, and you are not going to have the same school next year, because they are leaving."

Don Gill, standing and shifting from foot to foot, attempted to divert the conversation. He spoke of School Futures' heavy investment of cash and what it had meant. "For the first time," he said, "parents have a choice about where to send their kids." He tried to kindle some political feeling. "We are all part of a movement to change public education," he said. "Everyone knew it would be rough." But School Futures had done its part, he said, fronting $900,000 worth of salaries. "Did we break a promise?" he asked. "I don't think so." As he started to explain how the company was striving to export its lessons to Fort Lauderdale and Boston, a man in a T-shirt interrupted.

"Excuse me, sir," the father said. "It seems like you're missing the point. The main problem we have in this school is that the teachers' needs are not being addressed."

Gill suggested holding some meetings. But the parents had gone to plenty of meetings. "My son has turned into a monster being here," one of the founding parents said. "I'm his mother and I'm saying that." Another agreed. "Morale is low," she said. "The kids are feeling it and at this point they don't want to come to school."

Parents began trailing out of the meeting. A voice asked them to stop.

A man in an expensive-looking suit, with shiny shoes and a pocket handkerchief, had stood to speak. He introduced himself as the Reverend Jeffery Harris. It was the same Jeff Harris who had overseen the building project, but he was playing a very different role tonight. He was preaching.

"I'm assuming there are some Christians in this room," he said. "The word of God says that where there is order, there is peace." His spiritual appeal caught people's attention.

The new teachers who would come next year, Harris maintained, would be every bit as good as, or better than, the ones here now. "Everybody who was hired here shouldn't have been hired."

"No," Troy Brookins blurted out. "This is yet another insult by School Futures."

From the balcony came a new commotion. A disheveled man, perhaps schizophrenic, had wandered in off the street. He was screaming. They didn't want him in the church, he yelled. His voice seemed to register the suffering of the entire room. Pastor Brondon Reems—Cleveland's nephew—attended to him, and he was silent again. Below, the room was emptying.

Jeff Harris, recognizing his mistake in attacking the teachers, tried a true Hail Mary play. He asked the audience to pray with him.

Alan Foss, who was Jewish, figured that the evening's proceedings had strayed far enough across the church-state line. "This is a public school," he said, and stalked out. But Harris forged ahead.

"Heavenly Father," he prayed, "you have heard the wisdom of these parents and you've heard the responses. Wherever there is hardness of heart, I ask you to break it. Lord Jesus, those of us who are in agreement are praying to you. Minister to the hearts of these parents, of these teachers who have been offended by what they may see as insensitive administration and bureaucracy." He moved closer to the principal. "Father, I ask you to deal with Dr. Cleveland, and I'm going to lay hands on Dr. Cleveland."

This ritual was no small matter. The tradition stemmed from Biblical times, when holy men passed healing to the sick and expiated sins onto sacrificial animals through the touch of the hand. Even today, in many Evangelical churches, the Holy Spirit was thought to flow through the laying on of hands, accompanying baptisms and anointing with oil, and, occasionally, speaking in tongues. If anyone found it bizarre for the building contractor to invoke divine forces for the principal, that got lost in the overwhelming surreality of the entire scene. The Reverend Mr. Harris placed his hand on John Cleveland's shoulder. From the back, Brondon Reems called out, "Yes, brother." Surprised and bemused, Cleveland leaned forward to receive the blessing. Harris's voice rose. "I'm asking you, Lord Jesus, to work a miracle here if a miracle is necessary." Most in the sanctuary bowed their heads; one woman raised her arm up before her, as if to draw in the divine force Harris was releasing. "I pray for his strength," Harris concluded, "as he goes forth to do this job, Jesus."

One of the kindergartners, sitting with his teacher, Ms. Bade, was confused. "Why is that man putting his hands on the principal?" he asked.

She searched for an explanation. "Because," she said finally, "he needs help."

The new promise that night was that Dr. John Cleveland was going to address the complaints and charges the next day, Thursday, in his office. It might have been nice to think that holy powers were going to fix the problems of the E. C. Reems Academy and its principal, and the vast communication gap with San Diego. Instead, on Thursday and Friday, Cleveland managed to be almost completely absent from the Reems campus. It was another broken promise, but it didn't matter much. Few had really believed it anyway.

Except, that is, for Cleveland's bosses. They still entertained the possibility that the new principal had the situation in hand. With the end of the year on the horizon, though, they decided to check for themselves. For half an hour to an hour or more, Don Gill and Gene Ruffin interviewed each of the teachers at Reems. The executives entered the building in almost comically high spirits, but sobered up in a hurry. The allegations against Cleveland took root, as did the steady complaints about San Diego's failure to communicate with the teachers. By day's end, Ruffin and Gill were no longer blaming everything on Laura Armstrong's failings and the district's reluctance to write checks. They were intimating that Cleveland would not return next year, and they admitted that their own company had not done its part well. As the teachers explained that day, the promises that School Futures had made—of a high-performance school freed from bureaucratic problems—had been shattered. The teachers, as a result, had lost much of their joy in their work, likely with consequences for the children.

But of course, the school was not in business to keep its teachers happy. Its customers, as School Futures liked to put it, were the parents. And their opinions on whether the school had held up to its word varied widely. To many of them, E. C. Reems had not grown into the school they had been promised a year earlier, when Brian Bennett was barnstorming Oakland to proselytize for School Futures. In fact, the school's shortcomings recalled the parents' original complaints about the regular public schools. They spoke of a dirty building and filthy bathrooms, which so repulsed some children that they held their bodily needs in check all day. Parents complained that teachers did not set high enough standards, or got so bogged down with the worst behavior problems that academics fell to the wayside. Moreover, the qualities that were supposed to make this school special—the widespread parent involvement, the parent and community power over policy and direction—fell far short of what some parents had expected. For some, the school was not even completely safe; fights and intimidation may have been rarer than in the regular schools, but they still existed.

Many others, though, saw a brighter picture. William Stewart and Jasmine McGehee, together, had four children at the school. Like many parents, they stood at a distance from the chaotic changes there. Relatively pleased with the school, they appreciated the teachers' commitment and caring, even if Dr. Cleveland said many of them didn't have credentials, and they believed their children were progressing. Also like many parents, Stewart liked nonacademic aspects of the school: its small size, and the fact that there was only one entrance, which helped keep strangers out. He faulted himself for not doing his share of volunteer work, but he and McGehee cheerfully looked forward to sending their children back to Reems the following year. While other parents regretted that this "Academy of Technology and Arts" had no computers and no art classes, they were patient with a school that was less than a year old. It was true that many of the positive aspects the parents saw lay far from the school's academic core—its primary reason for being. Although not generally sophisticated consumers of curriculum and pedagogy, parents in the Reems neighborhood echoed interviews and surveys across the country: they wanted an orderly, safe school that felt like home to them. If the school was quiet and free of fights, many would be satisfied.

Perhaps the most intriguing parent opinions at E. C. Reems belonged to Margarita Soto and Bob Latson, the improbable dynamic duo of parents who were among the most enthusiastic volunteers. Latson had been a constant presence at the school until March 24, when he was arrested. The same man who had so effectively brokered a peace agreement between the teachers and their employers was charged with beating and torturing his fifty-eight-year-old girlfriend. Now an inmate at Santa Rita County Jail, half an hour's drive from Oakland, he acted as if he found the grim, sterile lockup a charming weekend getaway, and spoke at length about the school. He saw too much division at the Reems Academy, and viewed it—as it stood that year—as doomed. While he saw the move from Webster Elementary as a good one, Latson—himself schooled in England and Texas before graduating from Castlemont High in Oakland—wasn't sure if the Reems Academy had made gains for his son. He only knew that there had been no loss.

Margarita Soto agreed. She couldn't say whether Reems ultimately offered a better solution. But her plans answered the key questions all too clearly. She and her husband were planning to move to California's Central Valley at the end of the school year. Had E. C. Reems been an excellent school, she said, they might well have stayed in Oakland.

As much as Margarita Soto and her fellow parents might vote with their feet, however, the ultimate power to enforce promises belonged to the Oakland school board, the body charged with determining whether the school was doing what it had promised to do in its charter. If not, it was the board's duty to shut the school down. In academic areas, that review would wait until the school was five years old and the charter was up for renewal. That arrangement made sense, in light of evidence suggesting that charter schools become more educationally effective after their start-up struggles are over. In other areas where charters were bound by law, however, the school board could move much faster. That fact was to gain sudden relevance in the last few months of the school year, as the E. C. Reems Academy found itself locked in an unexpected struggle to survive.

The possibility of a shutdown order suddenly became real at several charter schools in Oakland in early May. The threat came just as kids at E. C. Reems and Dolores Huerta were beginning the standardized tests—which themselves would measure whether the charters were keeping their promise of better education. The new threat to the schools' existence, though, had little to do with the learning and performance of children. The real reason behind the move was politics.

On May 4, Cheryl Hightower, the district's deputy superintendent, hand-delivered a letter stating that every Oakland charter school would have to offer proof that its teachers held valid teaching credentials and had undergone a police background check based on their fingerprints. Those steps should have been complete before school opened, with records on file. California law required fingerprint checks on every public school teacher in the state, following the rape and murder two years earlier of a high schooler by a campus janitor with a criminal record. Charter schools were included in the requirement. As for credentials—certificates of completed teacher training—they had not been required at California charters in the early days. Charter advocates, however, had given up that freedom in exchange for the teacher unions' assent to an increase in the number of charter schools. Teachers with no training, like Valentín Del Rio, could get "emergency credentials," but if they hoped to teach for more than a year, they had to take education courses and work toward a proper credential.

It would have been nice to imagine that the district's sudden interest in the teachers' paperwork stemmed from a latent but heartfelt desire to protect its students from incompetents and criminals. In truth, this investigation, with barely a month left in the school year, grew out of the disputes of grown-ups. A teacher at the American Indian Public Charter School had tipped the district off to the fact that few teachers there had the proper paperwork. This, alone, might not have constituted a crisis for the district under normal circumstances. Many, many laws govern the schools, and the district was regularly exposed for its own violations. But politics forced the superintendent's hand. Jerry Brown, the mayor, had submitted proposals for a pair of charter schools he hoped to create: a military academy and, perhaps reflecting his former "Governor Moonbeam" reputation, an arts school. The proposals, both strikingly thin and lacking even such basic details as a budget, were getting tough questions from district office. Brown had charged that the existing charters weren't held to equal scrutiny, and the newly appointed superintendent, Dennis Chaconas, could not ignore the charge. And so his deputy, Cheryl Hightower, rode from one charter school to another like a commandant on an inspection tour.

John Cleveland had never thought to check the status of his teachers' credentials and fingerprints. As he discovered, though, much of the paperwork was missing. Perhaps, he speculated, it had vanished with the principals who had been ousted from each school. And now that he and the district were asking about the paperwork, the answers were worrisome. One teacher had an out-of-state credential, which carried no value in California, and at least one held no credential at all, not even an emergency one. The fingerprint situation presented even more of a mess. Evidently, the teachers had been fingerprinted, but the state had rejected their prints because of confusion over the official names of the two schools. (School Futures had assigned the schools placeholder names in the charters, and subsequently renamed them.) By the time the confusion had been sorted out, the fingerprints were out-of-date, and they were never submitted again. For many of the teachers, therefore, no criminal background check ever had been done—clear grounds for shutting down the school. Hightower's letter, delivered on May 4, demanded proof of credentials and fingerprints by the following week.

The schools, meanwhile, were immersed in their most crucial moment: the Big Test. The actual testing followed a formidable test-prep mobilization closely resembling what one often saw in the regular public schools. Valentín Del Rio's students had spent about two hours per day taking and reviewing practice tests in the week leading up to the real thing. (Most other classes did somewhat less; a few did more.) The final weeks of prep devoured much of the mornings, leaving the students sufficiently exhausted that their teachers imposed little real work in the afternoons.

In most classes, the test itself took place amid a fair semblance of quiet, order, and procedure-following, but there were exceptions. The most striking occurred in Cherlon Simms's class. Simms had persuaded a couple of mothers to help her proctor the test, and did nothing when one of the mothers roamed the room, checking and correcting answers. The mother would stop off at one table and then another, administer a reproving look for the mistakes she pointed out, and then leave it to the child to seek a better answer. It did not seem to register that this might be considered wholesale cheating.

In the kindergarten class, the five-year-olds had made a mockery of the system on the October pretest. Now they reveled in an encore performance. "Please find the picture of the meal," cajoled Theresa Bade, who under normal circumstances maintained good order. "You should not be talking to your friends at all." The children barely heard. "I'm six years old!" "I'm five!" Paul was showing off his answers to his tablemates; someone was trying to pull Janeece's test book away. Some kids were actually filling in bubbles on the test sheet, although randomly. Adam, one of the few on task, had located the piece of bread in the question and was ready to go on. He made up his own directions. "When you're finished with bread," he announced brightly to the class, "turn the page." The frustrated Bade couldn't help laughing.

Amid the heavy demands of testing, Principal John Cleveland moved sluggishly to deal with the district's threats over fingerprints and credentials. Cleveland evidently believed he could sweet-talk his way out of the problem, phoning the right people and postponing the day of reckoning. An article in the May 27 *San Francisco Chronicle* put an end to that strategy. "Oakland Charter Schools Missing Credentials," trumpeted the headline. "Chaconas threatens closings over lost records." The article revealed what only Cleveland and a handful of others had known: that his two schools, plus a couple of other charters, had their necks strung over a chopping block. The *Chronicle* reporter reached Don Gill, who suggested the problem had to do with missing paperwork, rather than actual uncredentialed teachers:

> OAKLAND—Four of Oakland's seven charter schools may be forced to shut down, unless they can come up with proof that their teachers have credentials and have had fingerprint background checks.
>
> At a time when Oakland Mayor Jerry Brown is trying to get the school board to grant him contracts to start two new charter schools in Oakland, most of those already in the city appear to be violating state law, Superintendent Dennis Chaconas said yesterday.
>
> The Oakland school district has sent warning letters to the American Indian Public Charter School, which opened in 1996, and three new charter schools that opened last fall: Oak Tree Charter School, Ernestine C. Reems Academy of Technology and Art, and Dolores Huerta Learning Academy. . . .
>
> The files at Dolores Huerta and Ernestine C. Reems "disappeared," said Donald Gill, vice president of school operations for the School Futures Research Foundation, which operates the two schools. The Foundation was started by Wal-Mart heir John Walton, a religious

conservative and main supporter of the voucher movement to use taxpayer dollars to send children to private and parochial schools.

The 20 teachers among the two School Futures schools have either full or emergency waiver credentials, Gill said, but someone walked off with the file—intentionally or by mistake.

"We will reproduce the documents in time," he said.

The article noted that closing a charter school was an extreme step, thus far taken at only 6 of California's 250 charters. But it emphasized that the superintendent wasn't afraid to act, saying that if the schools failed to produce the paperwork, the school board would revoke the charters at its June 8 meeting. He even talked about preparing the district "to absorb hundreds of kids it wasn't planning for," and promised "that he would add more portables to house the charter school refugees."

Ominous though it sounded, the closure threat bolstered the idea behind charter schools. That, after all, was the bargain that was supposed to make charter schools better: they had to perform, or else get shut down. Yet Oakland's attitude also hinted at a growing danger: the tendency of districts to focus on legal "compliance" rather than quality education. Certainly, it was the district's job to enforce the law, particularly where the safety of students from potential criminals was involved. Yet there wasn't the slightest indication of a felon in the ranks of any charter faculty. In truth, these bureaucratic problems had little effect on children. The fingerprints had been transmitted to the state, but got tangled in a confusion of school names. The teachers who lacked credential paperwork were among the best at E. C. Reems. The matters that really affected the children—the quality of curriculum and teaching, the discipline—held little interest for the district. That situation mirrored the national picture, where charter school shutdowns were extremely rare. Only 4 percent of charters had been shut down by 2000, and those closures typically stemmed from problems like finances and management, not lack of learning among the children. And in Oakland, the timing of this move was plainly suspect—weeks short of the end of the school year, but just as Jerry Brown's charter proposals were wending their way through the school board's review.

The public attention to the problems at E. C. Reems and Dolores Huerta sent School Futures into a sudden spasm of activity. Don Gill and School Futures' good-natured accountant, Fil Guzman, flew to Oakland and camped out in the superintendent's office, handing over documents and promising more. Teachers were dispatched in mass batches to get their fingerprints checked again, leaving the schools badly understaffed. At E. C. Reems, on June 2, the fingerprinting combined with an informal sick-out by some angry teachers to nearly shut down classes. Most students simply hung out on the yard playing foursquare, finally becoming so bored that a few actually asked permission to go inside and study quietly. On the yard, where one teacher tried to supervise perhaps a hundred children, playing turned to chasing, chasing to shoving, and shoving to moments of actual violence. John Cleveland watched for a while, grumbling that the teachers should make the children behave better, and then left to get fingerprinted himself.

Ultimately, though, School Futures' belated frenzy paid off. That required a bit of artful dodging over the precise credential status of at least one teacher, who hadn't actually passed the required basic competency test, despite several attempts. But these details were swept away by the company's apparently genuine desire to get right with the district. The district imposed an informal standard where any more than three major violations would lead to closure. School Futures' problems were credentials, fingerprints, and some missing financial documents—and that was only three violations. Reems and Huerta got their death sentences commuted. Another Oakland charter wasn't as lucky. At Oak Tree, amid a feud between the staff and the principal, some teachers refused to be fingerprinted, knowing their action would assure the school's closure. Their action culminated an ugly row in which the principal there was accused of repeatedly deceiving the district over the credential status of his teachers. At American Indian, the problems looked even worse. Attendance in some classes had fallen to just a handful of children, and some teachers had ceased teaching entirely. But that school won a reprieve, pending an improvement plan, largely because it had not defied the school board so openly.

•   •   •

With the advent of June, the school year was nearly over. At Dolores Huerta, the closing weeks were marked by a series of festive occasions. A final family volunteer day brought out dozens of parents to pretty up the campus, in preparation for the school's ceremonial dedication. That event brought out no less a light than the school's namesake, Dolores Huerta. Huerta—Cesar Chavez's longtime partner in labor organizing—enjoyed an esteem from many Mexican-American parents not unlike the admiration that many African Americans held for Rosa Parks. And if Huerta saw any irony in placing her name on a school run by a company that condemned unions, she kept it to herself.

The program of speeches and merrymaking turned out to be the most unifying and uplifting moment in the school's short history, and it left parents and children glowing for days. Some of the teachers had nagging concerns that they still had no contract for the following year, three months after teachers in the district received theirs, but even that could not darken their joy. Then, a handful of days later, the school held a "graduation" ceremony for the kindergartners, complete with lustrous canary-yellow caps and gowns. The smiles could have powered a small city.

E. C. Reems had its moments of joy, too, but it seemed to pay a higher price for them. Nazim's most shining hour dawned on June 8, in class just after the all-school talent show, which itself marked a high moment in a largely grim time. In the middle of a math lesson, in an effort to award attention to Nazim for doing something academically useful, Valentín Del Rio invited him to teach the class. Part impresario, part mimic, and part math whiz, Nazim handled the challenge with hammy, rapid-fire genius.

"I need a hand"—that was teacherese for I'll pick someone who raises a hand—"to tell me what the next step is," Nazim called to the class, as Del Rio ran to round up adult witnesses. The boy was teaching long division, dividing 7 into 7,899. "Oh, oh, oh," the students called, entranced, hoping to be picked by Schoolmaster Casey to answer the problem. He chose Asia to work the first step; she got it right. "Good job," he beamed. "We pull down." He pulled down the next digit. "So now what do we do?" Smiling infectiously, he jotted calculations on the dry-erase board, finished the problem, and set up the next. "I need a hand to come up here to do this problem. Girls first," he commanded. He selected Shaniqua, and looked to Del Rio for support. "Did I do a good job?"

Susan cut in to answer first. "You a good teacher," she marveled.

Del Rio wanted the room quieter. Suddenly, Nazim turned dictator. "Put your hands down," he snapped. Every hand rocketed down. "Can I have quietness please?" Nazim resumed teaching, but as Lamar was working the problem, Nazim heard a side comment from Susan. He could not be biased by her admiration. "That's a put-down," he accused, pointing his marker into her face. Del Rio tried to help out, but Nazim didn't want interference. "Mr. D, ain't I the teacher?" he chided.

"Yeah," Del Rio said. "I'm sorry."

A grin back on his face, Nazim started a subtraction problem. "Lemme show you all how to do this," he said, using his fingers to handle the computation.

For Del Rio's class, it was one of the most joyous moments of the year. An entire class sat amazed. Del Rio complimented Nazim on his skills in front of the class.

"I should be a teacher," Nazim said, smiling thoughtfully to himself. "But I can't take all this nonsense."

School let out at E. C. Reems on Thursday, June 15, amid a heat wave of historic proportions. The previous afternoon, downtown San Francisco—the same place whose summer Mark Twain famously recalled as the coldest winter he ever spent—had recorded its highest temperature ever, 103 degrees. At Reems, the entertainment during after-school care that afternoon consisted of staff members hosing down the overheated and exhilarated children. Across MacArthur Boulevard, shirtless teenage boys opened a fire hydrant, danced in the street, and spun muscle cars in the slippery flood. Now, on the fifteenth, one could feel another scorcher building even at 7:30 A.M. On the play yard, kids already were rationing icy runnels of condensation from water bottles that had spent the night in the freezer.

It is hard to find a child of elementary school age who does not thrill to the kickoff of summer vacation. The kids at E. C. Reems were no exception—ebullient, exhausted, excited. One first-grade girl had stayed up much of the night before. How late? "I don't know," she explained cheerily. "I don't know how to tell time." Yet even for the children, there was a bittersweet tinge to this last day. Many of them had fallen in love with their young, high-hoping teachers, and the large majority knew they would never see those teachers again. Of the fourteen teachers at E. C. Reems, only three— Wilma Cornish, Theresa Bade, and Athena Lee—were planning to return the following year.

That statistic made the final day a thoroughly melancholy time for the eleven departing teachers. Many had invested great hope and energy in the place, only to end up feeling that they had no home there after all. No one sank deeper into that melancholy than Valentín Del Rio, who had formed deep and strong connections to many of his students. He was overwhelmed by the sense of departure and loss, and the knowledge that he would not be able to watch his students' progress in future years. He took some satisfaction, though, in the fact that the parents of his "tough cases" had pushed hardest for him to stay. The exception was Nazim's family. Mr. Casey had pulled Nazim out of school for the last week, still angry after another parent had gotten involved in disciplining the boy. Indeed, Nazim was a source of particular regret for Del Rio. He had done so much extra for the boy, and for what? So Nazim could misbehave, except for a few good moments, and then disappear? Del Rio had wanted to give up on Nazim, but he just couldn't—he continued to care. It probably helped Nazim, he figured, but left Del Rio with pain. "For me to feel this hurt," he said, "it tells me that I went too far."

In all, Del Rio was glad he had become a teacher. If he could have done it over, though, he remarked, he would have taught within the district. "My advice to any brand-new teacher is," he said, "don't go to a brand-new charter school."

Robin wanted to know whether they would have to do any work on this, the final day of school. "Yes," Del Rio said, decisively, crisply. The class let out a cry of revulsion, the same one they used for nasty smells. Del Rio pressed on. "We have a test," he explained. "A final on everything we've learned." The kids were not fooled, even momentarily.

Robin had another idea. "Teach fifth grade, Mr. Del Rio," she advised, "and tell us what school you're going to!" Del Rio tried to console them. "You guys need to get to know other teachers," he said in a quiet voice. He was an emotional man, and it meant something to him to know that his first students loved him. The class didn't seem convinced that they needed to get to know any other teachers. "You guys can't be with me forever!" Del Rio said. Robin was quick to respond: "Yeah we can!"

As the final minutes of the day rolled in, though, the party mood vanished. LaShay remarked on the change.

"Mr. D," she asked, "are you sadful that you can't teach us no more?"

"Yeah," he said.

Then, wearing a wan smile, Del Rio plunged into the Farewell Address.

"I hope that you guys had a good year this year, aside from all my yelling," Del Rio said. "I hope you took it as more than just yelling. I hope I helped you guys become better people." He talked about the fifth grade, where they were heading. "You can't give up because something's hard," he advised them. "I hope that's what you got out of this class, to be a good person, to make right choices."

Del Rio passed out awards, posed for pictures. Reyna, a sweet, Spanish-speaking girl whom he had worked very hard to help, cried silently. She accepted her award certificate and hugged him for a long time. Then she pressed the certificate to her face to blot her tears.

•   •   •

Four days later, at midmorning on Monday, June 19, a black-and-white Oakland police patrol car pulled up in front of the quiet, nearly vacant E. C. Reems Academy. John Cleveland accompanied a skinny, bored-looking cop to the scene of an apparent crime—the school office. Enormous plastic garbage bags bloomed with shredded paper, presumably from school documents of some sort, in half a dozen bright colors. Several file drawers stood empty, and the computer, the printer, and a raft of office supplies had disappeared. Most bizarre of all, a portable storage locker sat, padlocked and sphinxlike in its stolidity, on the blacktop outside. The cop, however, looked less than intrigued by the mystery; he'd clearly seen much more interesting crimes. "What you wanna do?" he asked, fingering the metal box that served as both case and clipboard for his crime reports. The shell-shocked Cleveland lacked some information needed to prosecute a crime, such as who actually owned the computer equipment. He let the cop write out a report for the records, and tried to recover himself. "I just—" he began, then stopped, lost in thought, shaking his head. He pressed a hand to his chest. "That's not my upbringing," he said. "If I was going to leave a place, I'd just leave."

The thefts, or vandalism, or whatever it was that had happened, marked the final act in a sad drama that unfolded over the ending of the school year. That final act began on the last day of school, after the students left, as the teachers adjourned to a popular bar in North Berkeley for a bit of parting conviviality. Cleveland, if he had heard about it, knew better than to show up. But Laura Armstrong was there. Things started off on a cheery note, as the teachers giggled over a cast list for an imaginary blockbuster: *E. C. Reems: The Movie.* The teachers behind it just happened to be portrayed by sexy Hollywood stars—Angelina Jolie, Gwyneth Paltrow, Angela Bassett, Cameron Diaz. By contrast, John Cleveland was relegated to the "cameo" list, played by Sherman Helmsley, the former George Jefferson on *The Jeffersons*. School Futures suffered rough treatment, with Gene Ruffin played by O. J. Simpson, Don Gill by Steve Martin, accountant Fil Guzman by Jackie Chan, and Joan Collins as Bernadine Hawthorne. But seven hours later, the scene at the venerable Berkeley bar had become morose. Laura Armstrong, festive and almost flirtatious for much of the evening, no longer could maintain her trademark self-control. Separated from her divine mission and cut loose by her guiding star, Ernestine C. Reems, Armstrong had been stretched to the breaking point. Surrounded by the faculty she had chosen for the school that was no longer hers, she had grown silent. Finally, someone noticed that she was quietly sobbing.

The next day, as the teachers were clearing out, even the building itself seemed to join in a general feeling of despair and loss, sagging as if in sympathy with the teachers' spirits. The staff arrived that day to find a thinly disguised ultimatum from Cleveland, in apparent expectation of mischief: a long checklist of paperwork and classroom materials that teachers would have to turn in to get their paychecks. As the depressing day wore on, a toilet overflowed upstairs. Water flowed unchecked into the hallway, soaking into classroom carpets and through the floor, creating rain showers in one of the first-floor classrooms. Someone had called the principal about the flood, but no one came to fix it. Indeed, the place had the feel of a barracks on the day of abandonment by an army in retreat. Then the school's fire alarm freaked out, magnifying the sense of crisis with flashbulblike strobe lights and occasional, creepy beeping.

The crisis, however, didn't reach full flower until the next day, Saturday. Laura Armstrong and her most loyal staffers were still clearing out their materials when the church handyman arrived to change the locks. The teachers flew into a rage, and Armstrong left. By day's end, the mysterious clues—the storage locker, the shredding—were all that remained. What had happened was left to Cleveland's imagination. The garbage bags filled with ribbons of paper remained a mystery, a final symbol of the trashed trust between the teachers and what was supposed to be a community school.

•   •   •

On July 17, a month after school let out, the state of California announced the results of the Big Test, ending the suspense for everyone hoping to critique or brag about E. C. Reems and the other charters. The newspapers livened up the debate by offering strikingly different interpretations. On Friday, July 21, the *San Francisco Chronicle* headlined, "Charter Schools Test Well." The subheadline ran, "They outperform public neighbors." The story singled out E. C. Reems, noting that its reading scores in the lower grades outranked the nearby competition, Webster Elementary. But a day earlier, San Francisco's afternoon paper, the *Examiner*, had headlined, "Charters fare no better than traditional schools on tests." That story chose a different, and surprising, standard: comparing the inner-city charter schools to the statewide public school average.

It was indeed tricky to make comparisons between schools, especially in a charter's first year. As the *Chronicle* story noted, differences can result from varying student bodies as much as from the quality of teaching. Even so, the scores at E. C. Reems and Dolores Huerta offered reasons for both satisfaction and concern. Reems, which served one of Oakland's poorest neighborhoods, had fallen below the average scores of the district as a whole. But it had substantially outdistanced some neighborhood schools, from which it drew many of its students. The children also had achieved considerable gains since the October pretest; in several grades, the percentage of students scoring at the national average vaulted from the teens to the twenties and thirties. Oddly, however, one grade stuck out for its terrible scores: fourth, the one that Valentín Del Rio and Yasmine Alwan taught, the one that included Nazim Casey, Asia McGehee, and Malory Stewart. In that grade, only 7 percent read at the national average, and only 9 percent did math at that level.

Dolores Huerta offered a still more complex picture. For all the wonderful sense of community participation and cooperation, the school did not manage to rise above the neighborhood schools with their achingly low scores. (Huerta's poverty rate—63 percent—

ran lower than some area schools, but more of the children at the charter lacked fluency in English.) In reading particularly, the numbers galled: only 9 percent of third graders, 13 percent of fourth graders, and 4 percent of fifth graders at Huerta read at the national average. Math scores ranged from 18 to 25 percent. The scores were so low, in fact, that they were difficult to distinguish from those at the much-maligned Jefferson. Yet within Huerta, the span of scores dazzled. Two children from one professional family had reading scores in the ninety-ninth and ninety-sixth percentile, while the two children of a poor, drug-addicted mother scored in the first and fourth percentiles. In Del Rio's class at E. C. Reems, too, the numbers ranged widely. Nazim scored in the fourteenth percentile in reading, outdoing a handful of children with single-digit scores, while four students reached the forties, fifties, and sixties.

The complicated questions, of course, concerned why—why a school like Dolores Huerta could not outscore a dysfunctional place like Jefferson; why a place like E. C. Reems, with its neophyte teachers and virtually no professional development, did indeed outperform its low-performing neighbors; why the fourth grade was such a black eye for Reems, when two of its most committed teachers had been assigned to that grade. To some extent, the lack of a pattern exposed the folly of trying to draw meaningful conclusions when only a few dozen children were tested at each grade. Beyond that, however, the numbers proved the obvious: for instance, the dangers of comparing unequal groups of kids. In addition to mismatches in income, previous school performance, and knowledge of English, the two groups differed because one had gone out of its way to choose a new school, and one hadn't. Evidently, though, neither charter had worked any miracles in its first year. And perhaps that shouldn't have been surprising. Neither school did much in the classroom to set it apart from the regular public schools.

Within the charter world, people sometimes said that a school's first year was about survival. Mistakes in the first year might be forgiven, but the stakes would grow in a second year—a time when Reems, and to some extent Huerta, would be starting again practically from scratch. Reems, where only three teachers were returning, needed to hire nearly an entire staff, and both schools needed principals. At Huerta, the staff loved their school, but had suffered; of the eight teachers there, seven contributed to a grievance against their second-round principal, John Cleveland. (The complaints focused on Cleveland's manipulative management style, and particularly on sexist, racist, and anti-Semitic comments he allegedly had made.) Yet the teachers wanted to stay with their school. School Futures rewarded their patience with delays in offering a contract until July, four months later than the district. Nonetheless, the teachers waited—a testament to the sweet, cohesive spirit of the school, if not to School Futures' supposedly superior business practices.

By late July, little doubt remained that School Futures had broken key promises to OCO, to the parents, to the teachers, to the community. It was true that the company had invested philanthropic dollars and built schools that parents preferred to the district's offerings. On the other hand, School Futures repeatedly had failed to find quality leadership; failed to provide sufficiently attentive management; and at least in the case of Dolores Huerta, where many of the OCO members had children, failed to deliver the promised test score gains.

Moreover, the company seemed incapable of admitting fault, of taking responsibility for its broken promises, and of learning from its mistakes. Indeed, history looked poised to repeat itself. Teacher hiring had to wait until a new principal, who had been picked to run E. C. Reems, arrived from Kansas City. That wouldn't happen until August 14. No principal had yet been found for Dolores Huerta. As usual, the schools found themselves caught up in a rush to accomplish tasks that should have been done long before. After watching that pattern for more than a year, the people who had brought School Futures to Oakland—OCO and the Center of Hope Community Church—finally called the company to account on July 31.

The ostensible reason for the meeting, at OCO's dowdy office, was to confront the amazingly long-lived problem that the two charter schools still had no governing board, a year into their existence. This created a question of whether the schools even existed, legally speaking, and left them in jeopardy of shutdown by the district at any time. At the meeting, Don Gill and Jeff Harris—the consultant and Gene Ruffin's best friend—faced off against Ron Snyder, the executive director of OCO, and Herma Ross from Center of Hope. The discussion began civilly enough, shortly after six P.M., with proposals for Snyder and Harris to sit on the school's board. But the calm quickly evaporated. With Ruffin absent, no real action could be taken, a familiar situation that added to Snyder and Ross's frustration. Soon, the discussions devolved into statements of exasperation over poor communication, mismatched visions, and trading of blame. The conflict gained extra heat from news that School Futures had ordered changes to the language of the charters. The executives had decided to substitute "advisory" boards for controlling ones, a step that would put all the real control in the hands of School Futures.

What no one at the table knew was that Brian Bennett, School Futures' negotiator, had quietly blocked that move. Bennett, whose main job was helping to create new schools, had been fired a few weeks earlier as part of John Walton's effort to stub out any further expansion. Before he left, though, he saw to it that the changes to the charters died silent, painless deaths. More than a year earlier, Bennett had made lavish promises of community control, and he was not about to write legal language contradicting that (even in the very unlikely event that the Oakland school board would approve such changes). So despite repeated orders, Bennett merrily did nothing.

The discussion grew more contentious when Harris asked why the board had not been formed. "Ask School Futures," said an aggravated Ron Snyder. Don Gill got hot. "Ask OCO," he shot back. "Your name is on this, too." Accusations sailed back and forth. Time for hiring teachers was drawing short, but the new principal wouldn't take office for two weeks. Even Harris agreed that there was good reason to wonder about School Futures' assurances that everything would be OK. Gill promised that the new principal, Lisa Blair, would move quickly into action, but Herma Ross from the Center of Hope was tired of promises. "We have no idea when she's coming, what her plans are—we know nothing," she said. Gill sputtered that she already had a plan, but Ross cut him off angrily. "I understand, Mr. Gill, she has a 'plan.' But by Jove, here we are again, three or four weeks from school, and as far as I know, she ain't here. When Gene Ruffin sat in that room, he said that we would select a principal"—she banged the table as she ticked off the promises— "have them hired, and they would be here. They're not here, and I don't know when they're coming." She feared they would be scraping up bottom-barrel teacher candidates, and she growled that there had been no communication to warn of the crisis.

Gill dodged again, blaming the long-ago-fired Laura Armstrong, who "built the foundation for no communication." But he promised that Lisa Blair would stand as a new kind of principal. Unmoved, Ross focused on the bottom line: "When is she going to get here, and what is she going to do? You're telling me that's two weeks away, and I'm telling you that's not good enough."

Ron Snyder agreed. His anger rising, he demanded that School Futures place someone in Oakland every single day until Blair arrived. "In the absence of a principal, somebody has to be in charge," he said. "We can't rely on somebody that's in Kansas City that's not talking to us. Somebody has to be in charge of making this school open. Who is that?" Gill conceded he was the one in charge of that particular detail, but when Snyder asked whether he would show up in Oakland every day, Gill simply laughed. "I didn't know we were in that state of a crisis," he said.

Gill promised to handle the issue, but refused to commit his promises to writing. Exasperated, Herma Ross expressed herself in the plainest English. School Futures was a fine organization, she said, but "its management style sucks." She promised to carry her complaints directly to the CEO. Even Harris unloaded on Gill. "Legitimate doesn't describe the concerns that they have, because it goes beyond legitimacy," he drawled. "They ain't getting back from you what they need to hear."

"I get you, Jeff," Gill said. "But I got one hour's notice to get here, very little idea about what the agenda is. If these are issues, we go about solving them, but I don't sense—"

Snyder cut him off. "They've been issues for a long time," he said, drawing out the word *long* in his controlled fury. "They've been issues for a long time."

Ross looked into Gill's eyes. "I really need you to understand, we are not going to continue down this path," she said, enunciating carefully, "because this is utter, sheer chaos. You are not on the side of the parents or the students."

Snyder wanted to know why the School Futures m.o. involved eternal tardiness. "Don't you see what we're saying—that this should have happened six months ago?" he asked. "We are always faced with this last-minute, crisis-oriented decision making." The usually courteous senior director was nearly shouting. "As a result, this school is not going to be the kind of school it deserves to be this year."

"I don't believe that," Gill said evenly, as he packed his briefcase. "I believe we're going to have a great school."

Gill's words framed the challenge. A rough first year had passed, but that surprised no one who knew charter schools well. Now, though, as E. C. Reems and Dolores Huerta moved into years two, three, and beyond, the questions turned sharp: Would these little academies deliver on their promises of a better education? Would they open the horizons of children? Would they be great schools?

Chapter 10

New Year, Old Hopes

The E. C. Reems and Dolores Huerta Academies opened for a second year on September 5, 2000. The second year was to feel painfully familiar, in many ways: a last-minute rush to hire teachers; deep distress over student behavior; plenty of distractions from the core mission of solid instruction. Indeed, in some areas, the problems were to turn worse; teacher turnover skyrocketed, for a time, while some other longtime frustrations remained. Yet, for all the familiarity, this year would upend some central conceptions—about control, independence, choice, politics, community, and about who held the moral high ground. By year's end, the charter picture would puzzle all the more. Yet at the same time, the coming years were to produce signs of hope, that a broadening of school choices might mean better chances for a good number of children.

The second and third years of the charter school also helped to answer some key questions about their trajectory and promise. As with charters across the country, parents and policy makers would demand an accounting of Reems and Huerta: Would these schools achieve some degree of calm and stability? Would they help to open the way for wider improvements in the district as a whole? Would they deliver better student performance? Would their founders learn lessons from the experience, or tire of creating new schools? Ultimately, were these little schools worth the effort they required? From the great initial investment, was there a payoff in hope?

Even with all the drama and pain that had marred the first year, the families who had struggled to create the two little charter schools did not give up their dreams. As the second year dawned, the enrollment rosters demonstrated the parents' belief in the charters as a superior alternative. At E. C. Reems, roughly 90 percent of families returned for the second year. (Webster Elementary, down the street, held on to 83 percent of its students.) At Dolores Huerta, which was enrolled to maximum capacity, the scene was even more dramatic. The less-than-dazzling test scores had scared off no one. So high was the demand for spaces, in fact, that the waiting list numbered 180 children—larger than the school itself.

In recruiting a principal and then teachers, both schools suffered from the same abbreviated schedule that they had a year earlier. With principal positions open at both schools—School Futures had decided that one principal couldn't run two schools, after all—the daunting task of finding a skilled educational leader presented itself twice over. School Futures, however, limped when it needed to sprint. The company should have started searching for a principal in January, if not sooner, but it conducted interviews in mid-July. As if to underline how little the company had learned from its earlier carelessness, it limited the interviews to thirty minutes, which might have been appropriate for the secretary's position, but not what amounted to the CEO of a complex small business. The applicant list was equally thin. Where there had been half a dozen interviews the year before, this time there were three. (John Cleveland applied for his old job, but never showed up to the interview.)

Ultimately, School Futures chose a polished, cheerful woman named Lisa Blair to head up the Reems Academy. Blair had flown in for the interview from Kansas City, where she managed workforce development for the local chamber of commerce. She had never been a schoolteacher or administrator, but she had taught for years at the University of Southern California, and she recently had been elected chair of the board of a School Futures charter school in

Kansas City. Moreover, her charming, businesslike manner promised a smooth reliability long absent from the principal's office at E. C. Reems. Peering calmly over professorial reading glasses, unruffled by the daunting challenge, she quickly won approval. For Dolores Huerta, the company could find no one, so that school went—as usual—without a principal. Yet, by some miracle, when September 5 rolled around, every classroom at both schools had a teacher.

But filling all the positions didn't mean an end to staffing problems. At E. C. Reems in the first months of the school year, many teachers proved no match for the students' behavior. Soon, the school was beset by disturbingly high teacher turnover. It was also to lose one of its most troublesome students, quite early on.

Thanks to an odd choice to maintain the same class rosters from the previous year, all of Valentín Del Rio's students ended up with a teacher named Diane Sullivan, a former real estate agent who had sought a new career that would serve the community. Even in matters of simple instruction, Sullivan may not have been an ideal choice. (She admitted, for example, to some confusion over the precise number of states in the United States.) But concerns over teaching and learning quickly paled next to the daily trials of civility and order. Nazim led the pack. By lunchtime on the first day, Sullivan had moved him to a seat up front. On the second day, she wrote a note to Wilma Cornish, the onetime third-grade teacher, who had been promoted to the newly created position of dean. The note asked Cornish to call Nazim's grandfather, in light of his harrowing behavior. "Nazim has used all kinds of words to fellow students about them and me," the note said. It listed a surprising variety of vulgarities Nazim had flung, and concluded, "He talks constantly in class and doesn't do all the work. One girl cried today, because of him."

By the time the school year was ten days old, Principal Blair had lost patience. Laura Armstrong, a year earlier, had broken her own promises in order to keep Nazim at the school. Lisa Blair had less tolerance, and Nazim presented even more severe problems now. At a sit-down conference with Casey, Blair made clear that she wanted Nazim out of her school. The grandfather did not object; he had spent much of the previous week sitting next to his grandson in class, and he was dismayed by Sullivan's lack of control. Nazim spent his last day at E. C. Reems on Friday, September 15; he then returned to the regular public school system, at a campus near his home called Burbank Elementary. Nazim's departure was not recorded as an expulsion; like at least one other student, he had been "counseled out."

Unfortunately, the situation in Sullivan's class was not an isolated problem. In a quick conversation amid the preopening rush, Principal Blair had decided to keep the previous year's classes together. Groups of children who had had weak teachers the previous year now could exercise well-practiced techniques of chaos. For a handful of new, well-meaning teachers, it was slaughter. Although calm reigned in the classrooms of experienced, skilled teachers, that fact was painfully overshadowed by the rout of several neophytes. In a school with fifteen classroom positions, a distressing total of five teachers had departed by Christmas. Stubbornly, Sullivan remained, but it was no great favor to the kids. Amid the tumult in her classroom, she pondered a friend's advice to establish control by verbally abusing her students. Mercifully, she eventually dropped the idea.

Perhaps the most disturbing situation of all, though, involved the fourth-grade class that had run out Emily Deringer early in the school's first year. With the new year, the class had been assigned to yet another white twenty-something with good intentions and little training. In October, that teacher quit. By the time a new teacher arrived, enrollment in the class had dropped to seven, thanks to withdrawals and transfers. Yet even that tiny group proved too much for the new recruit. The teacher shouted and blew a police whistle, in some weird caricature of a drill sergeant, as his nine-year-olds mostly ignored him. Finally, in April, Lisa Blair put an end to the spectacle, dismissing the teacher and folding the remaining kids into Sullivan's class.

The view from outside, however, contrasted markedly with the internal scenes of mischief and teacher turnover. For all the changes on the staff roster, Lisa Blair had brought a sense of calm, affable professionalism to the school office. She was there every day and was friendly, a combination that placed her above either of her predecessors in the eyes of many. She carried an air of competence to her meetings with outsiders, and she spoke honestly about the school's shortcomings. A grant-writing genius, she scored thousands upon thousands of dollars to bring in computers and even a low-power radio station. For all the trouble in some of the classrooms, the academy's public relations had improved noticeably, to the delight of parents, the church, and School Futures.

Despite the newfound calm, the E. C. Reems Academy by the end of its second year had made only modest progress toward its initial promise. Perhaps the saddest aspect was the fact that, as a charter school, it was doing so little to take advantage of its freedom to try new and different approaches in the classroom. The staff met together only rarely and briefly, and the school engaged in little training of its faculty. The teachers assisted each other too rarely; those with experience were more apt to go home at the end of the day than to instruct their newer colleagues. Despite its freedom from the fetters of a giant bureaucracy, the school had failed to find noticeably superior teachers, to create a longer school day or year, or to devise stronger strategies for teaching children. Indeed, School Futures had no plans to establish a longer school year, in contrast to Brian Bennett's original promises.* The school still lacked a special-education program. Moreover, with a noneducator at the top, and no real head teacher, there was no one to lead an exploration of innovative educational ideas. E. C. Reems was following the same course as so many other inner-city schools—charter and regular—that lacked a clear vision: falling back on what each teacher happened to know.

Like her predecessor, Principal Blair had plenty to distract her from improving the teachers' work in the classroom. Beside the be-

---

* School Futures, which continued to charge its schools a 10 percent management fee, said there was not enough money in school budgets to provide for extra days.

havior problems, she had inherited a school with a woeful financial history. According to an audit the previous June, E. C. Reems had overspent its $1.2 million original budget by $213,000, due in large part to the school's failure to file paperwork that would have brought $200,000 in state class-size reduction funds. School Futures kicked in a "loan" of $113,000, on top of $200,000 in private grants, yet the school remained $101,000 in the red, in addition to the new debt to the company.

At Dolores Huerta, the second year brought relative classroom calm, but a political situation that made one wonder whether the world had suddenly turned upside down. Most of the teachers returned for a second year, despite a patience-trying summer; School Futures waited until August to offer contracts. The school once again had no principal, until early November, when the company elevated the fifth-grade teacher Jorge Lopez to the head position. Lopez (no relation to Lillian Lopez) had taught for only one year and had no administrative background, but he had won many fans among the parents for his easygoing, hardworking style in the school's first year. Approachable and kind, he embodied the family and community ethic that had enveloped the school since its first days. Test scores notwithstanding, families and teachers faithfully adored their small, safe, happy school.

Within the classrooms, the year unfolded smoothly. Jorge Lopez, despite his scant experience, created a level of training and support for teachers that had not been seen before at either school. He built a link to a private school where more experienced teachers acted as mentors, allowing the Dolores Huerta faculty to visit classes there, and arranging seminars for teachers nearly weekly for much of the year. He also took halting steps in the direction of observing and evaluating teachers, an absolutely crucial activity that Huerta had not known previously.

Yet the tiny school failed to close the curtain on the political opera that always had dominated adult life there. Aware of his inexperience and his uncertain political standing, principal Lopez had sought guidance from another charter principal. That man, who ran Oakland's American Indian Public Charter School, had rescued the disastrous program there and restored it to health. But he proved a divisive figure at the already divided Dolores Huerta. Lopez spent more and more time at American Indian, and came under fire for not being at Huerta to attend to the daily scares and injuries that punctuate school life. As it became evident that School Futures planned not to rehire Lopez for the school's third year, divisions deepened. One faction backed Lopez, while the other sided with School Futures, igniting a civil war.

Furthermore, a controversy surrounding the school's new governing board made matters far worse. After his rise to the principalship, Jorge Lopez had formed a governing board for the school. Its chair was a former president of the Oakland school board, and its number included parent Lillian Lopez and a thoughtful lawyer who was writing a dissertation on charter schools. School Futures, however, declined to recognize the group as the governing board of the school. After blaming a series of principals for failing to create governing boards, the executives now argued that Jorge Lopez did not have the power to establish such a board. Indeed, they were hostile to any idea that gave a separate board, rather than School Futures itself, real power over the school.

As the second school year drew to a close, the warring parties prepared for their biggest battle yet over control of Dolores Huerta. But with spring at hand, it was time for that great milestone in the life of both schools, the standardized test, a yardstick that presumably would measure the effect of all the additional teacher training. But the results would not arrive until August. By then, much would have changed.

•   •   •

Charter schools do not live in a vacuum. Beloved by politicians, they are inevitably political tools. Their performance—as judged by standardized tests, inevitably—interests the press and policy makers as much as it does the parents. Charter advocates promise that these schools can change the larger system for the better. Oakland offered a fine vantage point to see whether that would happen. Indeed, by the spring of 2001, Oakland had become as exciting a laboratory for charter schools as any city in the nation, having given birth to fully a dozen such schools. These schools ran the full gamut of quality, mission, and experience.

Several Oakland charters offered signs of promise. In hard-hit West Oakland, an astute group, after years of planning, had created a true community school with an afternoon enrichment program and plans for classes for adults. Opening, wisely, with only fifty students, the school was handily outscoring the regular district school across the street, despite an unusually high special-education enrollment. Another charter was helping dropouts achieve their high school equivalency degrees. The same school was gearing up to build an elementary school, its long planning process drawing upon some of the country's best educational minds. And, not far from Reems, a team headed by the architect of California's charter law had established a new school to replace the defunct Waldorf charter, and scores were rising. These were bright spots—schools that took matters of teaching and learning and educational vision seriously, hired strong teachers, and saw a payoff in the form of achievement.

Unfortunately, several of Oakland's charters had not enjoyed similar success. E. C. Reems and Dolores Huerta were joined by other charter schools in their scrambles and squabbles over money, organization, planning, and hiring of qualified teachers and principals. Oakland's oldest charter, one of the first in the nation, was trundling into its eighth year amid stubbornly mediocre student performance. The school had been through three campuses, five principals, and more than its share of controversy. Three other charters had been closed outright, thanks to internal disputes, falling enrollment, and money problems. And then there was the weird case: a charter school approved by the school board in Fresno—some 150 miles away—that was operating a "satellite campus" in a city recreation center in Oakland. The school was run entirely by Muslim teachers, with most girls in Islamic headdress, and with some lessons in Arabic, though witnesses maintained that no prayer was happening.

Amid growing press curiosity, Jerry Brown's administration kicked the school out of the city facility, and it ultimately collapsed as a state inquest was brewing.

In sum, Oakland's charters—though clearly of varying quality—had not, as a group, performed noticeably better than the regular schools, or at least not yet. That complicated the question of what political effect they might have. Across the country, likewise, many experts felt that the bulk of charter schools had yet to demonstrate meaningful academic superiority. Even so, charter schools were making themselves felt in district offices, often by attracting significant numbers of students away from the big system. To be sure, in Oakland—where just over a thousand students attended charters, in a district of fifty-four thousand—the numbers made only a small dent. But more and more people were lining up to create charters. And while small in enrollment, the charters cast an outsized political shadow. They constituted a measure of the acute hunger in the inner city for schools that were small, safe, and responsive to parents—places that felt like family. Surveys showed parents were happier at charter schools than at the schools their children had attended before, and most charter schools had waiting lists for enrollment. While the research on charters varied, they clearly were pushing some districts toward reform and toward better customer service, especially where they threatened significant proportions of district enrollment and budget.

In Oakland, charters became a tool for Jerry Brown, who talked constantly of shaking things up inside the school district to make people pay attention. And likewise, they became a bargaining chit for the district superintendent, Dennis Chaconas. Early in his administration, Chaconas had announced his backing for the small-schools plan that OCO had been urging. But the ferment—and fear—stirred by charter schools helped him to win support for the small schools plan from the teachers' union and his own vast administration. (In district small schools, unlike in charters, teachers would have collective-bargaining protections, small-schools advocates told the union.) Now, that project was progressing at an impressive clip, with a handful of such schools poised to open just a year after the school board cleared the way for them to exist. The charter schools may not have been delivering world-class results. But they were having an impact on the political landscape.

From OCO's vantage point, the charters had brought power, but not without a touch of irony. The success of the small-schools plan testified to the political muscle OCO and its education partner, now called the Bay Area Coalition for Equitable Schools, had gained from the charter school effort. Yet by spring 2001, OCO's own role in the charters stood vastly changed. Two years earlier Lopez and the rest of OCO had joined with School Futures when they concluded that the then-superintendent and her system had no real interest in small schools, could not be trusted, and would not listen to individual parents like her. School Futures, by contrast, had seemed responsive, quick to act, and genuinely concerned about the inadequate educational offerings foisted on Oakland's poor children.

Now, however, the situation had completely reversed. The new superintendent, Dennis Chaconas, huddled with OCO parents in a long Saturday morning meeting early after taking office. He ousted a raft of principals at low-performing schools—including Lopez's old nemesis, Mike Hopkins at Jefferson—and appeared thoroughly excited about the small-schools plan. Chaconas really "got it," in a favorite phrase of Lillian Lopez's, and she and others now trusted the district. School Futures, on the other hand, was now playing the district's traditional role: aloof, unreachable, unaccountable for vague promises, and acting without urgency on schools that were not performing well. So, in hushed tones, Lopez and others at OCO began murmuring about doing the unimaginable: asking the district to take over the little charter schools that OCO had helped to start. Two years after the community group had fought so hard to leave the district, it was poised to complete a perfect circle.

A series of dramatic changes within School Futures, however, staved off that powerfully ironic step. The changes had begun the previous Christmas, when CEO Gene Ruffin's difference of vision with the School Futures board reached its logical conclusion. A letter from board chair John Walton announced that Ruffin was leaving "with the intention of developing a for-profit educational management company." Don Gill stepped in as interim CEO. Two months later, in another letter, Walton announced that he himself was stepping down as chairman of the board, and that a new CEO had been appointed: Neil Derrough, a onetime president of CBS Television Stations. Derrough had taken part in education discussions through a San Diego business consortium, and described schools as a longtime "pet" interest. He took on the School Futures post as a part-time job, while continuing his position at the University of California, educating principals about business practices.

The change in management at School Futures, by all accounts, brought calm and logic to the company's operations—and therefore muddled the politics at Dolores Huerta even more. Lillian Lopez had once liked the idea of cutting ties with School Futures, but now hesitated under better management. Moreover, she wondered whether, without the company, the families could find and pay for a building. So, in summer 2001, she met with Derrough—turning her into a traitor in the eyes of some parents who vehemently supported Principal Jorge Lopez. That angry judgment extended to Lopez's organization, OCO. To those parents, OCO's leaders no longer represented the massed voice of the families. They had become apologists for rich suits at a faraway, double-dealing corporation.

An odd three-way war among School Futures, OCO, and the Jorge Lopez loyalists played out in a series of meetings. At perhaps the most dramatic of those sessions, Neil Derrough offered apologies for the mistakes of the past, promising not to repeat them. Derrough acknowledged that the company had made its decision to remove Jorge Lopez without parent "input," in admitted violation of the charter. Yet many parents directed their anger at OCO—in the person of Lillian Lopez. After a long hour of argument, Derrough wondered out loud whether the problems were too deep for School Futures to continue running Dolores Huerta. But no one was quite ready to cross that bridge, and instead, the discussion shifted to the notion of a new governing board to oversee the school.

The difficult experiences in Oakland apparently didn't dim the passion of the many people who had arrived there determined to create new charter schools. Gene Ruffin, the former School Futures chief, and his best friend, Jeff Harris, had formed a company called Good Schools for All. The new company, which bragged of big-name board members such as martial-arts film actor Steven Seagal and motivational speaker Deepak Chopra, was a nonprofit, but contracted with a for-profit Ruffin venture called Ed Futures. Together, the two companies managed fourteen schools. GSFA followed Ruffin's longtime scheme of wooing black churches as places to establish schools. Its record, however, raised questions about how much Ruffin had learned from School Futures' mistakes.

A survey of the press in 2001 indicated that Ruffin was finding his way into some very familiar trouble. For example, a headline from Florida's *St. Petersburg Times*: "Parents Rue Their School Choice." The story focused on Bethel Metropolitan Christian School, a private school funded by a Florida voucher program and managed by GSFA. "Parents at Bethel said the school has no books, no uniforms and has not provided special education services their children need," the story reported. "They said the school is understaffed and several teachers have left. And they said the school has verbally and physically abused their children for misbehavior." In two school districts in the Sacramento, California, area, GSFA charters got shot down over equally familiar concerns. "North Sacramento officials have said that the revocation was justified because GSFA had committed numerous violations of the charter, state law and accounting principles, and acts of fiscal [mismanagement]," the *Sacramento Bee* reported.

Ruffin described the complaints as isolated and politically motivated, and noted some parents had defended the attacked schools. A remark from Ruffin's old boss at Xerox, David Kearns, however, offered perspective. Kearns, the CEO credited with rebuilding Xerox to compete successfully with the Japanese, had later entered the school arena himself, becoming deputy secretary of education in the Clinton administration and a great fan of charter schools. He continued to get along well with Ruffin, but his one general criticism of

Ruffin was telling: that Ruffin had always been better at the marketing of a product than at the details of building it.

Another big-picture man, Jerry Brown, likewise remained bullish on charters, despite the mixed Oakland picture. He persisted in campaigning for his two charters—a military academy and an arts school—after his plan with the for-profit Edison fell through. Yet he had to take extraordinary measures to win approval for his military school. Even though Brown himself had appointed three members to the ten-member Oakland school board, that panel rejected Brown's charter, with one of his own appointees casting the final vote and calling the proposal racist. Under California law, school boards elsewhere in the region could have approved a charter in Oakland, too, but Brown had a hard time finding one that would vote for the military school. Ultimately, he ended up at the very top—the state school board. There, no less a figure than the governor himself—Gray Davis, who had served as Brown's chief of staff when Brown was governor—spoke in favor of the school, assuring approval. The school opened in 2001, and quickly dismissed 35 of its original 200 students, all for behavioral reasons during an opening out-of-town "encampment." By November, the school had shrunk to 158 students, but for the remaining cadets, it appeared to provide quality teaching and a sense of calm. Brown's arts academy was to open the following year.

Also amid the forthcoming charter applicants was Laura Armstrong. Working with the teachers still faithful to her—Alan Foss, Christine Landry, and Carol Fields—she drafted a new charter for submission to the Oakland school board, convinced that the Lord's vision for her had not been denied, just delayed. (Previously, she had tried to join forces with the faltering Waldorf school, a plan that proved futile when the Waldorf charter got revoked.) Armstrong won a $35,000 grant to support development of the school. But it was not to be. After the fiascoes at E. C. Reems and the star-crossed flirtation with the Waldorf group, Armstrong's name inspired little respect among the authorities responsible for approving the charter. And an anonymous caller had tipped the district that Armstrong's claimed doctoral degree did not exist. Moreover, the charter itself was full of holes, including doubts over the validity of signatures and the accuracy of the budget. "I feel a moral obligation to protect our children from programs that don't sound sound," one high-ranking district official said. The superintendent recommended a *no* vote, and the school board heeded his advice.

Bishop Ernestine Reems also entertained expansive charter dreams. She was thrilled with the new principal, Lisa Blair, and felt the academy that bore her name would eventually grow into "a model school for the whole world." She also remained deeply optimistic about the prospects for charter schools to make positive change for inner-city kids. She purchased a building across the street from the school and was pondering plans for a high school there—perhaps as a charter school, or perhaps as one of the new small schools. If her plans worked out, the babies of E. C. Reems would never have to return to the regular district system.

Brian Bennett, the onetime negotiator for School Futures, hadn't given up on charters, either. Joining with two other School Futures refugees—the former accountant and the former personnel man—he formed a consulting firm to create charters and private schools.

Meanwhile, OCO, with a cadre of new leaders and professional staff, focused their fight on the small-schools effort, which had blossomed. With millions of dollars from Microsoft founder Bill Gates, and support from the new superintendent, the Small Autonomous Schools—built on the inspiration of Debbie Meier—marked the culmination of all the efforts at Jefferson and of the leverage the charter schools had provided. With five schools opening in 2001, they represented an enormous victory for this powerful, multiracial coalition. Now, they would face the same question as the charters: Would these small schools be better schools?

•   •   •

In the summer of 2001, the state of California released standardized test results for the charter schools' second year. At E. C. Reems, far from the bold promises of improvement, scores had actually fallen from the previous year. The *Oakland Tribune* headline told the story: "Some Charter Schools Fail to Make the Grade." "At the Ernestine C.

Reems Academy of Technology and Arts," the article said, "every grade could not match the scores from 2000." That statement wasn't strictly true, but it came sadly close to the mark. Almost regardless of how one counted, scores were down. In the class that once belonged to Del Rio, the numbers were especially devastating. At the end of the first year, 7 percent of the fourth graders had read at the national average. Now, in the second year, when they were fifth graders, that number was down to 3 percent. In several grades the scores were barely above those at Webster, the vast, sad district school that the families had left behind.

At Dolores Huerta, by contrast, scores rose in every grade, in both reading and math. Sadly, however, particularly with so few students taking the test, Dolores Huerta's scores remained difficult to distinguish from those at Jefferson.

All the same, as a new school year began in September 2001, the scene offered reason for hope. The New Small Autonomous Schools opened, building on the plans of teams of teachers working for more than a year. All found it harder going than they had expected, and all had to contend with the same difficulties as other urban schools, including exhaustion for teachers and even parents. Yet it wasn't long before the district superintendent, Dennis Chaconas, remarked that all of them showed more promise than the local charter schools. The Small Autonomous Schools were slated to expand in the coming years.

Meanwhile, other signs of exciting change had blossomed. A long- and well-planned charter school, sponsored by the East Bay Conservation Corps, rose from the ashes at the building that once belonged to a defunct previous charter. And in another exciting turn, KIPP— the school that had so energized the OCO group back in their visit to the Bronx in 1998—laid plans to establish a school in Oakland. With help from both OCO and the Small Autonomous Schools group, a KIPP-trained principal planned to open a school in Oakland in July 2002, as part of a far-ranging national expansion plan.

In fall 2001, both of School Futures' Oakland charters began their third year with governing boards and full-time principals. The company hired an instruction chief, and at E. C. Reems Principal Blair rededicated herself to improving the quality of teaching, especially in light of the lower test scores. The school had calmed enormously, especially with the addition of an effective full-time counselor for students. The high teacher turnover dropped sharply, as did student suspensions. The special-education enrollment climbed to about a dozen, signaling a change in the school's illegal policy of shutting out or failing to serve special-needs students. Blair also instituted a new, schoolwide reading program. Yet she conceded that the teachers needed more support. Blair had never taught, and her dean hadn't passed the basic competency test. Neither had the expertise to give the teachers the training they needed. It remained to be seen whether this more orderly school would develop that capacity.

In a twist of coincidence, Barbara Purdom—whose first year of public school teaching at the vast, troubled Webster Elementary is chronicled earlier in this book—got hired at E. C. Reems in 2001. She started off as a third-grade teacher, but was moved—with a single day's notice—to replace a first-grade teacher who quit in October. Her comparisons of the two schools were revealing. Purdom found that she was freer to use her education and wide knowledge—she had trained as a computer scientist before entering teaching—than she had been at Webster, and also felt more appreciated personally. Yet she found it harder to obtain resources, ranging from textbooks to substitutes. She met weekly with other lower-grade teachers, and the whole staff met roughly monthly, for generally useful teaching workshops. At Webster, she said, there had been almost no such training. Overall, her comments suggested more attention to teaching practice, a key development.

Dolores Huerta entered its third year amid continuing power struggles. The school remained riven by calls for new board elections, amid talk of a shadow board that wanted to assume control. A lawyer who had served on the defunct previous board wrote to the district, asking it to rescue the school "from what appears to me to be a hostile corporate takeover." Many parents had no say in the selection even of the parent members of the board, while much of the selection power was exercised by School Futures. The board then drew up bylaws for itself that were questionable on both legal and logical grounds, including provisions that anyone wishing to attend a meeting must ask for permission days in advance, "and describe their interest and reasons so the chairperson can, if appropriate in the chairperson's sole opinion, make reasonable accommodations for them." Given that the meetings were, by law, public, the position was almost certainly illegal. Much of the action was taken in meetings held with little or no public notice, apparently in violation of the open-meeting laws governing public schools.

Dolores Huerta's principal, like the one at Reems, looked poised to bring stability to the place. Kenneth Reed, a onetime United Parcel Service supervisor, had entered teaching in 1998. A reassuring presence, he allowed teachers to concentrate on their craft rather than worrying about the fate of their school. Yet Reed's scant experience in education raised questions about his capacity as an instructional leader. He was working on a master's degree in education, but when he accepted the principal's post, he still held only an emergency teaching credential.

The situation at both schools suggested the same possibility that some experts saw nationally: that after a year or two of battling for simple survival, charter schools tend to stabilize, perhaps opening the field for academic improvement. The key question, at the Oakland charters and nationally, was whether key players such as parents and school boards would be satisfied with stability, by itself, or would demand more. In Oakland, both schools were smaller, safer, and more welcoming than the district "competition." Without outside help, though, both arguably lacked the resources to forge excellence in their classrooms. School Futures, while better managed and more focused on instruction, acknowledged the depth of that need only grudgingly.

School Futures, under its new leadership, was quite serious about making other sorts of changes in the name of "downsizing." By spring 2002, it was cutting ties with three of its San Diego schools. Donald Gill, the operations chief who came on board just as School Futures was arriving in Oakland, was to leave the company as of summer 2002. And officials at the company were also actively weighing an end to their long-troubled relationship with their Oakland charters, E. C. Reems and Dolores Huerta. If School Futures could not get full control of the schools, by reducing the governing boards to mere advisory boards, it was likely to "return the schools to the community," in one official's words. But as abrupt as that transition might be, the schools were not likely to close. More likely, they would take the same ironic turn that some Dolores Huerta parents had demanded: the schools, along with their buildings, would be absorbed by the Oakland Unified School District.

•   •   •

Some months earlier, as the charter schools were nearing the end of their second year, Lillian Lopez went to lunch with an acquaintance on a brilliantly sunny Wednesday. Seated in a nearly empty basement café at Oakland's City Center plaza, they got to chatting about the schools.

In the past her greatest fear had been that the school might close. To her, that would have meant the loss of something truly precious. "It's like we won the lottery," she said then. "It's this little safe school in a horrible neighborhood. It's actually functioning like a community."

But now, in 2001, Lopez was consumed by the woes at Dolores Huerta. She recited them with a good-humored sort of irritation: School Futures' decision to oust Jorge Lopez, the school's third principal in two years, after doing little to support him; the woes of the governing-or-advisory board; the possibility that one of that board's members might take legal action against School Futures to win formal control; the possible gambit to pry the charter away from School Futures and fold it into the district. With the late-night calls of concern and complaint, and the anger directed her way by so many parents, the battles over the school had left her, at times, utterly exhausted.

Her lunch companion wondered how, with all the troubles, her son Alex was faring in the charter school. At the thought of her son and his cozy little school, Lopez brightened visibly.

"Good," she said. She thought for a moment, and smiled. "A lot better than he would have done in Jefferson."

Chapter 11

What We Should Do

In 1997, when Lillian Lopez and William Stewart set out to find better schools, they harbored no grand dreams of changing American education. They merely believed their children ought to have a decent and welcoming place to learn, without leaving their own neighborhoods and without forsaking public schooling. In the pursuit of that maddeningly elusive goal, Lopez and Stewart, like hundreds of thousands of other American parents, found their best hope in a daring experiment with a new type of school. By its third year, their experiment was turning out in ways that they could not have predicted. Nonetheless, their experience highlights both the unique strengths and the challenges of a charter school. That experience holds lessons about how our nation might build better schools for children like Alex and Malory and Asia and Ronrico and Jasmine and Nazim—children who have grown up with less, materially, than other American children, but who are no less deserving of a shot at comfort, choices, and happiness.

Charter schools are defined by their uniqueness. It is odd, therefore, to talk about a "typical" charter school. Moreover, since most charter schools are quite young, the research about them is largely preliminary, making it hard to talk about "results" in a meaningful way. In addition, the special focus of numerous charters—on the homeless, dropouts, or special-needs students, or themes like the arts—

further complicates the picture. Yet, with all that said, E. C. Reems and Dolores Huerta embody many features and patterns common to these upstart little academies, particularly in the inner city. Certainly, there are better charter schools. KIPP and the East Palo Alto Charter School demonstrate how much an urban charter can achieve. But—as indicated from observation, interviews, and the nascent research—a good number of inner-city charters likely have some important points in common with Reems and Huerta.

First, some positive qualities set these schools apart. They offer crucial things that their district neighbors often don't. They are welcoming and open; they are places where parents say they have a voice, after feeling shut out at district schools. They have a sense of community about them.[14] (Indeed, while parents generally become more involved in charters than they were in their previous schools,[15] some evidence suggests charters also draw off the most engaged parents from regular schools.) In charter schools, often, values and morality seem like more comfortable concepts than they might at a regular school. They are smaller, by far, than their neighbors, which permits many of their other good qualities. And, perhaps most important, they are safe. Many parents weigh this more heavily than anything else, and justly so. In all these ways—in smallness and community and safety and morality—E. C. Reems and Dolores Huerta were better schools, to the parents who chose them.

Moreover, the benefits of these two Oakland charters went beyond the four-hundred-odd students that they served. It didn't happen in exactly the way that some charter advocates might have hoped—where academically superior schools force the district to buckle down and improve through pure competition for kids and dollars. Events didn't go that way because, at least in their early years, these two charters never offered demonstrably better teaching than their neighbors. Nor were the numbers of children leaving the district a real financial threat; on the contrary, the departures to charters reduced overcrowding in the district and thus the pressure to build expensive new schools. Yet even so, the charters did provide political leverage for reform. Under a district superintendent who was friendly to an innovative small-schools plan, charters helped break a logjam against change. It appears that charters have had a similar impact in numerous districts, especially when they have drawn off meaningful amounts of district funding, though studies on the matter conflict.* In some cases, though not always, it seems that the changes districts make in response to charters carry real benefits for children.

Yet E. C. Reems and Dolores Huerta also embodied many of the weaknesses sometimes seen in urban charters. For example, they squandered potential advantages in assembling a strong staff. In a highly competitive market, charter schools enjoy some advantages in recruiting, keeping, and motivating good teachers. They have the freedom to create more livable working environments, and can add inducements like merit pay for excellent work. Indeed, creative teachers say they find charters attractive because they represent reform, freedom, and autonomy.[16] Yet both Oakland charters damaged their chances by starting their recruiting late, and then failing to treat teachers well through pay and contract arrangements. (That lousy treatment became a victory for the teachers' unions, which had issued dire warnings about what can happen without collective bargaining.) The schools also had far too little time to

---

* An authoritative Rand study in December 2001, "Rhetoric versus Reality," which was based on "an exhaustive review of the existing literature," takes an unenthusiastic view of the effect of charters on districts. The study argued that "it appears that the general stance of public schools with regard to charters is to ignore them or deny their relevance to the conventional public schools." Other studies differ. A report by the Manhattan Institute (Paul Teske, et al., "Does Charter School Competition Improve Traditional Public Schools?" June 2000) argued that "charter competition has not induced large changes in district-wide operations," but that "principals adopt more innovations at their school in direct proportion to the competitive enrollment pressure." A federal study (John Ericson and Debra Silverman, RPP International, "Challenge and Opportunity: The Impact of Charter Schools on School Districts," June 2001) reported that in response to charters, "all districts reported that they had changed the way they conducted their operations and more than half changed aspects of the education they offered in district schools." That included 61 percent of districts that made changes to their educational offerings. Eric Rofes ("How Are School Districts Responding to Charter School Laws and Charter Schools?" [Berkeley, CA: Policy Analysis for California Education, April 1998]) found the majority of districts making small changes, and a minority of them making significant changes.

plan their academic program, rules, and culture, and to forge a cogent vision among the staff. By the same token, for all the apparent benefits of independence, these charters did not prevail in the close-fought struggle for visionary, expert principals. Even without a rushed hiring process, the painful truth is that there simply aren't nearly enough brilliant principals to go around. And while freedom from the bureaucracy is widely seen as the charter's great advantage, that, too, carries a cost. The principals found themselves loaded down with financial, business, logistical, and administrative tasks that a district otherwise might have handled. Sometimes that came at great cost, such as when Reems failed to provide federally funded free breakfasts, and lost $200,000 over forgotten paperwork. (Financial woes comprise one of the most oft-cited problems for charters, but the hefty bankrolls of School Futures protected its charters from the ruin that might otherwise have resulted.)

The Reems Academy in particular also confirmed the fears of many charter critics when, especially in its first year, it drove away special-education students. The national evidence, while contested, suggests that the Oakland school may not be alone in avoiding such hard-to-teach children.[17] In addition, parents at that school pushed to kick out every family that didn't fulfill its volunteer hours, and a number of them voiced support for parent-delivered corporal punishment. Those facts suggested that the school should have worked harder to balance its unusual levels of parent involvement and control with guidance by educators. (There is no evidence that charters are more hospitable to corporal punishment, but it certainly is an issue that such schools should be aware of as they consider the meaning of parent control.) Finally, the schools found themselves thrown into chaos repeatedly amid disputes over who was really in charge—a frequently cited problem at charter schools, especially those without powerful governing boards. Forming boards can prove troublesome for charters,[18] but Reems and Huerta were rare in going without governing boards for two years.

Despite such solid grounds as the absence of a governing board, the Oakland district was loath to shut down these charters. These little schools enjoyed vehement support from many parents, as well as from an influential community group and a well-known church. Moreover, the school board would have faced charges of hypocrisy if it had moved to close schools that already performed at or above the level of the district's own schools. For similar reasons—absent scandals of finance and mismanagement—school boards nationwide have been hesitant to shut down low-performing charters. When boards hesitate, though, they do charter advocates no favors, because they are removing a key argument in favor of charters: that if the school doesn't deliver on its performance promises, it will cease to exist.

Yet despite only modest early performance, the Oakland academies remained fully enrolled. Nationally, too, parents are lining up to join charters, most of which are filled to capacity and have waiting lists.[19] In fact, despite quite mediocre practice in many Reems and Huerta classrooms, parents generally seemed fairly satisfied with the schools. That raises questions about another key argument of charter advocates, called "market accountability." This theory holds that parents will force charters to perform well by pulling their kids out of bad schools and sending them to good ones. Among other things, that idea relies on two questionable assumptions: that parents will be sufficiently sophisticated consumers of education, and that enough school choices will become available.

Arguably, the central issue is the bottom-line performance of the children at these schools. This is not the only valid purpose for schools, but I believe it must rank as the most important. As the preceding chapters demonstrate, E. C. Reems and Dolores Huerta—like nearly every charter school—were created at the cost of enormous effort and struggle. For School Futures and its benefactor, John Walton; for the district; for parents and teachers and the school board and the state and still others, the building of these charter schools took a great investment of time, political capital, emotional energy, and cash. Had they returned academic gain?

At these two schools, as at charters across the country, it was too soon to say anything definitive. It is not unusual for charters to spend their first year, or even their first few years, struggling for stability as an organization before they develop academic strength. To be sure, School Futures had suggested it could deliver academic superiority with little delay; clearly, to judge by the first two years, that didn't happen. This should have come as little surprise, considering that the charters weren't doing much instructionally to set themselves apart from their district neighbors. Perhaps more important, however, there was reason to question whether E. C. Reems and Dolores Huerta were building the capacity to improve themselves academically. Neither school employed a qualified, experienced instructor to lead teachers. On the other hand, School Futures' hiring of an instructional chief in 2001 suggested some promise in that area.

The key point, however, is that neither school took real advantage of the extraordinary latitude a charter provides. Some of the best urban schools in America are charters. Such schools follow the lead of KIPP, East Palo Alto Charter, and their philosophical kin. At the helm of such schools stand principals who are also excellent teachers. Those principals carry in their minds a precise sense of what an excellent lesson looks like, and frequently, those principals retain some teaching duties. They act as true instructional leaders. Moreover, excellent charter schools benefit from a well-defined vision that the entire staff understands and shares. That clarity of vision, in turn, stems from extensive and careful planning *before* the school opens. (KIPP, for example, gives its new principals a year of training and planning time as part of its national expansion.) The shared vision also results from a recruiting process where principals search for teachers who are not only smart and dedicated, but also philosophically aligned with the school's mission and methods. Teachers in these schools see instruction as their key, defining task and focus serious energy on continual improvement of their craft. In addition, many such schools start quite small, often with only a couple of classes at a single grade level. These schools also sweep in resources—including large numbers of adults—to support an intensive approach, often including substantial extra time in class. At such thoughtfully designed schools, built around a coherent, powerful, instruction-focused mission, students stand a good chance to make real educational gains.

Not all charter schools follow that model, of course. Nationally, the evidence on student performance in charters is mixed. A handful of early studies offer arguments on both sides of the question of whether charters typically improve student performance. Moreover, it is crucial to note that a charter school is not an instructional strategy—a "reform"—in itself. It is a new structure for a school that dictates nothing about what happens in the classroom, though it may permit a greater range of possibility there. With those disclaimers, it seems fair to say that despite some standouts, the bulk of charter schools have yet to demonstrate clear academic advantages over regular schools. Nonetheless, some researchers see reasons for cautious optimism as these schools mature.* Perhaps, then, the real question for charter schools in general is the same as for E. C. Reems and Dolores Huerta: Where will they end up when they have matured a bit? Will they find stability as comfortable, homey schools that are not educationally exceptional? Or will they be something more?

---

* Studies of charter school performance are, of course, tentative because most charter schools are so young. Nonetheless, numerous studies have turned up conflicting data on the subject of charter school performance as compared to regular public schools serving similar student populations, suggesting that charters have yet to demonstrate clear academic advantages. Most up-to-date, as of this writing, was the Rand study. Rand found that "achievement results in charter schools are mixed, but they suggest that charter-school performance improves after the first year of operation. None of the studies suggests that charter-school achievement outcomes are dramatically better or worse on average than those of conventional public schools." Nonetheless, the report noted that "parental satisfaction levels are high in virtually all voucher and charter programs studied." Various state studies (for example: Jerry Horn and Gary Miron, "Evaluation of the Michigan Public School Academy Initiative," January 1999; Miron and Nelson, "Autonomy in Exchange for Accountability: An Initial Study of Pennsylvania Charter Schools," October 2000) have found evidence, at turns, that charter students outperformed or underperformed students in host districts. As for the question of curricular innovation, at least two studies (Christopher Lubieski, "Charter School Innovations in Theory and Practice," 2001; Horn and Miron, 1999) suggest this is an area where charters have fallen short of early hopes.

If it emerges that charters, and particularly inner-city charters, have not risen substantially above their neighbors in academic performance, the challenge for them will become all the more urgent. Legislatures and voters may not tolerate investing so much time, effort, and money without meaningful academic gains. Charters must keep their key promise: to educate children well. Several key changes would markedly increase their chances of success in that effort.

The charter school idea is of immense value in education. For people with robust, tradition-breaking ideas about how to make a school work—particularly in places where schools generally don't—the charter concept stands as a beacon. In a charter, educators have a chance to realize their visions without battling a system that, at every turn, has the capacity to take away bits of the school's specialness. For these reasons, charters can help fulfill one of education's most pressing needs: the creation of a workplace that will attract skilled, sharp teachers and principals. Yet if the Oakland experience teaches a single lesson, it is that, at least in academics, there is nothing about the word *charter* that makes a school instantly or magically good. The charter, really, provides nothing more than freedom—a blank slate—combined, ideally, with strong accountability. A charter school merely reflects the ideas and the quality of effort behind it. In many urban charter schools, as in many of their district neighbors, that powerful, coherent vision is lacking.

There is a danger here: namely, that the power of the charter idea could be dissipated in a sentimental movement that goes the way of the alternative schools of the sixties and seventies. Often based on innovative thinking, those schools cast a momentary glow—a time of real benefit for some children, largely thanks to young, creative teachers willing to work extraordinarily hard in schools that embodied the newest, most exciting educational ideas. Today, the alternative schools are a pale shadow of decades ago, remembered mainly as a wonderful, sweet, but largely obsolescent period piece. Charter schools could face a similar danger; though the bulk of those that already exist may be here to stay, the opportunity to create new ones could dry up quickly. Many charter schools run on the heat of a bright new idea. Particularly with the high costs of start-up, including facility renovations and purchases or leases, they absorb hundreds of millions of dollars in government and philanthropic grants. For the moment, their academic results are largely unknown. (And even after the "too-soon-to-tell" period ends, their results will be debated sharply, given the difficulty of comparing charter and non-charter students.) Yet it seems plausible to imagine that with such an enormous investment of effort and cash, if the record of urban charters proves lacking—or if only a comparative handful of children benefit—charters will quickly lose their luster, and with it their public and philanthropic support. Ultimately, charters could come to be remembered like the alternative schools: a pleasant experiment that didn't really last.

The charter idea is too valuable for that to happen. I believe, however, that by adopting a few key principles—some of which would require significant changes—states could heighten the chances of success, the wide benefits, and the equity of charter schools. Namely:

- **A new focus on quality.** States could improve the effectiveness of charter schools markedly by setting up a system that focuses more clearly on high-quality teaching and learning. Today, a large proportion of charters are awarded by local school boards or by "authorizers" such as universities, in a process that sometimes rests more on politics than on good schooling. Particularly before local school boards, which frequently view themselves as under attack by the very charter schools they are asked to approve, the process can be painfully political. In other places, financial arrangements allow local districts to make substantial money from the charters they approve through "administrative" fees. And in places like California, state law has placed the burden on school boards to approve charters unless the board can demonstrate that the school is truly unworkable. Such arrangements apparently rest on the notion of permitting an

experiment which can be shut down later if it fails to produce a high-quality school. Some, in fact, rely largely on parents to force bad schools to close by simply leaving, and
thus causing per-student funds to dry up. Experience, however, teaches that closures over academic quality (rather
than financial or legal problems) are quite rare. Meanwhile,
districts complain of the added workload of monitoring
charters, an important task that often amounts to an un-
funded mandate from the state.

An independent board to approve charters and then oversee them could remedy many of these problems. Numerous
experts see the best hopes in boards whose sole purposes are
the creation and monitoring of charter schools. An independent state charter board, appointed by the governor or the
state department of education, would help to remove the
battle over such schools from the local political fray and
from the financial inducements local boards face. Such
boards would implement an entirely new approval and funding process directed at improving the quality of education in
charter schools. For such boards to work well, however, they
must have a well-defined mission focused on school quality,
as well as adequate funding. The existence of a single-purpose
state board is not an automatic ticket to strong schools.

- **Higher standards and fair funding.** The current arrangement for funding charters—where schools receive relatively
  little money until they actually open—hampers the key task of
  planning extensively and carefully *before* children arrive.
  (Without funds, schools cannot pay the salaries and other
  costs associated with that planning process.) Moreover, even
  when the school opens, many states give charters less funding than regular schools, in many cases, or fail to cover facility costs. A new approach to approving and funding
  charters could help to fix these problems. Charter oversight
  boards would work via a two-step process. First, charter
  candidates would present a detailed outline of their instructional plans. Schools with convincing proposals would win
  substantial planning grants—enough to support a small staff

through one or two years of planning the school. (The logic here is that charter organizers ought to be focused primarily on core education matters, and that only charters with strong educational programs ought to open. Some states, as of 2001, already were wisely moving to increase such planning grants.) After a planning period, candidates would return with a full charter, which the oversight board would examine closely for its educational coherence. Only those that met high standards in that regard would receive approval. Once approved, charters would get their fair share of per-student funding, including facilities money. After approval, charters would be required to demonstrate that they had made a good-faith effort to notify families in their community of their existence, and of their vision, in terms parents can understand easily.

It seems likely that this new bargain with charters would reduce the total number of schools approved, while increasing the amount of money supplied to those that meet the standards, resulting in a more intelligent use of largely the same dollars. And it would help to avoid the process of approving, and later perhaps closing, schools based on mediocre ideas—a process painful to families and educators alike. The counterargument, of course, is that approving fewer charter schools will keep more children locked in low-performing or dangerous district schools. This is an achingly potent argument. Yet I believe that an investment in the quality of charter schools now will pay off better, for more children, over many years.

- **Better support.** States and cities can take other steps to assure that charters fulfill their potential as laboratories for better education. For one, states or state-supported charter consortiums should offer a menu of reasonably priced services to handle tasks that are not central to the schools' mission, and which charter schools often perform poorly. These might include payroll, accounting, purchasing, transportation, maintenance, cleaning, food service, and legal work, among other items. No charter should be forced to purchase any of these, but having them easily available would free schools to focus on their central mission of instruction. Some states and communities, fortunately, are already moving in this direction. (In some places this means purchasing services from host districts, but often mutual distrust or the district's bureaucratic problems prevent this relationship from thriving.)

Of course, the real work of a school rests on how teachers work with students, and what they teach. It seems bizarre that after laboring for a century to devise better ways to teach our children, we now see the best hopes in setting schools completely on their own. Charter schools should be independent without being isolated. High-quality, ongoing professional training for teachers is irreplaceable, as is access to expertise, new ideas, and materials. Consortiums or even districts could offer such crucial support, which charters would be free—but not required—to purchase.

- **Tougher accountability.** All this new support for charters ought not to come for free, however. The same state agency that would approve the charters would be charged with maintaining tough accountability—not just in handling money and teacher credentials properly, but in what counts most: high-quality work in the classroom. These boards would also closely monitor the process of admitting students, checking that charter schools are not avoiding special-needs children. Likewise, these boards might review expulsions of students, a step that currently gets very little oversight in some places. Such boards ought to have unlimited rights of unannounced visits to schools and should conduct detailed reviews at least every two years. These boards should also make their expectations—that is, how the schools will be graded—quite clear. Schools found wanting in their teaching and learning practices would have to draft improvement plans, complete with fixed deadlines, and then meet those plans in order to stay open. (This would be an improvement over some accountability systems, where no middle ground exists between doing nothing and shutting a school down.[20]) Yet such reviews would include a supportive aspect, where skilled educators would offer principals recommendations for better instruction and expert professional training. These same detailed reviews of a school's practice also would provide the basis for another as-yet unmet promise of the charter movement: the sharing of effective ideas hatched in the freer atmosphere of the charter schools.

No matter how successful individual charter schools become, they still would represent an interesting but terribly limited experiment if the only children who benefited were the 1 or 2 percent who actually attended a charter school. This leads to key questions: How can other schools for urban children be made better, and what part can charters play in that effort?

Answering those questions requires a few moments' thought about what, really, is wrong with urban schooling. The current conversation, in the media particularly, has not been especially enlightening on this point. The press and public often view urban school systems like corporations which, if they are not producing good bottom-line numbers, simply require new and better management. Few seem troubled by the obvious flaw in this analysis—that despite the astonishing regularity of ousting and replacing superintendents, not one inner-city school system has generated the "results" of a typical suburban system. Other popular scapegoats include supposed legions of lazy, uncaring teachers, who wear that label despite laboring in arduous conditions for much less pay than they could earn elsewhere. (It is, however, absolutely true that inner-city kids, who need good teaching the most, are denied their fair share of the best teachers.) And still other popular explanations link poor urban school performance closely to the admittedly daunting organizational woes of the big urban school districts. Such systems undoubtedly hurt children when they waste money and fail to hire and retain good teachers and deliver books and materials to classrooms. Yet, as the urban charter experience teaches, creating an effective classroom takes much more than freedom from the arthritic creakings of a giant bureaucracy.

For these reasons, the frequent talk of "failing school systems" in the inner city sounds a bit simplistic to me. Are there any "succeeding" inner-city systems? Are there any whose graduates are as well prepared as their suburban counterparts for a competitive career marketplace? Are there any that have provided the same range of life choices open to those who can afford the ultimate "school choice"—the ability to live in a wealthy neighborhood or pay for an exclusive private school? The answer to these questions, surely, is no. We must therefore look beyond the rhetoric of simple "accountability" in our existing system and ask what more profound changes we must make in order to do more for children in neighborhoods of poverty.

The reasons why so many children aren't learning in inner-city schools remain the subject of debate and controversy, and rightly fill volumes of their own. But many of the reasons are not mysterious, though they go beyond the commonly discussed problems of lacking materials, inadequately trained teachers, and crumbling buildings. For one, many children simply don't show up at school regularly, whether because they choose to go truant, have to baby-sit for younger siblings while a parent works, or live in families marred by such chaos that their parents don't send them to school. Other home problems take more insidious forms; in homes with few books, or where parents don't read to children, youngsters are not exposed to letters and words enough. Many children who speak no language other than English arrive at school with painfully tiny vocabularies. Disciplinary chaos in the classroom, too, may have some roots at home, especially when parents don't demand good behavior from their children or don't support a teacher's efforts to instill discipline. That distrust between home and school may have entirely rational roots; many parents learned to doubt whether a sometimes segregated, often troubled school system had their best interests at heart when they themselves were children. But the result is a school where children can cause mischief rather than learn.

Teachers, frustrated or exhausted by a daunting workplace, sometimes quit trying hard. Some become nasty or unfeeling. Others turn on their colleagues, even separating into racially divided camps. Still others adopt patronizing attitudes, acting as if any work at all from a poor child is wonderful. And even the children themselves, in many urban schools, play a caustic role when they mock other children for studying. Any solution that is to improve urban schools must deal, somehow, with all of these problems. Charter schools can be a part of that.

As Lillian Lopez knew, there is probably nothing more important than the skills of a child's classroom teacher. For a school as a whole, it is the principal who makes the greatest difference. Our systems must create incentives to draw the best teachers and principals to the schools where they are needed most, and to keep them there. Obviously, pay is one of those incentives. Likewise, schools need to motivate teachers to keep doing excellent work, and must be able and willing to remove teachers who remain ineffective after high-quality support. Charter schools can be a proving ground for merit pay and other strategies to motivate teachers, and their existence can help to break through ossified resistance to any but the most traditional contracts.

Charter schools also can play a role in creating a different school atmosphere—one more attractive to teachers. Currently, teachers in inner-city schools complain, frequently and justly, about a workplace and schedule that treats them with little respect, sometimes including supervision requirements that prevent them from going to the bathroom for hours at a time. More corrosive, however, is the sense of being involved in a fruitless enterprise. (Imagine being a surgeon in a hospital where most of the patients died.) Charter schools can pave the way as smaller schools where adults and children are treated with respect, and where, one hopes, innovative approaches combined with substantial support will lead to greater educational success.

I believe, however, that achieving that elusive sort of success in inner-city schools—large or small, charter or not—will require far more than mere merit pay, bonuses, or even improved teacher and principal recruiting. I believe that achieving such success will take a willingness to recognize that schooling is a vastly larger, more complex task in inner cities than in wealthy communities. Currently, as measured by the extra time, effort, and cash that we put into inner-city schools, the task there might be presumed to be, say, 10 percent larger than in the suburbs. But the size of the disparities demonstrates the absurdity of that figure. (For example: In the affluent city of Piedmont, entirely contained within the borders of Oakland, fully 88 percent of ninth graders read at the national average, and a mere 0.6 percent drop out of high school. In Oakland, by contrast, only 15 percent read at the national average, and 22 percent drop out.) If this country is serious about bringing inner-city kids into the game, it must make more dramatic changes than the ones currently on the table.

I believe that inner-city education must be redefined not as a 10 percent bigger job, but perhaps 200 percent bigger. Effective charter schools like KIPP are leading the way in this effort. Such schools act on the understanding that children who come from homes with few books, and whose parents have limited education, need more effort to reach the same goals as more fortunate children. These schools recognize, for instance, that eight A.M. to three P.M., five days a week, for 180 days a year, isn't enough. They are expanding the day, week, and year to include more academic class time. They also make no apologies for an explicit effort to develop habits of hard work and commitment that are so rarely demanded, or seen, at other urban schools. Such innovation, in schedule and culture, can be achieved more easily at charters than at district schools. Yet, strong schools also resist the notion of innovation for its own sake. Not all innovations are improvements, and some excellent strategies may look quite traditional.

Our strategies must transcend a collection of superb model schools. Improvements in urban education cannot rely in the long term and on a wide scale on individual teachers and principals who work extraordinarily long hours. While the norm at superstar schools, this is unlikely to form the basis for wide reform. Here, however, a serious investment can make a real difference—not throwing money at the problem, but providing proven reforms. With a longer school day and more personal attention, it may take many more adults to make an effective urban school; that will be expensive. Charter schools will not be alone in demonstrating effective ideas in this area, but they certainly can play an important pilot role. Again, however, accountability counts here. The public doesn't just have a right to expect results for additional investment; it must demand them.

To drive toward truly widespread achievement for inner-city kids, however, I believe that we must be more ambitious still. I believe that together with inducing good teachers to work in the inner city, this nation must be more willing to share its currently best classrooms—in its more prosperous communities—with the children who need them most. In the book *All Together Now*, Richard Kahlenberg and Richard Leone argue persuasively that every American child—including every poor child—has a right to an education in what they call a middle-class school, a very different agenda from the forced busing of a generation ago. They offer compelling evidence that economic integration, using schools of choice, will accomplish what racial integration did not. They point out that poor kids perform better in middle-class schools than middle-class kids do in schools of concentrated poverty. Our current efforts to improve schools for poor kids, they lucidly explain, amount to attempting a better execution of the "separate but equal" doctrine. I think this critique makes common sense. How much harder do we make the struggles of both teachers and children when we concentrate all the least-prepared students into the same schools? Can we not see the merit and beauty in Horace Mann's notion of economically integrated "common schools"?

Of course, threaded through all of this is the issue of political will. It has never been easy to build a consensus in this nation to invest heavily in the needs of its poorest citizens. And now, that challenge looms even larger than it has in the past. As I write this, in November 2001, national priorities are profoundly altered from just a few months earlier. The events of September 11, 2001, instantly relegated the education of poor children—until that day among our most urgent concerns—to a secondary matter. Yet, in another sense, that work has become more urgent still. Terrorists seek to fracture a society; good schooling can bring it together. Perhaps more than anything else we can do, educating the urban poor will help to make us "one nation, indivisible." It is a battle we cannot afford to lose.

Not long ago, the *New York Times Magazine* ran a cover piece by the able journalist James Traub entitled "What No School Can Do." The article, which caused a stir among educators and thinkers of every stripe, argued that schools do more to mirror than to change social circumstances. Drawing largely on data from New York City, Traub claimed that good schools don't do much to help poor kids, and bad schools don't hurt them much, either. The argument didn't just stick a thumb in the eye of urban teachers; it scorned what I have called in this book the American dream. It suggested that public schools no longer can fulfill their key role in a democracy: equipping children to thrive, as long as they are willing to work hard, but regardless of where they were born or how much money their parents have. It suggested that now, in an age when we are attempting the unprecedented task of providing an academic education to virtually all children, the schools are largely irrelevant.

I disagree. I believe that schools can and must play a central role in educating those communities that now stand removed from the opportunities of the world's wealthiest society. To be sure, I believe that schools ought not stand alone in this struggle. Government at all its levels, as well as churches and community groups, can do more. We must work harder to help poor communities grow jobs and solid families and realistic hopes for a decent future. We must work harder to extend early childhood education, to strengthen families, to create more jobs, to bring peace to streets and homes, and to help people avoid or quit dangerous, addictive drugs. Every step we take in that direction is a step toward making the work of teachers and schools easier.

At the heart of the action, however, lie schools, and particularly schools that live outside current definitions and boundaries. These schools, contrary to the pessimistic claim, can make a difference. I base this belief on more than just the hundreds of good schools, and handfuls of great ones, that are defying actuarial predictions of failure calculated by race and income. I base my belief on an understanding of the different compact that schools and families can fashion in places where parents and teachers and principals achieve unity on a school's vision. Such schools can build on that unity to forge an ethic of striving, of hard work toward grand goals, that so many urban schools lack today. These good schools don't just educate children; they make communities and families stronger. Charter schools, with their promise to alter definitions and boundaries, belong at the center of this fight.

Ultimately, I believe we must ask ourselves: Just how serious are we about making changes for the better in our inner cities? How much are we willing to alter the way schools look and behave? How hard are we willing to work, and how much are we willing to sacrifice, to open the horizons of children born into material poverty? How much are the comfortable of this nation willing to share?

As we ponder those questions, I hope that we will hold young people like Alex, Asia, Ronrico, Malory, Jasmine, and Nazim close to our thoughts. They are our children.

In ways subtle and grand, the effort to build better schools in Oak-land transformed the life of every person involved. Sometimes, too, those changes upended common assumptions about schools of choice and "regular" district schools. As of the end of 2001, this is where the experience left some of the people whose stories are told in these pages.

Valentín Del Rio, the young, dedicated, ill-prepared teacher from E. C. Reems's first year, carried through on his promise to find a job in the Oakland school district. He was hired to teach fifth grade at Markham Elementary, a moderate-sized school near Eastmont Mall. By standard definitions, it was a high-poverty school—nine out of ten children qualified for a free lunch—and it scored a one on the state's one-to-ten performance scale. Markham suffered from the same sort of distrust between parent and school so commonly found in the tough parts of Oakland. On a visit there, it was little surprise, passing through the office, to find a mother livid with accusations that a teacher had twisted her child's finger.

Yet Del Rio had found a home. His physical situation was a marked improvement: a larger (if portable) classroom with its own heater and air conditioner, plus a good-sized play yard where the kids could release their energy. "I got it made," he chortled. His skills at maintaining discipline, learned mostly by trial and error, had improved enormously. Turnout at the school's open house night was strong, and parents of his students were supportive. He also appreciated his largely Latino class. It was true, he conceded, that the staff at Reems had been more united than his Markham colleagues were. But charter schools, he had concluded, were no good for first-year teachers, comparing the experience to being thrown into a lion pit with no weapons. Here at Markham, he said, nearly everything was better—and he never had to worry about whether he would get paid on time. As of 2001, he was preparing to start a two-year teacher credential program, as a foundation for what could turn into a potential career in education.

In another switch that seemed to favor the much-maligned district, Donald Evans—the star principal of School Futures' most impressive charter, in East Palo Alto—was successfully wooed by Dennis Chaconas, the Oakland superintendent. Evans spent the 2000–2001 school year as principal of Burckhalter, a smallish elementary school not far from E. C. Reems. Chaconas had always planned to bring Evans inside the central administration, but wanted him to serve as a principal for a year in hopes that he would see how troubled the system was. Oddly, however, Evans seemed to learn the opposite lesson. In an experience that reversed the supposed rules of charters and districts, Evans cheerily announced that he was more effective as an Oakland public school principal than as the head of a charter school. In an observation that may have had something to do with his status as a golden child in the district, Evans explained that all the extraneous business—building maintenance and gardening and such—got taken care of with a simple call downtown. (With dilapidated buildings and frozen boilers common in the district, one wondered whether every principal had it so easy.) Free to focus on the central matter of instruction, Evans liked his job just fine, and left it only reluctantly in the summer of 2001 to take a position downtown, overseeing a number of smaller elementary schools throughout the district.

If there was one person whose new job made hash of everyone's previous understandings, though, it was Carole Quan, the short-time Oakland superintendent who had left OCO and Jefferson's HOPE teachers so frustrated. Quan, in semiretirement, started working part-time for an Oakland nonprofit group called ARC Associates. The group won a grant to establish a sort of clearinghouse to provide technical assistance to Oakland's charter schools, and the project became Quan's sole focus. To some, it was stunning to see Quan—who as superintendent had been criticized as a defender of the existing system—helping charter schools and talking about services without bureaucracy. Quan explained that once one stepped outside the system, things looked a little different. When she was superintendent, she conceded, she saw the debate with OCO as a distraction from the main priority of reforming the big system. Now she saw that discussion as valuable, as a tool to involve parents in their children's education. And perhaps, she said, these little schools could improve children's education in meaningful ways.

As for Mike Hopkins, the principal who undercut the original small schools plan at Jefferson, retirement arrived unceremoniously. The new superintendent, Dennis Chaconas, removed him from the Jefferson principal's post in 2000, moving him to a classroom teaching position at another school. A year later, Hopkins retired, a month short of his maximum potential pension.

At OCO, meanwhile, the education battle took a series of turns, ultimately ending in success with the creation of the small autonomous schools the HOPE teachers had fought for. Matt Hammer had left the organization to head its sister in San Jose, but that didn't mean he had left the fight for better schools. The San Jose organization PACT helped to force the departure of a local school superintendent whom many parents considered ineffective. Much as he had done in Oakland, Hammer was working to help people see the education situation for what it was: a crisis. He had gained more than just experience in Oakland, though; he had gained perspective as well. Charter schools alone, he now felt, did not force change in the larger system. But paired with effective community organizing, they could.

A sad story surrounded Bob Latson, the jovial, ever-present father who had brokered peace between School Futures and the E. C. Reems staff in the school's first year. Latson, one of the most beloved figures at the school, had been arrested in the late spring of 2000 for savagely beating and terrorizing one of his girlfriends. In interviews, he did not deny the incident, but quibbled with details of the case against him and defended it as a crime of passion. On November 29, 2000, at 7:50 P.M., while at Santa Rita County Jail, he crumpled to the floor of his cell. A deputy who witnessed his collapse from the other side of the housing "pod" radioed for help, and paramedics responded to the jail. They began CPR and heart defibrillation, but by the time they loaded him into the ambulance, Latson had no respiration and no pulse. At 8:48 P.M., at a hospital near the jail, he was pronounced dead. The coroner reported no evidence of foul play.

News of his death cannonballed through the community that had populated the school's first year—the Laura Armstrong school. His funeral was so well attended that mourners spilled out onto the street, and those who had already paid respects had to be asked to leave so that others could view Latson's body and say their final good-byes. As the service ended, one person seemed unable to tear herself away, returning again and again to the coffin. It was not Latson's mother, nor his sister, nor even a longtime girlfriend. It was Margarita Soto, the woman with whom he had joined forces to distribute food and good will, first at Webster Elementary, and then at E. C. Reems. It was, for her, as if she had lost a brother. Outside, as she mourned, her son was keeping Bob Latson's son company. In their year at E. C. Reems they, too, had become the closest of friends.

Mercifully, less trauma accompanied the next years for William Stewart, his girlfriend Jasmine McGehee, and the four children they were raising together. Stewart did have some drama in his life, to be sure—a custody battle with his late wife's family over daughter Malory, with school as one of the inevitable battlegrounds. (Malory was not getting good grades, and her late mother's family charged that

Stewart was not doing enough to get special help for her.) Yet he and McGehee remained tolerant of, if not thrilled with, the performance of the school. He wasn't around as much, having found a job at a pest-control company where he worked long hours, and his main complaints about the school concerned field trips that returned late. Overall, he gave the school a C-plus; he could see it trying, but felt the curriculum was not as advanced as he had expected. He was not pleased with the discipline problems in Malory's class. But he figured a more stable set of teachers would improve the school over time, and he was happy to see more attention to physical education. He was also glad to see the school making plans for a ninth grade, because he did not want to throw McGehee's oldest, Ronrico, into the uncertain world of the district high schools. Ultimately, he and McGehee had the opportunity to vote with their feet, and they voted to stay at E. C. Reems for a third year.

As for the famously troubled child of Asia's class, Nazim Casey, life remained all too eventful. Expelled, for all intents and purposes, in the second week of the school's second year, Nazim enrolled at Burbank Elementary, a short walk from home, a school coincidentally run by the former principal of an Oakland charter school. Nazim was assigned a teacher out of his grandfather's happiest dreams: a no-nonsense, male disciplinarian who also commanded a competition-level crossing-guard squadron under full-fledged military strictness. The teacher had inscribed a daunting seventeen rules on the board ("1. Stop fighting and talking a lot. . . . 13. Keep hands and feets to yourself. . . . 17. Stay out of other people buisnes. . . ."), but he also displayed a genuine caring for Nazim. Nonetheless, Nazim continued to make noise and cause mischief with his classmates. Administrators soon placed Nazim in a schoolwide therapy group of sorts for behavior problems, which made little obvious difference. What truly proved essential, however, was the district's remarkable decision, after a number of flare-ups, to assign Nazim his own full-time aide. Young, charming, and pretty, she rather miraculously kept Nazim focused on an academic target. She was aided in that campaign by a new weapon: drugs. Nazim's grandfather had long opposed drugging, but a visit to a support group for grandparents raising children had changed that. There he picked up a pamphlet that described the behaviors of attention deficit/hyperactivity disorder. It seemed to have been written with Nazim in mind. Casey was particularly struck by the mention of children who raise their hand in class for questions even when they have no idea of the answer.

The doctors prescribed a couple of drugs for Nazim, the most potent a Ritalin look-alike called Adderall. For a time, the change in Nazim's behavior was quite noticeable, but it seemed to wear off over months. He finished a fair year at Burbank, but in summer school he ran into trouble. In the later weeks of summer, on a day when his teacher happened to be absent, he got into a fight over a basketball foul, and then tried to pull away from staffers who were escorting him to the principal. Thanks in part to his history of such trouble, and the low tolerance of misbehavior in summer school, he was expelled. In the fall of 2001, in an attempt at an entirely new approach, he enrolled at a private Catholic school near his home, his tuition covered by charity. There, the principal and his teacher made strong commitments to help him, despite his difficulties. His behavior, however, remained a struggle, and his survival at the school was not assured.

The three dismissed principals of the E. C. Reems and Dolores Huerta Academies all had tough stories to tell. For John Cleveland, the charters represented his last job in education. Shortly after his brief tenure at the two schools came to an end, the state revoked Cleveland's teaching credential. The action apparently resulted not from the numerous grievances generated in his short tenure at School Futures, but from a sexual harassment case in his previous job, in a San Francisco school. The state action prohibited him from working in a public school unless he could get the ruling reversed, a move that he voiced no interest in pursuing. (Both he and his sister, Bishop Ernestine Reems, attributed his workplace woes to discrimination against African Americans. Bishop Reems asked that Cleveland's accomplishments, including the many highly successful graduates of the Hope Academy, be noted along with his shortcomings.) On July 1, 2000, John Cleveland officially retired from education, and later began working in a real estate office in the Oakland hills. Prominently displayed on the office coffee table were thick, glossy-bound booklets of test scores for every school in the area.

Felicitas Coates, the first principal of Dolores Huerta Learning Academy, rejoined the district following her firing by School Futures. She taught in the independent study department, teaching high schoolers who did not attend the regular schools for reasons ranging from pregnancy and motherhood to safety fears. She was planning to retire in January 2002, and was entertaining offers to teach in Thailand, China, and Spain. She looked back on her brief charter experience as a "total mistake."

For charter heartache, though, few could match Laura Armstrong. It took her more than a year to recover from seeing her dream die at the school named for her guiding star, Bishop Ernestine Reems. Ultimately, she decided that E. C. Reems was not the school she had been destined to oversee, and decided to open another charter school. At the same time, she wanted to abandon Reems's church, but could not tear herself away. So in her personal world, she did her best to forgive. So great was that effort that, apart from necessities, she hardly left her house for months after her firing.

In September 2000, the onetime principal returned to teaching in Hayward, the suburb where she lived, but she had not given up what she believed to be her destiny. Still backed by some faithful parents and teachers from E. C. Reems, she submitted a new charter in Oakland, much of its language lifted directly from a sample charter distributed by an agency that gives charter schools technical help. Her dreams went further than a single charter, though; this school would be the first in a network controlled by a nonprofit corporation that she would start. Those academies, she explained, would serve as "training schools" at which teachers would become highly skilled. But the charter was rejected; once again, Armstrong's school dream had disappeared. Ultimately, she contented herself teaching near her home in Hayward. "I'm ready to go back in the system," she said. "I'm tired."

In June of 2001, events in Armstrong's family helped her to complete what she called a "full circle." Armstrong's brother was forced to put his four-year-old daughter into foster care. Armstrong and her mother intervened and persuaded child protection authorities to award custody to Armstrong's mother. Armstrong, who had visited the girl frequently at her brother's in Sacramento, already had established herself as the girl's godmother. Now, she assumed a role closer to actual motherhood. Armstrong—whose surgery in 2000 had left her unable to bear children—began visiting Arizona frequently to spend more time with the girl. By the end of the year, Armstrong was pondering a plan to move back to Phoenix. Leaving Oakland would mean the end of a divinely wrought journey, but after two years of depression, pain, and healing, Armstrong was nearly prepared to take that step.

"I was led by God to live out here for the purpose of attending this church and teaching in this private school," she said, referring to the long-defunct Hope Academy. "I almost feel like my time is just about up here." She could not leave, she said, until she had recovered completely from the trauma of her separation from E. C. Reems. Now, though, she had a new mission. A day before New Year's, she remarked that she looked forward to becoming a "second mother" to her goddaughter.

"I think," Armstrong said, "I have a very important role to play in her life."

Endnotes

Introduction

1. Bruce Fuller, "The Public Square, Big or Small," in *Inside Charter Schools*, Bruce Fuller, ed. (Cambridge, MA: Harvard University Press, 2001), page xviii

2. Steve Farkas, Jean Johnson, and Ann Duffet, with Patrick Foley, "Trying to Stay Ahead of the Game: Superintendents and Principals Talk About School Leadership," Public Agenda, 2001, page xix

3. David Tyack and Larry Cuban, *Tinkering Toward Utopia* (Cambridge, MA: Harvard University Press, 1997), page xx

4. Charles W. Eliot, quoted in *Left Back*, Diane Ravitch, ed. (New York: Simon and Schuster, 2000) 87, page xxii

5. James Earl Russell of Teachers College, quoted in *Left Back*, page xxii

CHAPTER 2: The Taste of Hope

6. David Tyack, "The One Best System," page 34
7. All quoted in "The One Best System," page 34

CHAPTER 6: Weak Links

8. U.S. Department of Education, "Charter Schools and Students with Disabilities: Review of Existing Data," November 1998. At *www.ed.gov/pubs/chartdisab/enroll.html*, page 164

CHAPTER 7: Comparisons

9. E. Bettinger, *The Effect of Charter Schools on Charter Students and Public Schools* (Occasional Paper No. 4) (New York City: National Center for the Study of Privatization in Education, Teachers College, Columbia University, 1999), page 199

10. The National Bureau of Economic Research, "Would School Choice Change the Teaching Profession?" August 2000. At *http://papers.nber.org/papers/W7866*, page 200

11. Christopher Lubienski, "Charter School Innovations in Theory and Practice" (a paper presented at the Educational Issues in Charter Schools Conference, Washington, D.C., November 2001), page 202

CHAPTER 11: What We Should Do

12. Katrina Bulkley and Jennifer Fisler, "A Review of the Research on Charter Schools." (A working paper for the Consortium for Policy Research in Education, University of Pennsylvania, in press), page 297

13. Bulkley and Fisler, in press, 297

14. Gary Miron and Christopher Nelson, "Autonomy in Exchange for Accountability: An Initial Study of Pennsylvania Charter Schools," October 2000. Surveys indicate that charter school teachers, while younger, are better educated than their district counterparts (Caroline M. Hoxby, "How School Choice Affects the Achievement of Public School Students," 2001), page 299

15. The largest charter study (RPP International, Fourth-Year Report) says charters enroll disproportionately low numbers of special-education students—8 percent in charters, versus 11 percent in other schools. Likewise a sweeping Rand study in 2001 found that "students with disabilities and students with poorly educated parents are somewhat underrepresented" in most school choice programs. Other studies argue, however, that charters underreport their special-education enrollment (U.S. Department of Education: "Charter Schools and

Students with Disabilities: Review of Existing Data," November 1998, at *www.ed.gov/pubs/chartdisab/enroll.html*), page 299

16. Paul Hill, et al., "A Study of Charter School Accountability," Center on Reinventing Public Education, June 2001, page 300

17. "The State of Charter Schools 2000: National Study of Charter Schools Fourth-Year Report," RPP International, 2000, page 301

18. Bulkley and Fisler, in press, page 308

Acknowledgments and Author's Note

I owe my greatest debt of gratitude to the parents, students, and teachers at the E.C. Reems Academy of Technology and Art, and the Dolores Huerta Learning Academy. Over three sometimes difficult years, these families and educators invited me warmly into their classrooms, offices, and homes, sharing their time and the details of their lives. In particular, I am grateful for the unwavering generosity of the people I imposed upon the most: Valentín Del Rio, Laura Armstrong, Felicitas Coates, and the families of William Stewart and Jasmine McGehee; the Lopezes; and the Caseys. My thanks also to the staff and families at East Palo Alto Charter School, Webster Elementary, Jefferson Elementary, Garfield Elementary, the KIPP Academy, and the many other schools I visited, as well as the administration of the Oakland Unified School District.

Matt Hammer, Ron Synder, and numerous other staffers and leaders at Oakland Community Organizations always found time to answer my questions, despite the heavy demands of their schedules, and helped to make sure that I was present and informed at all events of note. The School Futures Research Foundation also made its operations, practices, and documents open to my journalistic inquests. Brian Bennett, Don Gill, Lisa Blair, and Gene Ruffin, among others, were generous with their time.

It is hard to imagine how this book would have been written without the help of my able research assistant, Joanna Kaplan, who gracefully marshaled thousands of fluttering sheets of notes into impressive order. She also proved herself a master of many other disciplines, from finances to interpreting. I am thankful, also for the research help of Christopher Tucker, who has shattered my stereotypes of professional hockey players.

This book would not have come into being without the generosity and far-ranging interests of the Open Society Institute. I am especially indebted to Gara LaMarche, Gail Goodman, and Joanna Cohen. Bonnie Nadell, my agent, was brilliant. Tracy Brown, my editor, and everyone else I have had the opportunity to work with at Ballantine Books, have made this process an absolute pleasure. I thank them all for believing in this book, and for putting such fine effort behind it.

Hamilton Cain combined valuable assistance in structuring this story with unflagging support and kindness. It is a markedly better book for his help, and any weak verbs that remain are the fault of my own insolence. Jacob Levenson also did yeoman's work on the structure and tone of this book, and offered unfailing moral support, as did Eric Klinenberg. In addition, I remain indebted to the many others who patiently read and thoughtfully commented on drafts of chapters, including Victor Peskin, Tamara Fox, Alexandra Hernandez, and Meredith May. Jay Mathews, a North Star for any education journalist who is paying attention, offered valuable advice and encouragement. I count myself lucky for his guidance.

Some of the great lights in the world of education, and particularly in school choice, aided me unstintingly with their expertise. Among them were Peter Schrag, Paul Hill, Patty Yancey, Katrina Bulkley, Diane Ravitch, Joe Nathan, Paul Berman, John Ericson, Bruno Manno, Luis Huerta, Scott Hamilton, Sy Fliegel, Debbie Meier, Bruce Fuller, Bob Blackburn, and California's charter school mavens, Eric Premack and Laurie Gardner. I am grateful to all of them for their efforts to educate me and to keep me on the right track, and especially to those who labored through reading and commenting on early drafts of this book.

A small army of able journalists assisted me when I needed to be in two places at once. My thanks in particular to Angela Hill, Jessica

Scully, Heather Blonkenfeld, and Anita Chabria. In addition, Sgt. John Bradley provided crucial help navigating the criminal justice system, and Rachel Rosenkrantz lent her talents as a pseudonymist.

Noel Cisneros, the justly Emmy-awarded television journalist, offered invaluable resources for my research. Father Jay Matthews and Paul Cobb kindly shared a wealth of Oakland history. Thanks also to Bishop Ernestine Cleveland Reems, who made time for numerous interviews and spoke with warm candor.

Finally, and with great enthusiasm, I thank the most reliable and thoughtful supporters of my work: my family. My father, Daniel, my mother, Lisbeth, and my sister, Lisa, have encouraged me daily, and all have lent their formidable knowledge, talent, and wisdom to supporting me in this three-year effort. I remain moved and grateful.

•   •   •

A few notes on sources and methods:

Most of the information in this book is taken from my own direct observation. Events that I did not observe are based on extensive interviews with people who were present, and sometimes on video or audiotapes, in addition to documentary records.

I went into this project assuming that I would play no role at all in the events that I observed. This proved impossible, from both practical and moral standpoints. To take a simplistic example, an adult who stands by and does nothing while children fight or damage property is not playing a neutral role by any means. Particularly in the period after the bulk of the research for this book was complete, I chose to try to play a different role: one of a responsible adult citizen in whatever school I happened to be in. At the same time, I strived to do nothing that would affect the overall course of the school. At E. C. Reems I participated as a tutor in the after-school reading program. I have spent time tutoring Nazim Casey Jr. and taking him on weekend outings, mostly after the initial year of research was over, and have been included in the decisions his family made about his education after his move to Burbank Elementary.

As part of my research for this book, I visited the KIPP Academy in New York and was, like the OCO group, deeply impressed. I told the KIPP organization that I wanted to assist in the effort to create more such schools, including one in Oakland. I have been honored to play a role in that effort, particularly in Oakland, and was paid for that work.

Mayor Jerry Brown declined interview requests for this book. Portions of the book regarding him are based on my previous interviews with him, other published interviews, his own writing, and the extensive comments of his staff and others who have spent time with him.

The San Francisco Unified School District, its lawyers, and the San Francisco City Attorney's Office labored arduously to impede the release of public documents regarding the legal case against John Cleveland. I trust that everyone involved in that scurrilous effort understands that action of that sort aids predators in finding new victims, and I appreciate the work of the talented James Wheaton in breaking San Francisco's artificial and unfortunate logjam. Dr. Cleveland walked out of an interview regarding some of the allegations against him and declined to speak further, making it impossible to get his response to some of those allegations.

Many of the names of children in this book are pseudonyms, as are the names of Ms. Sullivan, Ms. Cowan, Robert, Candace, and LaTanya.

A portion of the proceeds of this book will support the education of some of the children mentioned in these pages.

Index